125.00 / 9.98

Powell's Elephant Treaties (NoDJ)

125.00/9.98   **NDJ**

Political Science & International Rela   103253

ELEPHANT TREATIES

Elephant Treaties

THE COLONIAL LEGACY
OF THE BIODIVERSITY CRISIS

Rachelle Adam

University Press of New England
Hanover and London

University Press of New England
www.upne.com
© 2014 University Press of New England
All rights reserved
Manufactured in the United States of America
Designed by Mindy Basinger Hill
Typeset in Adobe Caslon Pro

University Press of New England is a member of the
Green Press Initiative. The paper used in this book meets
their minimum requirement for recycled paper.

For permission to reproduce any of the material in this book,
contact Permissions, University Press of New England, One Court
Street, Suite 250, Lebanon NH 03766; or visit www.upne.com

Library of Congress Cataloging-in-Publication Data

Adam, Rachelle, 1951– author.
Elephant treaties: the colonial legacy of the biodiversity crisis / Rachelle Adam.
    pages   cm
Includes bibliographical references and index.
ISBN 978-1-61168-499-5 (cloth: alk. paper)—
ISBN 978-1-61168-500-8 (ebook)
1. Biodiversity conservation—Law and legislation—History.
2. Wildlife conservation (International law)—History.
3. Environmental law, International—History.
4. Imperialism—History. 5. Elephants—Law and legislation—History. I. Title.
K3488. A93 2014
346.04'69516—dc23   2013026567

5 4 3 2 1

I dedicate this book to those extraordinary individuals who devote their lives to the wildlife of Africa. By their courage in the face of danger and even terror they remind us that against overwhelming odds, we can still influence the present course of events. These people have made the difference to the elephants of Africa, and perhaps are all that stand between them and the irreversible descent into oblivion.

Contents

Acknowledgments ix

List of Acronyms xi

CHAPTER ONE Introduction 1

CHAPTER TWO Colonial Beginnings 13

CHAPTER THREE Decolonialization 58

CHAPTER FOUR Disillusionment 98

CHAPTER FIVE Epilogue and Renewal 126

Notes 139

Index 183

Acknowledgments

In writing this book, I owe a great deal to the research librarians at the Harvard University libraries, who were generous with their knowledge and time, and particularly Frederic Burchsted for introducing me to the Harold Coolidge papers. I also thank the librarians at the Wildlife Conservation Society at the Bronx Zoo for their assistance in accessing the archival material housed in the society's library. And for its ongoing support throughout my doctoral research, I gratefully acknowledge the generosity of the Leonard Davis Institute for International Relations.

I thank both Peter Haas and Nicholas Robinson for their kindness in making the time to meet with me and discuss the research at its initial stage; and especially Francoise Burhenne-Guilmin of the IUCN Environmental Law Center (ELC) for her generosity in answering my many questions, and in forwarding hard-to-find sources. In particular, I thank Tamar Ron for her unflagging enthusiastic support and key insights, and especially for her generosity in sharing her rich and unique experiences of African nature.

Above all I thank my doctoral advisor, Professor Tomer Broude of Hebrew University's law faculty, for his key part in the making of this book: for his patience in reviewing the never-ending drafts of my thesis; his constructive criticisms and bringing to my attention sources that proved crucial; and his insights that always cut right to the core of the problem, as well as his wise advice that got me back on course.

Acronyms

ACIWLP American Committee for International Wild Life Protection
ASP African Special Project
CBD Convention on Biological Diversity
CBNRM Community-Based Natural Resource Management
CCTA Commission de Coopération Technique en Afrique
CEPLA Commission on Environmental Policy, Law and Administration (formerly IUCN's Commission on Legislation; today, IUCN's World Commission on Environmental Law)
CEQ Council on Environmental Quality
CITES Convention on International Trade in Endangered Species
CMS Convention on Migratory Species (Convention on the Conservation of Migratory Species of Wild Animals)
ECOSOC Economic and Social Council (of the UN)
ED Executive Director (of UNEP)
ELC Environmental Law Center (of IUCN)
EPA US Environmental Protection Agency
FAO Food and Agriculture Organization of the United Nations
FFI Fauna and Flora International
GC Governing Council (of UNEP)
GEF Global Environmental Facility
ICBP International Council for Bird Preservation (Birdlife International)
ICEL International Council of Environmental Law
IGO Intergovernmental organization
IRDNC Integrated Rural Development and Nature Conservation
IOPN International Organization for the Protection of Nature (Office International de Documentation et de Correlation pour la Protection de la Nature)
IPCE International Parliamentary Conference on the Environment

IUCN International Union for Conservation of Nature (World Conservation Union)
IWGC International Working Group on Conservation (UNCHE)
NGO Nongovernmental organization
NIEO New International Economic Order
OAU Organization of African Unity (today the AU, African Union)
PAU Pan-American Union
PC Preparatory Committee
PSNR Permanent Sovereignty over Natural Resources
SPFE Society for the Preservation of the Fauna of the Empire
UN United Nations
UNCED United Nations Conference on Environment and Development
UNCHE United Nations Conference on the Human Environment (Stockholm Conference)
UDHR Universal Declaration of Human Rights
UNEP United Nations Environment Program
UNESCO United Nations Educational, Scientific and Cultural Organization
UNGA United Nations General Assembly
UNSCCUR UN Scientific Conference on the Conservation and Utilization of Resources
WCC World Conservation Congress
WCS World Conservation Strategy
WCED World Commission on Environment and Development
WHC World Heritage Convention (Convention concerning the Protection of the World Cultural and Natural Heritage)
WSSD World Summit on Sustainable Development

ELEPHANT TREATIES

CHAPTER ONE

Introduction

Prologue

As a government lawyer for Israel's Ministry of the Environment working my way through the maze of international biodiversity conventions, I soon learned that the way to get them swiftly ratified was to answer the perennial question, "What do we have to do if we join?" and simply tell the truth: no more than what we are already doing. Pointing out the flexibility that these conventions provided with such qualifying phrases as "to the extent possible" or "as appropriate" was usually sufficient to persuade decision makers that no major policy changes were needed. Hence the government could ratify a convention confident that by doing so, it could gain legitimacy in the eyes of the international community, while at the same time no other country could protest that it was not in compliance. In this state of affairs, the Ministry of the Environment succeeded in completing Israel's ratification of the major biodiversity agreements,[1] enabling ministry officials to participate (dependent on budgets) in endless conferences in which governments compete in their rhetoric on saving the biosphere and its biodiversity. Global environmental governance operates through these conferences, which have become a way of life for thousands of government, IGO, and NGO officials.

Meanwhile, the clock was ticking, and the goal that governments had set themselves in 2002—to stop biodiversity loss by 2010—was edging uncomfortably closer. Leaving government and moving over to the NGO sector, I attempted to leverage those same biodiversity agreements to protect Jerusalem forestland, but quickly discovered that they were poorly equipped to contend with the core factors driving biodiversity loss. Although the agreements address direct drivers such as habitat loss, pollution, and invasive species, the critical and underlying determinants go far beyond, to the unforgiving and formidable threats of overpopulation, overconsumption, and the arch-demon—unsustainable growth devouring Earth's biosphere. Moreover, in trying to use these agreements to promote NGO objectives, questions arose regarding their appropriateness as governance tools that I was hard-pressed to answer. Simple observations revealed that outside of Antarctica and the marine environment, biodiversity issues are *land use* issues—what a country does within its own territorial jurisdiction. And despite ubiquitous declarations supporting international cooperation for global biodiversity, no one outside of Israel seemed particularly perturbed by the loss of its biodiversity, never mind cooperating to protect it. Israel's biodiversity was obviously a domestic-scale issue of concern only to Israel.

A Dilemma of Scales

Alarmed over escalating rates of species extinctions, scientists crafted the enigmatic term biodiversity as a concept encompassing the complexity of life on earth. It was part of a strategy to convey the urgency of the biodiversity crisis, to make people ponder its meaning and to provoke their curiosity, in the hope of gaining broad support in tackling it. Biodiversity is chiefly defined by its holistic quality; it addresses the components and processes of the biosphere as an entirety, in contrast to traditional nature conservation, which has focused on individual species and habitats. The term is meant to express not only ecosystems and species diversity, but also the diversity within them. This richness of biodiversity is of critical significance to the effective functioning of ecosystems, dependent on the variety of species, their genetic diversity, and their natural processes. In turn, the survival of humans and other species depends on well-running ecosystems that supply essential goods and services. In confronting the present biodiversity crisis, the maintenance of any population's genetic diversity is critical for strengthening its resilience to the threats that confront it, and its chances of surviving the current wave of extinction.

Although biodiversity is not yet a concept familiar to the general public, the term coined in 1986 for a key scientific conference was enthusiastically adopted not only by scientists but by environmental lawyers: by 1987 a proposal for an international convention for biodiversity had already reached the international agenda. Though I initially revered biodiversity conventions as sources of inspiration and promise, my work with them eventually disclosed their weaknesses and flaws, marked by a "dilemma of scales" hovering persistently overhead. From a legal perspective, biodiversity comprises a national resource; yet ecologically, biodiversity is the living stuff of ecosystems crisscrossing the earth's surface, weaving the web of the biosphere. Political reality has bluntly and grossly ignored the interconnectedness of the biosphere by drawing national borders that arbitrarily slice through it. Rather than following the natural boundaries of watersheds or other ecosystems, these borders were forged by warfare and politics.[2] After successfully enclosing its portion of the earth's surface, and without an international principle holding states accountable for their own biodiversity, each state is a priori free to do with its own share of the biosphere as it pleases. Thus the commonly held view that stopping biodiversity loss requires the coordinated action of the international community, although ecologically wise—and politically achievable if the world were governed by a centralized global government—contradicts its national scale. Thinking globally does not seem to work for protecting biodiversity.

Confronting scales of environmental problems was part of the process of the 1972 United Nations Conference on the Human Environment (UNCHE, or the Stockholm Conference). Its earliest preparatory meeting in 1970 noted that "the number of environmental problems which are international by nature [. . .] is comparatively small. Those which are international in the sense of being of international concern [. . .] form the bulk of the problems."[3] Elinor Ostrom observed the multiplicity of scales pertaining to environmental issues in general and biodiversity in particular. She pointed out that although "[m]uch of the literature on biodiversity stresses the global nature [. . . ,] many biological processes, however, occur at extremely small scales [. . .] [and] an overemphasis on the need for large-scale institutional arrangements can lead to the destruction or discouragement of institutional arrangements at smaller to medium scales."[4] Current legal critique of biodiversity conventions notes the implications of biodiversity's national scale for international law. John Kunich has written extensively about the law's failure to successfully confront biodiversity loss, which he attributes, among other factors, to national sovereignty and the narrow self-interests of nations.[5] Christopher Stone has similarly observed that "as long as a nation is chewing up only its own insides, it is not, in the eyes of international law, doing anything it can be sued over."[6] Stone further argues that international cooperation in solving environmental issues is not always required, and bilateral or unilateral action can be more effective.[7] Tony Brenton, in *Greening Machiavelli*, maintains that biodiversity agreements are unnecessary because "we are talking here about conservation of resources within national borders. The most effective and flexible way to do this is [. . .] through individual arrangements with the countries concerned than through global agreements."⁸ British conservationist Richard Sandbrook offered the most succinct critique of international conventions for biodiversity:

> We should not elevate matters to the global level if they are best dealt with nationally. Do we really need international law when national resources are at stake? [. . .] Legal agreements do not stick anywhere [. . . .] Perhaps we have been seduced into thinking we are making progress by the disease I call "conventionitis."⁹

A Story of Africa

In light of biodiversity's local-national scale, how did international law come to address biodiversity issues that touch the deepest roots of sensitive state sovereignty? How did biodiversity loss make its way onto the international agenda as a burning global issue? What *international* problems were biodiversity conventions meant to solve? Seeking clues to these puzzles, I undertook an initial review of the five major biodiversity conventions, which swiftly revealed that all of them were the work of IUCN (International Union for Conservation of Nature, or World Conservation Union). Because four of these conventions were on the agenda of the 1972 Stockholm Conference (UNCHE), this iconic conference was a logical entry point for this book. Yet reaching back further into the past, the narrative disclosed that IUCN had been working on international biodiversity conventions prior to and independently of UNCHE. Moreover, the earliest treaties for territorial species predated IUCN itself by almost fifty years, going back to 1900 and focusing on Africa at the height of European colonialism.¹⁰ Alerted to this largely untold story, I set out to expose the roots of biodiversity treaties on the premise that revealing their history would throw light on the puzzles I set forth. Completing the journey into this past, I offer three linked claims. First, the biodiversity crisis of today became an international issue because it was originally a colonial issue; and second, it became a colonial issue because of biodiversity's asymmetric global distribution—Europeans colonized non-European lands to access and exploit their unique natural resources. Third, and finally, to legitimize the colonizer's seizing of what the colonized possessed, European powers created what they called *international conservation* conventions but were actually *colonial* conventions. They applied only to colonial territorial possessions.

This book proffers an iconoclastic history of international biodiversity agreements. A sweeping historical overview from the vantage point of the European colonial milieu that spawned these treaties, reveals their origins in the legal cover for European takeover of Africa's biodiversity. In contradiction to the widespread account that such treaties emerged circa 1972 from a global "tsunami" of alarm over a rapidly declining biosphere, in reality they stretch back in time to the "colonial confrontation" between Europeans and non-Europeans.[11] Although universally framed as the global megaconference that launched international environmentalism, the Stockholm Conference was preceded by other UN-sponsored environmental conferences, as well as a vibrant colonial history of conservationism encompassing a rich cast of characters. Powerful colonial states, conservation organizations, and unique individuals who made the ultimate difference play leading parts in the unfolding saga.[12]

Marking its location in time and space, this book centers on colonial Africa. At that time, although Africans had exploited their fauna for millennia without reaching a crisis of extinction, within a few decades of their arrival Europeans wreaked havoc on African wildlife, leading to a sharp downward spiral in numbers.[13] And as colonialism drove biodiversity loss, the European craving for non-European natural resources was, in turn, a factor driving colonialism. Biodiversity-poor European countries sought the natural resources of biodiversity-rich non-European lands as raw material for their industries and to nourish the global trade fed by these resources.

Africa runs thematically and powerfully throughout the narrative as the motivating and ultimate concern of conservation conventions. The earliest convention was a hunting and trade agreement for African fauna. It arose from the conviction shared by Great Britain and Germany that only European colonial cooperation could prevent the elephant's extinction. Seventy years later, the next generation of conservation conventions emerged from IUCN's conviction that newly independent African nations could not protect Africa's nature, justifying IUCN's intervention. The use of law to both exploit and protect nature entwines within the story as a core element in colonial conservation policy promoted by both government and nongovernment actors.[14] These actors created species conventions to counter the effects of the colonial encounter on African fauna: its overexploitation, which threatened lucrative profits from the ivory trade; cultural clashes over "humane" hunting as opposed to "barbarous and savage" hunting; and land enclosures to protect fauna, producing harsh results for local populations. Drawing on positivist jurisprudence as the godfather of colonialism, Europeans had assiduously wrought international law into the justification for the invasion, conquest, and rule of non-European peoples and their lands, cloaked by a "civilizing mission." European powers deemed their colonies sovereign-less, clearing the way for exploitation of the colonies' natural resources.[15] Sovereignty was an exclusively European institution, and membership in the club of international law was open only to "civilized" states that shared interests, values, and culture.[16] "Positivists developed an elaborate vocabulary for denigrating non-European people, presenting them as suitable objects for conquest [. . .] all in furtherance of the civilizing mission, the discharge of the white man's burden."[17]

But the story is not entirely grim. Just as colonialism triggered massive biodiversity loss in Africa, it also launched the institutions to counter it. Paradoxically, while colonialism dictated the use of positivist international law, its civilizing mission formed the ideational context from which sprang constructivist discourse and debate. The earliest territorial conservation treaty was the work of European colonial powers, yet it also served as an entry point for conservation organizations that went on to initiate further conservation treaties, eventually leading to today's biodiversity treaties. Moreover, though irretrievably intertwined with colonialism and formulated primarily to protect European profits in the ivory trade, Great Britain's objective in the use of international law was not only instrumental; Britain profoundly believed in its normative obligation to protect African fauna as the self-appointed trustee of what it defined as a unique imperial legacy. Thus the colonial experience legitimized by the discipline of international law was composed of a richly diverse tapestry of dialogue and ideas diffused among an array of actors. The themes of civilized and uncivilized, sovereign and non-sovereign, bearers of the white man's burden and trustees for imperial legacies, were concepts forged by both state and non-state entities, creating a distinctive colonial constructivism. Despite their flaws and troubling origins, these early conventions symbolize the deep passion of remarkable individuals for Africa's endangered wildlife.

Colonial Constructivists

This book primarily tells the story of conservation organizations and their pursuit of international conventions to promote their values and beliefs — as well as their reputations and influence. It starts out with a brief narrative of some of the giants on whose shoulders these organizations stand. Beginning in the seventeenth century, European scientists operated as transnational networks of colonial constructivists united by concerns over the impact of colonialism on conquered lands. Ironically, and displaying the recurring theme of devastation versus conservation, colonialism was the critical element in the development of these early epistemic communities.[18] European empires became communication networks for like-minded colleagues located in colonial outposts. A body of scientific knowledge, based on observations, data, and specimens collected throughout these empires, spread through epistemic networks and launched scientific societies and academies. Colonial constructivists shaped norms that would become standards of behavior for future environmental activists. They lobbied colonial governments, holding them accountable for environmental devastation. They drafted early environmental laws that would serve as models for environmental legislation throughout the rest of the world. Working strategically, colonial constructivists used the fear tactic to prod governments into action by plying anxieties over drought and famine. Inspired by natural law, their mistrust and dislike of colonial rule went beyond environmental concerns; many of them opposed colonialism because of its devastating impact on indigenous populations and, of course, because of slavery.

Continuing along the historical continuum, international conservation organizations first appeared around the start of the twentieth century. Pivotal to the narrative is their role as the compelling force that drove international conservation law. Well integrated into the colonial milieu, conservation organizations shared the prejudices of society at large regarding non-European populations of colonized lands, which led to the ensuing justification of the civilizing mission. Toward the end of the continuum, IUCN emerges as the key player in the narrative. IUCN is a leading international conservation organization, acclaimed in particular for its expertise in biodiversity issues.[19] A hybrid government-nongovernmental organization with over 1,000 members, since its founding IUCN has been setting the international agenda for biodiversity issues. Staffed by both scientists and lawyers, and harnessing a unique resource of thousands of experts working voluntarily in six different commissions, its work is internationally recognized as both cutting edge and highly authoritative. Beyond its achievements in crafting international conventions, IUCN was the creative force behind innovative institutions for nature, such as the Red Lists of threatened species and ecosystems, the World Commission on Protected Areas, and the Species Survival Commission. Wrought as an agent for change,

IUCN has achieved groundbreaking work in developing the principles, rules, and norms for the conservation and management of biodiversity and ecosystems.

IUCN was founded primarily by Europeans from countries still ruling vast territories in other parts of the world. It was born into colonialism and spent a great deal of time worrying about decolonialization. IUCN's roots had direct implications for its task of biodiversity treaty making. It had been nurtured on a colonial internationalism that engulfed the territories of European possessions while leaving the sovereign European metropolitan to its own national and regional laws. IUCN feared that new African governments lacked the capacity to protect what it perceived as a global and common heritage rather than an African one.[20] IUCN proceeded to protect Africa's biological resources and fauna in particular, deemed under critical threat, by means of international law. It created a body of international conventions that today comprise the institutional core of global governance for biodiversity.

Coupling international conservation law and international conservation organizations, this book traces IUCN's evolution from an enthusiastic promoter and supporter of international law to its gradually emerging awareness of the law's limits for saving Earth's biodiversity. While negotiating the Convention on Biological Diversity (CBD), developing states tossed out IUCN drafts and replaced them with a convention that entrenched these countries' right to development and developed countries' obligation to help them achieve this right. The colonial past hung heavily over these negotiations. Developing states scrapped global lists of species and ecosystems, which they viewed as thinly disguised attempts by their former colonial rulers to regain control of their natural resources. They succeeded in negotiating an agreement marked by amorphous and weak commitments, and held its implementation hostage to financial aid from the developed countries. There was no restructuring of states' identities; rather, states succeeded in transforming IUCN's norms. CBD is the last of the global multilateral biodiversity conventions.

Why a Colonial Legacy Matters

Does it or should it matter that the roots of international biodiversity conventions are firmly planted in colonialism? Has their colonial legacy made a difference to these agreements, and if so, how? Are there lessons to be learned from this story, or does it simply chronicle a short period in human history of less than a hundred years, that perhaps a hundred years hence our descendants will have forgotten anyway? Yet biodiversity loss is an alarming and formidable dilemma, accelerating out of control. This book's point of departure is the increasing impoverishment of our planet's biodiversity despite a significant number of international agreements meant to stop it or slow it down. The 2012 UN report *Global Biodiversity Outlook 3* "has determined that biodiversity loss continues in its downward spiral."[21] The 2005 Millennium Ecosystem Assessment established, "*with high certainty*, that biodiversity loss and deteriorating ecosystem services contribute [. . .] to worsening health, higher food insecurity, increasing vulnerability [to natural hazards such as flooding], lower material wealth, worsening social relations, and less freedom for choice and action."[22]

Common sense alone predicts that the current biodiversity crisis will become more severe in the coming years. On a finite planet threatened by a burgeoning human population and an even faster economic growth, the greater the number of individuals of our species and the more resources we consume, the less room and resources remain for other species. Threatening ecological chaos, with its ominous implications for life on Earth, biodiversity loss is a *humanitarian* issue. We are or will all be victims of biodiversity loss, but its earliest and most vulnerable victims are those who are the least to blame for its loss. The crisis afflicts primarily those populations who live most closely with nature, who depend directly on the services and goods of biodiversity and ecosystems, and who are the weakest and most marginalized of human societies.

With biodiversity loss defined as ultimately life threatening, biodiversity conventions continue to be critical items on the international agenda. Locating and isolating their historical roots evokes different perspectives on the institutions and actors involved, and in particular the international conservation organizations. Although they are key players in the global environmental governance of today, the historical narrative calls into question the common perceptions of these organizations as transformative forces in restructuring states' identities. And although such organizations are popularly visualized as global white knights for Earth's threatened biodiversity — transcending sovereign borders and narrow politics to promote global concerns and interests — doubts about them start to set in. The narrative divulges traces of their colonial legacy directing their work with an invisible hand, perceptible in the use of international law for power and reputation and in their own distinctive civilizing mission. Conservation organizations — and not only states — could be colonizers.

More generally, it is also pertinent to other environmental issues for us to question what makes an issue international, how these issues reach the international agenda, and what international problems biodiversity agreements were meant to solve. As succinctly framed by an early twentieth-century conservationist writing in the 1930s, "There is a magic sound about international action and its effectiveness is apt to be overestimated."[23] Although issues including ozone depletion and climate change are widely recognized as international, affecting all countries because by their nature they cannot be contained within political borders, are they truly such? Are all countries equally involved, and do their activities have a sufficient impact on the issue at hand so as to make their participation in the particular regime a must? Are massive multilateral structures absolutely necessary to address the problem? Asking whether climate change really requires an operating system of close to 200 member states, and tracing these operating systems back to colonial governing systems, could lead to rethinking this governance structure.

Yet above all, chronicling their past yields pertinent insights on the immense challenges faced by biodiversity conventions today. Viewing them as direct descendants of colonial conservation conventions shines high-beamed light into shadowy corners, and abruptly a larger and brighter picture emerges. Acknowledging their colonial legacy sharpens our understanding of the historical burden that they bear. Endeavoring to protect nature yet maintain it primarily as a resource for the betterment of chosen human societies, colonial agreements failed to protect both nature and the societies of "others" utterly dependent on it. International biodiversity law did not start out as law between or among sovereign states addressing the biodiversity of all. Rather, it was originally colonial law imposed on Africa by European conquerors. The law was international only in the sense that it applied to lands outside of Europe.

Strains of colonial ideologies linger within contemporary governance structures for nature. Exploring the origins of international biodiversity law, from the perspective of marginalizing the other so as to exploit the other's natural resources, reveals that the issues still concern biodiversity-poor countries versus biodiversity-rich countries. As was the case when they were colonial powers, developed countries do not need international law and governance to protect what is left of their own biodiversity; these institutions are intended for developing countries.[24] In spite of endless dialogue on the need for global cooperation to reverse biodiversity loss, today's global governance for nature evolved directly from European operating systems for Africa's megafauna.

More specifically, Africa's national parks are the same protected areas established by European colonial conservationists for wildlife; as a policy of separation between humans and animals was pursued, in many instances indigenous populations were evicted and excluded from these parks. Today's global biodiversity conventions are not the result of a measured, well-considered process to reach the most effective governance structure for biodiversity. Instead, they are the continuation of colonial regimes through which Europeans governed non-Europeans; and rather than mechanisms for global cooperation, they are meant for developing countries deemed to lack governance.[25] Today, a new "Scramble for Africa" is under way, and colonialism has most recently metamorphosed in Africa as "land grabbing." Trading land for foreign currency, African governments have become colonizers of their own populations, dispossessing farmers, pastoralists, and communities of their ultimate sources of sustenance. Africa's land and water are being sold to foreigners to grow food for today's masters of the world, threatening millions of Africans. As angrily noted by one African protestor,

> [W]hat gets under my black skin is the incredible amount of cynicism, myopia, greed and the blatant disregard of history, and the future, that it takes to lease arable land to foreign investors to grow food or biofuels at the direct expense of Africans. Colonialism seized both land and people. African leaders are now offering cheap land and labour to foreign investors.[26]

This book's basic premise is that biodiversity conventions are obsolete. Entrenching conservation norms based on nineteenth- and twentieth-century European colonialism, these conventions record a Eurocentric view of nature that meant excluding colonized populations in order to preserve nature. They document colonial norms of governing nature that have remained locked into today's international governance institutions, such as segregating humans from wildlife, enclosing lands as protected areas, creating lists of species protected (or unprotected) because of their significance to Europeans, and promoting international trade in species, again, that pivot around European interests. These conventions reflect a mindset that has become universal: development, growth, and the pursuit of wealth are sacrosanct, and nature will have to accommodate human society rather than human society accommodate nature. The anachronistic nature of these agreements, originating *under* colonialism, is sharply outlined by a comparison with human rights conventions, emerging *with the end* of colonialism. Returning to the dilemma of scales, by dictating governments' relations with their own populations, human rights conventions boldly intervene in key sovereignty issues once jealously guarded by states. Yet this expansion of government accountability to the welfare of humans living within its borders has not yet reached government accountability for other species. International biodiversity law's critical challenge remains to sweep away the stubbornly entrenched norm — and principle of international law — that what a country does with its own biodiversity is its business alone.

I chose the title of this book to express the deep frustration that has persistently dogged my work with biodiversity treaties, poignantly demonstrated by the tragedy of the African elephant. An extraordinarily sentient species, the elephant is spiraling toward extinction despite a substantial number of biodiversity conventions, a victim of its own tusks. These modern treaties, captives of colonial ones that sprang from the elephant's economic value to Europeans, still treat the elephant as a tradable object. The colonial legacy endures, and modern international conservation law cannot break free of the chains of elephant treaties. Given escalating biodiversity loss, relentlessly fuelled by never-ending colonial confrontations, and the incapacity of international law to counter these forces, rethinking current structures and scales of global governance is imperative. By opening windows onto the past, the following account of biodiversity conventions and the organizations that created them affords unconventional views of current governance institutions, spurring debate on alternatives. This book argues that these institutions have run their course, making way for the shift to scales of governance that minimize human disharmony with nature.

CHAPTER TWO

Colonial Beginnings

> For about 150 years prior to the beginning of this century an intellectual movement occurred which in many respects was one of the most revolutionary in all human history [...] The movement may be said to have culminated in the pronouncement of Charles Darwin's theory of evolution. The impact of this upon men's minds was greater than that of any pronouncement which one can recall [....] The only great danger, it seems to me, lies in the possibility that man may endeavour to disassociate himself, or consider himself exempt, from natural laws [...] [W]e must hope that the final half of this century may witness a re-awakening in the minds of people of the inestimable values that nature is capable of providing for us. —*International Technical Conference on the Protection of Nature, Lake Success, 1949*[27]

Trailblazers

In his opening address at the first UN-sponsored conference for the environment in 1949, conservationist Fairfield Osborn, author of the environmental classic *Our Plundered Planet*, evoked the rich past of international conservationism. Peopled with outstanding personalities, a historical narrative of the international conservation movement discloses that international conservationists of earlier times led professional lives surprisingly similar to those of today. While admittedly on a much smaller scale, these individuals attended ubiquitous conferences; drafted and negotiated international treaties; worried about compliance and enforcement; agonized over listings of species; and discussed astonishingly identical issues, such as overpopulation, consumption, climate change, deforestation, invasive species, the impact of technology and industry on the environment, and the loss of ecosystem services. The mid-twentieth-century IUCN and its founders stood on the shoulders of early twentieth-century conservationists and organizations, who, as Osborn recalled, stood towering on the shoulders of those who had preceded them.

Among these giants were scientists and naturalists who, by the middle of the eighteenth century, were alerted to colonialism's impact on the natural environment of European colonies. Colonial expansion entailed massive change in land use, triggered by the clearing of land and forests for settlements, farms, and plantations. The ensuing devastation was swiftly felt (particularly on small islands), leading to desiccation theories that linked decrease in rainfall and ensuing drought to massive deforestation.[28] Operating as agents for change, these scientists worked as pressure groups both within and outside colonial administrations, shaping norms for today's advocacy groups. As environmental and human rights activists, many were antislavery as well, distressed by the devastation and suffering that colonialism inflicted on indigenous populations.[29] They operated through vast networks encompassing European empires, within which they corresponded extensively with each other, traveled, and worked. They established scientific societies and academies as institutional frameworks for knowledge sharing and ongoing dialogues. Colonial exploration divulged extraordinary data and generated exciting knowledge and information, epitomized by Darwin's epic voyages on the *Beagle*, ultimately leading to *On the Origin of Species*.

Within the paradoxical duality in which colonialism both destroyed and protected nature, colonialism encouraged the expansion of these networks by creating environmental job opportunities—a demand for scientists with expertise in natural history. European global expansion required experts capable of synthesizing new knowledge forged by the discovery and exploration of previously unknown lands.[30] Scientists were needed to classify and assess the flora, fauna, geology, and climate of the colonial territories, both for commercial purposes and to address environmental and health concerns. In caring for the ship crews, they were required to have expertise in botanical remedies. As the naturalists on board, their task was to observe and document the natural history of the lands they visited on their journeys, conducting surveys of local flora and fauna and collecting specimens. These scientists became early conservationists, bonding together through a profound concern over the environmental devastation inflicted by Europe. To counter the impact of colonialism, with colonial administrators they devised strategies and engaged in tactics that have become standard fare for environmental activism—primarily the use of law. Leveraging their powerful social and economic positions, they lobbied colonial governments to enact and enforce laws that addressed environmental damage. Long-delayed legislation for forest protection on the island of St. Helena was finally approved, thanks to "pressure from Sir Joseph Banks and in knowledge of legislation already passed in Mauritius and St. Vincent."[31]

In Mauritius, Pierre Poivre promoted the use of law to regulate a wide array of environmental issues. A renowned French naturalist, botanist, and explorer, as well as a colonial human rights activist, Poivre was also the French colonial governor of Mauritius from 1767 to 1772, which enabled him to realize his other interests. Alarmed over the impact of deforestation on the island, he used his position to promote restorative policies implemented by an ambitious project for environmental legislation. To add credibility to his policies, Poivre brought in scientists as back-up support, employing them as staff scientists. Regulating land use through integrative watershed management, Poivre created mountain reserves to stop deforestation and soil erosion, and river reserves to prevent silting in rivers and harbors. Law as a response to environmental degradation became standard usage by which colonial governments of Mauritius would from then on counter environmental degradation.[32] Responding to the contamination of the island's water resources by effluents from the highly polluting indigo industry, in 1791 the legislature enacted an anti–water pollution law regulating the industry. The concern over water quality led to further legislation in 1798 regulating the island's fisheries. Mauritius's environmental laws were buttressed in 1804 with a series of innovative regulations that established an environmental police force.[33]

By the end of the nineteenth century, the Cape Colony had a substantial body of environmental law dating from the seventeenth century. Similar to Poivre's work in Mauritius, in the Cape Colony conservation legislation was the result of teamwork by scientists and government administrators. Concern over intensive land use and ensuing environmental degradation led in 1846 to legislation addressing soil erosion. Its architect was Ludwig Pappe, an Austrian medical doctor with an expertise in the botany of the Cape, recognized for its rich and unique diversity. The Cape botany was the subject of correspondence between Pappe and the renowned director of the Royal Botanic Gardens at Kew, Sir William Hooker. Fostering the support of the eminent botanist to promote Pappe's conservationist ideas, in 1856 the Cape Legislative Assembly adopted a revolutionary forest protection policy replacing private property rights with forest conservancies.[34] Demonstrating the dynamic network of conservationist-minded administrators, the colonial secretary of Mauritius, Rawson Rawson, was transferred to the Cape Colony and appointed governor in 1853. Pappe and Rawson represent the convergence of two major elements of colonial conservation policy. Pappe's key concern was extinction of species, while Rawson, with his experience from Mauritius in forest conservation policy, was chiefly concerned with deforestation and ensuing drought.[35]

In addition to scientists who advocated government intervention through their positions in colonial administrations, a scientist-explorer based in Europe but deeply influenced by the colonialism of his time was Alexander von Humboldt. Active throughout the first half of the nineteenth century, Humboldt possessed a holistic concept of the relationship between humans and the natural world, through which he visualized the world as a great, global whole. Deconstructing the "demonization" of nature—a common perception during his time: nature as a threat to humans to be subdued and controlled—Humboldt instead emphasized the threats that *humans* posed to nature.[36] Alarmed by the impact of European expansion observed throughout his extensive travels, he was vehemently anticolonial.[37] Yet Humboldt himself was not an activist. In contrast to European colonies where scientists were successfully persuading governments to tackle environmental destruction, in early nineteenth-century metropolitan Europe, environmental advocacy was waiting in the wings for Darwin's explosive work on evolution. It was published in 1859, a year after Humboldt's death.[38] Environmental advocacy began in colonial Europe, not in Europe itself. Nevertheless, Humboldt's writings and lectures certainly inspired emerging activists of the middle and late nineteenth century. His richly descriptive essays starkly revealed the impact of colonialism on both the environment and humans, while his pioneering work in ecology was widely read by other scientists and naturalists. One of them was Charles Darwin. Bonded by their explorations throughout the New World, the two great scientists corresponded extensively, with Darwin sending "data and other manuscripts to the older scientist and claim[ing] that he owed his entire career to his constant rereading of Humboldt's *Personal Narrative*."[39]

In contrast to the non-activists Humboldt and Darwin, other scientists were forcefully outspoken on the environmental devastation spurred by European "pursuit of wealth." Alfred Russel Wallace, Darwin's co-writer on their joint submission on the theory of evolution, was a fervent advocate for species preservation who had been profoundly influenced by his years of travel in Asia. In 1863 Wallace issued a warning that if nothing is done about nature conservation, "future ages will certainly look back upon us as a people so immersed in the pursuit of wealth as to be blind to higher considerations. They will charge us with having culpably allowed the destruction of some of these records of creation which we had it in our power to preserve."[40]

The eminent British ornithologist Alfred Newton was another scientist-activist passionately dedicated to preventing extinctions. His advocacy for endangered bird species depicts the rich tapestry of relationships between scientists, government, and law. A highly respected professor of zoology and comparative anatomy at Cambridge University, Newton was also a devoted campaigner for bird conservation, particularly those of oceanic islands.[41] In 1858 he founded the British Ornithologists' Union (BOU) together with the still-published journal *Ibis*. Rounding out his distinguished academic standing and advocacy work for bird conservation, by an amazing stroke of good luck he was the brother of Edward Newton, who had served as assistant colonial secretary of Mauritius and then as colonial secretary and lieutenant governor of Jamaica. Beyond his career as a high-ranking colonial government official, Edward Newton shared his brother's enthusiasm for birds. A respected ornithologist himself, Edward made full use of the exotic lands that he administered for the British Empire, for his own research and specimen collecting. His brother Alfred was a major beneficiary as the recipient of bird specimens from the far-flung islands of the empire, including one of the extinct Dodo. Pursuing the string of connections, Alfred was also a colleague and friend of Darwin, with whom he corresponded and shared scientific data, including his bird specimens. Working to thwart looming extinctions,[42] Alfred had been profoundly inspired by *On the Origin of Species*.[43] Newton's bonds to both Darwin and Wallace are revealed in the profound awe in which he read for the first time their joint paper on natural selection:

> Not many days after my return home there reached me the part of the *Journal of the Linnaean Society* which bears on its cover the date 20 August 1858, and contains the papers by Mr Darwin and Mr Wallace, which were communicated to that Society at its special meeting of the first of July preceding [. . .] I sat up late that night to read it; and never shall I forget the impression it made upon me. Herein was contained a perfectly simple solution of all the difficulties which had been troubling me for months past [. . .] I never doubted for one moment, then nor since, that we had one of the grandest discoveries of the age — a discovery all the more grand because it was so simple.[44]

Alfred Newton was the archetype of a modern environmental activist, employing tactics such as lobbying, drafting and promoting legislation, and strategic use of the media, which in his day was limited to newspapers. He advocated for conservation laws as a response to threats of extinctions. Harnessing public opinion to leverage government intervention, Newton played a key role in the enactment of the 1880 Wild Birds Protection Act.[45] Addressing species preservation on the international level as well, Newton had a hand in formulating government policy and legislation during the Scramble for Africa.[46] Part of the network of scientists striving to prevent extinctions, Newton had one foot planted firmly in the world of European colonialism, linked to his brother Edward the colonial administrator and the data that this association afforded him. And as a distinguished academic, Alfred's other foot was planted in nineteenth-century Great Britain of African expansion at what was probably the most auspicious moment for biological scientists—Darwin and Wallace's paper on the theory of evolution by natural selection.[47]

The First Elephant Treaty

It is wonderful how little effect natives with spears, traps and arrows have on game in a country, and how suddenly it disappears before the gun and the rifle.[48] —*Sir John Kirk, 1897*

A member of the small European community has to take out an expensive license to hunt, but the native [. . .] has few restrictions placed on his desire to kill, and moreover he kills regardless of age and sex or of rarity of species.[49] —*C. W. Hobley, 1930*

Distinct from local laws designed for individual colonies and in particular oceanic islands, international conservation law sprang from the Scramble for Africa during the latter half of the nineteenth century. It pivoted around the decimation of wildlife vital to European interests and was expressly designed to address trade issues that colonial governments could not handle unilaterally. An early example of the use of international law to combat territorial extinctions is the first "elephant treaty":[50] the Convention for the Preservation of Wild Animals, Birds and Fish in Africa, adopted in London in 1900. Although it has remained largely forgotten, the 1900 London Convention certainly deserves its place in the annals of international conservation as international law's first shot at regulating territorial biodiversity. Defined "as the first serious attempt at systematic international cooperation for the preservation of wild life,"[51] it incorporated innovative concepts of conservation policy that have since become part of the fabric of biodiversity treaty law. Hunting restrictions, protected areas, lists of protected species, and trade rules all formed the backbone of the convention. It stands out as the work of *governments*, distinct from later agreements forged primarily by nongovernmental organizations. Its story is a fascinating glimpse of an instance of German-British cooperation at the end of the nineteenth century.

The origins of the 1900 London Convention trace to an 1896 letter from Britain's prime minister and foreign minister, Lord Robert Cecil, Marquess of Salisbury, to the colonial administrators of Uganda and the East African protectorate, noting the following:

> My attention has recently been called to the excessive destruction, by travelers and others in East Africa, of the larger wild animals known as "big game." There is reason to fear that unless some check is imposed upon the indiscriminate slaughter of these animals, they will, in the course of a few years, disappear from the British Protectorate [. . . .] It will be for your consideration whether it would be advisable to deal with the subject [. . .] by establishing a close time, by specifying reserved districts, and by limiting the number of any particular class of game to be shot by an individual sportsman.[52]

Salisbury's letter points to growing government alarm over the precarious condition of African wildlife. By the last decade of the nineteenth century, this had become an issue of immense public concern.[53] Reports were coming in from colonial administrators, settlers, hunters, and travelers that documented the vast devastation of African fauna and warned of looming extinctions.[54] Scientists played a key role in raising the awareness of governments to the crisis. Edwin Ray Lankester, a renowned zoologist and director of the British Museum (Natural History), spurred the British government into undertaking the 1900 Convention. He served as the government's scientific advisor to the plenipotentiary conference in 1900, and was a member of the British delegation and a signatory to the final act. Lankester continued as scientific advisor for the convention after the conference as well.[55]

But the critical force behind the British government's wildlife policy in Africa was the tusks of the African elephant, the ultimate European exploitation of Africa's biological resources. The immense power that ivory held over rapacious Europeans, who considered it an infinite source of vast wealth, is hauntingly evoked by Joseph Conrad's epic work *Heart of Darkness*, told against the background of the African ivory trade and first published in 1899: "The word 'ivory' rang in the air, was whispered, was sighed. You would think they were praying to it."[56] As succinctly observed by Harry Johnston, the first commissioner (in 1891) for the British protectorate of West Central Africa,

"From a commercial point of view, the most valuable animal is the elephant. Ivory is our chief export."[57] Ivory was the chief source of revenues for colonial governments, the foundation of colonial trade. But by the last decade of the nineteenth century, revenues were falling, attributed to increasing scarcity of the greedily coveted resource—the dwindling number of elephants hunted and killed for their tusks. An article in the *Zanzibar Gazette* in 1895 predicted that "fifty years hence there will be practically no ivory at all, the present annual mortality of African elephants for ivory export, being about 65,000."[58] Historically, fifty years has been a popular estimate of the time remaining to the threatened African elephant: besides this 1895 article, in 1931 the British physician, naturalist, and explorer Major R. W. G. Hingston warned in his report *Proposed British National Parks for Africa* that "I doubt if any of the three pachyderms, the elephant, rhinoceros, and hippopotamus, will [. . . .] survive beyond the next fifty years."[59] And today the World Wildlife Fund website warns, "Most range states do not have adequate capacity to protect and manage their herds. If conservation action is not forthcoming, elephants may become locally extinct in some parts of Africa within 50 years."[60] Yet fifty years now seems an optimistic estimate; a recent report warns that given the present rate of killings, within ten years most of Africa's elephants will be gone.[61]

The ironic tragedy of the African elephant is that its apparently unstoppable fall into oblivion is directly linked to its own unique physical traits. African elephants are in mortal danger because of their tusks, a cruel trick of fate that has encumbered them with teeth highly valued by humans. They are also cursed by their huge dimensions: as Earth's largest territorial animal, weighing up to six tons, an elephant requires vast tracts of land as well as enormous amounts of food, which they consume at up to 450 pounds daily. But the elephants' shrinking habitats have become a critical threat to their survival in the wild, throwing them into bitter conflicts with humans that escalate into actual fights over land and land use.[62]

Many humans feel a great compassion for elephants; this is understandable in light of elephant behavior, which so reminds us of our own. Elephants are sentient beings. They are highly emotional. They live in matriarchal groups whose members care for each other. They love their babies and are devoted to caring for their young. They communicate with each other, including through a great deal of physical touch; they miss each other when separated, and they rejoice when reunited. Elephants care for their sick and wounded. They have a sense of death and a connection to the bones of other elephants, which they cover with earth and branches.⁶³ Yet compassion toward elephants is understandably not shared by Africans who have to deal with these massive animals in their own backyards. They fear elephants because of the physical threat they pose and the destructive foraging they can inflict, laying waste to homes, villages, crops, and pastureland.

Beyond the elephant-human conflicts provoked by habitat conversions to farmland, the key threat to elephants — during colonialism and today — is the ivory trade. Although it was firmly entrenched prior to the Scramble for Africa of the 1880s, under European control the ivory trade reached unprecedented dimensions. Europeans brought to Africa technologically advanced rifles, which rapidly and efficiently decimated elephant herds. They constructed railways that eased hunters' access to herds formerly protected by the sheer size of the immense African continent. On the return trips, trains transported enormous amounts of ivory ripped off the dead elephants, on their way to global markets. The mighty African elephant could not withstand the force of European technologies, and quickly succumbed. By the 1890s, only fifteen years from the beginning of the Scramble for Africa, the elephant was mourned as a species on its way to extinction. Over the past 100 years, the elephant population of 3 to 5 million elephants throughout Africa has declined to approximately 400,000.⁶⁴

Great Britain was not alone in its panic over the alarming decline in elephant populations and the implications for the ivory trade. A partner to this concern was Germany. In 1895 Major Hermann von Wissmann, a German explorer who had traveled and hunted big game throughout central Africa, was appointed imperial colonial governor for German East Africa. An avid hunter as well as a ruthless colonial administrator, von Wissmann was personally aware of the massive decimation of African fauna.⁶⁵ With his new appointment, he set out to draft a wildlife policy designed to curb widespread wanton hunting in German East Africa. His first step was the enactment of new game regulations establishing a hunting system based on licenses and fees, and incorporating his concept of reserves in which hunting would be totally banned. The regulations further barred the use of snares, nets, fire, and driving of animals, as well as the use of poisons (or, in other words, African hunting methods). Addressing Germany's grave concerns, the regulations also introduced restrictions on the ivory trade, prohibiting the killing of elephants with tusks weighing less than 3 kilograms and ordering the confiscation by the government of tusks already taken.⁶⁶ In a generous gesture of early environmental diplomacy, the German Foreign Office translated the new regulations into English, and in

1896 presented them to the British Foreign Office, which in turn distributed them to colonial administrators with a request for comments.[67]

The German regulations lasted only the two years that von Wissmann remained in office. Yet their legacy lingers as the inspiration for the first territorial biodiversity convention. Beyond the local scale, von Wissmann recognized that protecting the African elephant required international cooperation of neighboring colonial powers. Leveraging the growing alarm of both Germany and Great Britain over the future of the ivory trade, von Wissmann apparently persuaded Paul Kayser, director of the German Colonial Department, of the need to cooperate with other European powers in Africa. Kayser in turn persuaded the German Foreign Office to approach Great Britain with a proposal for an "international arrangement authorising the confiscation on the coast of all tusks under [a certain weight]" in order to prevent "the indiscriminate slaughter of elephants in Africa." By July 1896 the German proposal had reached the British embassy in Berlin, which forwarded it to the Foreign Office. As he had done with the German regulations, Lord Salisbury sent the German proposal for an "international arrangement" to colonial administrators for their response. In favor of the German proposal, in January 1897 Salisbury requested the British ambassador in Berlin "to communicate a copy of Mr. Sharpe's dispatch [. . .] to the German Government, and to ascertain whether they would be prepared to suggest to the Powers interested the signature of such an international arrangement."[68]

Alfred Sharpe had meanwhile replaced Johnston as commissioner for West Central Africa, and his response to the German proposal had apparently persuaded Salisbury to move forward with the convention. He first clarified in his answer to Salisbury that the primary threat to the elephants was the Africans and not the Europeans: "It is rather generally, and quite erroneously, supposed in Europe that the slaughter of elephants is due to a great extent to Europeans [. . . .] The number killed annually is trifling compared with the vast number which are constantly being mobbed and followed and killed by natives."[69] Sharpe then offered an analysis of the cooperation required among the countries involved, in protecting the prosperous ivory trade:

> My own opinion is, and always has been, that there is only one method by which we can stop this slaughter of elephants of all sizes, and that is that all the Powers who hold territory in Africa should agree to prohibit the export of tusks of less weight than, say, 15 lbs each. If this course was taken

by all the Powers, [...] the killing of small elephants would cease, as the ivory would no longer be of value to the natives [....] For one Power alone, or two, or three, however, to pass such a regulation as this would be useless unless all the others joined in [...] as it would simply result in the ivory of small size [...] going by new channels to the territories which have no such Regulations.[70]

By April 1897, Germany and Great Britain had agreed on convening a conference of European colonial powers as the next step toward safeguarding their take of the African ivory trade. Their objective was to restrict the hunting of elephants and the trade in their tusks.[71] The British had defined the agenda well ahead of time: prevention of export of elephant tusks weighing less than 15 pounds; establishment of reserves; "closed seasons" for all animals and a ban on killing females; hunting licenses for both Europeans and natives; the "enforcement of the provisions of the Brussels Act in regard to the supply of arms and ammunitions to natives"; and total protection for "useful" animals including birds.[72] Although the need to regulate the ivory trade had triggered the conference, so as not to scare off the more protectionist colonial powers, the British government's officially more soothing position was that the main objective of the 1900 Convention was to protect

> the wild animals, birds and fish of Africa [....] The Convention is drawn on the basis that each Power must reserve to itself complete freedom as to the actual administrative measures to be applied in its own possessions, and that the smallest possible interference with legitimate commerce should arise from the proceedings of this Conference [....] [W]e have every reason to hope that it will lead to the immediate issue of Regulations to secure [...] animals [...] now threatened with extinction.[73]

Responding to the French ambassador's complaint concerning why the French-held island of Madagascar had been included in the territorial coverage of the convention, it was important to Salisbury to drive home that "the only objective that Her Majesty's Government have in view in assembling a conference is to discuss, and, if possible, arrive at an agreement on the best methods of preventing the wanton destruction of animal life." Emphasizing that concern over wildlife stood behind the conference, Salisbury added that the island contains unique fauna "which naturalists are anxious to protect."[74]

Reviewing the 1900 London Convention reveals that its most blatant shortcoming was its failure to cover all of continental Africa. Article I of the convention delineated its geographical coverage between the 20th parallel on the north (sub-Saharan Africa) and "on the south by a line following the northern boundary of the German possessions in South-Western Africa," thus leaving out southern Africa.[75] Even at the time of its adoption, the convention's limited coverage, particularly to the south, was acknowledged as a major drawback, apparently the consequence of the ongoing Anglo-Boer War.[76] Article II defined "the most effective means of preserving [. . .] animal life [. . .] within the zone defined in Article I."[77] The first "means," set out in the first four sections of the article, was the "Prohibition of the hunting and destruction" of those animal species listed in the first four schedules of the convention, or other animals as determined by each "Local Government."[78] The article also called for the establishment of reserves "within which it shall be unlawful to hunt, capture or kill any bird or other wild animal." It also established closed seasons and hunting by license holders only; prohibited the use of nets and pitfalls as well as poison ("for the purpose of taking fish"), dynamite, and other explosives; and imposed export duties on hides, skins, horns, and tusks (but not the tusks of elephants).[79] A further precept prohibited "hunting or killing young elephants," backed up by the confiscation of tusks weighing less than 5 kilograms. Reflecting the chronic fear of rinderpest and other diseases that devastated wildlife, Section 12 of Article II called for "preventing the transmission of contagious diseases from domestic animals to wild animals." Article IV directed "the Contracting Parties [. . .] to apply, as far as possible, measures for encouraging the domestication of zebras, of elephants, of ostriches . . ."[80] Domestication was considered a guarantee of the survival of African's wildlife, and Europe's golden goose—the elephant—in particular. Eventually it became clear that the elephant's immense physical size, which required vast quantities of land and food, together with its slow-growing tusks, were insurmountable obstacles to the animal's successful domestication. Five schedules were attached to the 1900 Convention, categorizing fauna species according to an assigned level of protection, ranging from total hunting bans on giraffes, gorillas, and chimpanzees, among other species, to "harmful animals [. . .] which it is desired to reduce the numbers." Listed among "harmful animals" were lions, leopards, and otters.[81]

Although alarm over the decimation of African elephants had driven Germany and Great Britain to create a treaty for its protection, because of the protests of more protectionist European nations against rigorous trade restrictions, the elephant treaty gave surprisingly little protection to the elephant itself. It simply prohibited the hunting or killing of young elephants (or females accompanied by their young), sanctioned with heavy fines and confiscation of ivory weighing less than 5 kilograms.[82] Thus an elephant's fate was decided by the weight of its tusks. The absence of export tariffs on mature ivory tusks was a victory for Portugal, France, and Belgium; these countries had opposed such tariffs as parties to the 1892 Congo Basin Convention, which they had convened to regulate the ivory trade in their colonial territories.[83] Elephants appeared in Schedules II, III, and IV of the 1900 Convention; Schedules II and III prohibited, respectively, the destruction of their young, and the killing of their females when accompanied by their young. Schedule IV addressed animals of which only a limited number could be killed. The elephant did not appear in Schedule I, which gave total protection to the animals it listed, patently because the treaty was intended to protect elephants as objects of a lucrative trade rather than as a species to be protected for its own inherent worth.[84]

Despite recognition of the need for cooperation to stop the illegal ivory trade, and although the major consideration was to create an even playing field, the 1900 Convention did not establish an international regulatory system or institutions to monitor compliance.[85] Further, it was a convention exclusively for European powers; only they had been invited to participate in the plenipotentiary conference. Yet even though the independent African states of Liberia and Ethiopia had been rejected as negotiators and signatories, they were still expected to implement the convention, as were the governments of South African and Boer territories not even included in the geographical coverage of the convention.[86] Great Britain in particular stressed the convention's implementation by all colonial powers. Lord Salisbury urged Arthur Henry Hardinge, the governor of British East Africa, to "arrange with the Governors of German and Italian East Africa for [. . .] [r]egulations enforcing [. . .] the recent Convention."[87] Complying with the request, Hardinge wrote the East German colonial governor, prompting him to enact regulations prohibiting the export of tusks weighing less than 5 kilograms. Forwarding this letter to Salisbury, Hardinge noted that "[i]t is probable that until they [the German and Italian colonial governments] issue regulations similar to ours [. . .] our ivory trade will suffer from the strict application at British ports of the existing Regulations which I am instructing the Customs authorities must now be enforced."[88] Meanwhile the Italians, French, and Portuguese were making excuses about why they had not yet ratified the convention.[89] Yet, displaying its powerful normative effect, although the 1900 Convention never came into force, the years 1900 and 1901 saw a wide sweep of new regulations throughout European colonies (primarily British possessions) and the generation of reports on numbers and species killed.[90] Moreover, by calling on "the High Contracting Parties" to establish reserves "within which it will be unlawful to hunt, capture, or kill any bird or other wild animal," the convention authorized colonial governments to set up protected areas in their territories. Hence the first elephant treaty, the 1900 Convention, set the stage for a colonial conservation institution—national parks—which would be the focus of the second elephant treaty.

Yet despite this nod to the importance of protected areas for conservation efforts, the 1900 London Convention was primarily a hunting convention in acknowledgement of the then-critical threat to African wildlife. Prohibiting traditional African practices such as nets and pitfalls and the use of poison, the convention echoed the European view of Africans as cruel and barbarous hunters.[91] By restricting hunting and modes of hunting, authorizing land enclosures as reserves, and regulating trade, the convention impacted what Africans ate, where and how they lived, and how they sustained themselves.[92] As noted by the commissioner for Uganda,

> I can readily understand a feeling of strong repulsion arising at such barbarous extermination of animal life as it is perpetrated in some regions by fires and drives. But those practices are now driven back to tracts well beyond the range of administrative control [. . .] and there they probably use the same means to exterminate whole villages of human beings, as was done generally throughout these countries before the advent of the Government. Also [. . .] spears and pits are still used by natives to a limited extent to secure game for food and skin wraps. I am sure it would be unwise to exert much force just yet to stop the practice; it will not continue for any great length of time if the sphere of our influence goes on increasing at the present rate.[93]

Gently objecting to the imposition of hunting restrictions on Africans, the commissioner for Uganda strongly believed in the ultimate triumph of the civilizing missions. He was convinced that under British influence, traditional African hunting methods that so dismayed the Europeans were bound to come to an end. The chief justice of the Gold Coast expressed similar sentiments and concerns over the welfare of African populations. When consulted about the establishment of a new game reserve, he pointed out, "The natives depend on game for food and it would not be right to preserve the native fauna at the expense of the native landowners."[94] Displays of sensitivity to Africans' dependence on hunting to obtain basic needs were not isolated incidents. Controversies raged over which group was more culpable for the devastation of fauna—European hunters or African hunters. Arguments that heatedly blamed Africans for the decimation of animals were countered by equally impassioned arguments blaming the Europeans.[95] While many colonial game laws imposed hunting licenses and fees on Africans as well as Europeans, others imposed hunting restrictions exclusively on Europeans. The same was true for game reserves, which had also come under criticism "on agricultural grounds, on economical grounds [and] on the grounds of protection for the natives."[96]

Even as human activity was generally prohibited within the area of reserves, in many reserves Africans were allowed to continue their lives undisturbed, and in at least one case, a game reserve was returned to the Africans.[97] Colonial officials were blamed for non-enforcement of the game laws against Africans, or for enacting laws that simply did not apply to Africans.[98] And most significantly, a few British colonialist administrators were aware that the underlying cause of wildlife loss went much deeper than hunting, and that European colonialism, framed by a vision of "civilizing the natives" with the associated development, was the core of the problem. In his 1903 report on game conditions in Egypt and the Sudan, Lord Cromer noted that warring African tribes, by creating wastelands devoid of human populations, had caused the return and revitalization of wildlife:

> In these devastated areas, the game increased until its numbers were as great as the soil could support. The barbaric power [. . .] is the best game preserver. Legislation can protect game from the rifle, but is powerless to save it from giving way to civilization. The Pax Britannica can never do for African game [. . .] what the zulu impis, the masai moran, the slave raiders [. . .] have done in the past."[99]

Lord Cromer's observation that declines in wildlife populations were a result of the increase in human populations displays recognition and awareness of underlying factors in the loss of wildlife. Hunting as the traditional threat to African fauna was being replaced by a much more insidious threat, not only to Africa but to the rest of the world—habitat loss as a result of encroaching development. By 1931 this process had become sufficiently pronounced for one commentator to prophetically remark,

> The native [...] is being educated and civilized. He is receiving modern medical and sanitary attention which will both diminish infantile mortality and increase the average length of life. All this must bring about a growth in population, spread of cultivation, and wider settlement [....] The result of this on the wild life will be to drive it ever farther afield; and if we look ahead into the far future we must picture a time when the wild life of the continent will exist only where there happens to be a sanctuary.[100]

While the different camps pitted European hunters against African hunters, contesting which group inflicted the most harm, it was colonialism itself that devastated African fauna. European greed was backed up by technologically advanced weapons designed to kill large numbers of game swiftly and accurately from long distances. Subsistence hunting that had existed for millennia had not spurred the massive decimation of African fauna repeatedly described and documented by European travelers. Europeans brought in the rifles, and Europeans boosted the demand for ivory and other animal products. "[W]ho is to blame if it is not the Europeans, who offers rewards to the negroes, and furnishes them with up-to-date arms?"[101]

Yet blaming the Africans for impending and actual extinctions was a critical element of the European colonial ethos in Africa. The need to validate European policy generated new doctrines that globalized biodiversity, obliterating its local scale to disempower local populations. With the scramble for Africa in the last quarter of the nineteenth century, Europeans developed the concept of an "imperial heritage"[102] to implement their civilizing mission, a concept that evolved later in the narrative into the common heritage of humankind. They framed African fauna as an inimitable and unique legacy entrusted to the care of the colonial powers. To fulfill this great trust imposed upon them, Europeans pursued a policy of separating humans from wildlife, made operational through reserves and national parks from which the "uncivilized," "barbarous," and "savage" Africans were barred. To legitimize their racist policy, Europeans adopted the 1900 Convention that "epitomize[d] environmental imperialism and initiated the gradual exclusion of Africans from access to the wildlife resources of their continent."[103] Preserving wildlife for posterity was presented by Europeans as part of the white man's burden in the task he had assumed in civilizing Africa. In other words, African fauna was framed as a global heritage to justify taking it away from local populations, in order to deliver it to Europeans.[104]

Thus the 1900 London Convention, the first territorial conservation convention, was time and space specific to European rule over Africa. It was an agreement of European powers over the fauna of *another* continent. Independent African countries were barred from the negotiations, and "[i]nternationalism was confined to the circle of the 'civilized' European imperial powers."[105] The 1900 Convention exemplifies how Europeans shaped international law to deny Africans legal identity, and specifically to limit their access to their lands and their biological resources, under the guise of the civilizing mission. Unlike sovereign European powers protected by the consent doctrine that required their assent to being bound by international law, Africans had no right of dissent to laws imposed on them by Europeans. The colonial empire had triggered the destruction of African fauna and then devised international agreements in an attempt to clean up the mess that it had made. African fauna never recovered from the impact of colonialism.

A Society for the Empire's Fauna

[T]he character of our endeavour during the next ten years will do much to decide the fate of the wild life of the world. This may sound ambitious, but as some 70 per cent of the larger mammals of the world are in this Empire, the responsibility resting on those who claim its citizenship is not to be disregarded. This Society based as it is in the capital city of the Empire and with its twenty-five years' record of achievements behind, can, it is submitted, claim to be the correlating focus of wild life conservation for the [. . .] colonies [. . . .] [O]ur efforts to enlist the sympathies of our American friends [. . .] will develop into a great co-operative effort between the Anglo-Saxon races [. . .] throughout the civilized world. — *"Report of the Executive Committee,"* Journal of the Society for the Preservation of the Fauna of the Empire, *1930*[106]

Beyond institutionalizing what would become widely held conservation policies, the 1900 London Convention helped to launch international conservation organizations. The need to track its implementation signaled a legitimate entry point, and the challenge was taken up by the Society for the Preservation of the Fauna of the Empire (SPFE).[107] Established in response to British concern for the nature of *other* lands, SPFE deserves the title "earliest *international* conservation organization." It was founded in 1903 by Edward

North Buxton, who had gained national prominence as an activist in the movement against public land enclosures.[108] Most significantly, Buxton was an avid big-game hunter who had traveled extensively in Africa, eyewitnessing wanton and rampant hunting of African game. Alarmed by the destruction, and expanding his environmental advocacy from local issues to international ones, he established the new society as a counterforce. The particular crisis that triggered his initiative was the proposal permitting British colonial officials to hunt in the Blue Nile Reserve in Sudan, which meant the end of this fauna-rich area as a protected reserve. Strongly objecting to violation of the sanctity of Africa's reserves, Buxton organized a petition against the government plan signed by prominent aristocrats, colonial administrators, members of Parliament, industrialists, authors, and scientists.[109] With the success of this petition, Buxton convinced its signatories to continue their work for British colonial fauna by organizing on a permanent basis.[110]

From its beginnings, SPFE mobilized around a powerful membership of the ruling elite.[111] The first official encounter between the government and the new society took place in February 1905 with the colonial secretary Lord Lyttelton, who would shortly become an honorary member of SPFE.[112] The organization raised its major concerns over African wildlife and politely complained about lack of information on its status, particularly in West Africa.[113] In the context of a meeting between the British Empire's highest colonial official and a newly established *non*governmental organization, the encounter had a remarkable outcome. Disclosing SPFE's powerful influence, Lyttelton forwarded the society's demands for information to colonial administrators, and requested reports on the status of game in their respective territories, together with lists of species. Reponses started to reach London, and the Colonial Office forwarded them to SPFE, asking for feedback.[114] As a result, a further meeting took place in June 1906, in preparation for which—and in an astute political move—SPFE prepared its own report on the status of wildlife in Africa, drawing on data received from colonial administrators.[115]

By setting in motion this exchange of correspondence between London and colonial governments, SPFE succeeded in generating information that would entrench its status as a highly professional organization. Its ability to acquire, process, and use information, and wildlife data in particular, allowed it to develop a reputation for expertise on African wildlife. Surging ahead in establishing its name and reputation, SPFE gained recognition as a scientific advisor to governments. In 1919 King Albert of Belgium turned to SPFE for advice on setting up national parks to protect mountain gorillas in present-day Zaire and Rwanda, eventually protecting almost the entire habitat.[116] Working within a powerful network composed of like-minded members of Britain's ruling classes who shared concern over African fauna, SPFE's activists were the perfect insiders. Direct lobbying of top colonial administrators defined the organization's key working method, brought to a high level of expertise by lobbyists who were themselves government officials. In addition, SPFE drew on its own members who were also members of Parliament to raise government queries on African wildlife issues.[117] The society was continuing the legacy of Alfred Newton in combining tactics for advocacy and activism, together with scientific expertise, and innovatively using international law as a key component of its policy.

The expanding concern of conservationists beyond their own national borders was not limited to Great Britain. Swiss scientist Paul Sarasin was widely respected and recognized as a founder of the international conservation movement. Similar to other leaders in this movement, Sarasin began by promoting national conservation efforts, and establishing the Swiss League for the Protection of Nature in 1906 and the Swiss National Park in the Engadine in 1909. Beyond his concern for the fauna and flora of Switzerland, Sarasin envisioned a network of national conservation organizations coordinated by an international governmental body to achieve "global protection of nature."[118]

Sarasin distinguished between national and international protection of nature within the colonial context of his time. While European and other sovereign countries used national laws to protect their own natural environments, colonial possessions and other non-sovereign entities fell under the care of international law. To address these cases, Sarasin initiated the Advisory Commission for International Protection of Nature, the first intergovernmental organization for nature conservation.[119] With the death of the elderly Sarasin in 1929, the torch passed to Peter van Tienhoven, a Dutch scientist and a leading figure in the conservation movement during the first half of the twentieth century. He also established both national and international organizations and advocated international cooperation and conventions. Inspired by Sarasin, van Tienhoven conceived of a network of regional conventions ultimately evolving into a world convention for nature protection.[120] Drawing from their writings, international conservation law was created by European countries to both exploit and protect the biological resources of their colonial possessions. This law had no application to the biodiversity of the European metropole protected by national laws. International cooperation for biodiversity started out as *colonial* cooperation for nature conservation, forged by a few powerful nations running their empires from Europe.[121]

Colonialism shaped the thinking of both Sarasin and van Tienhoven, yet in a diametrically opposed manner. As a citizen of non-colonial Switzerland, Sarasin was openly critical, accusing colonialism of the "ransacking of Earth's riches and her creatures which, up to that time, had been living in a seclusion that protected their happy existence."

> A single species, man, is driving animal life everywhere with speed into hiding places [. . . .] Wherever the white race intruded upon such a scene we may hear the cry: "Ave Caesar, morituri te salutant." [. . .] I call to mind the fate of the inhabitants of Tasmania [. . .] who after 70 years after colonization has become extinct to the very last individual [. . . .] [A]ll those races have to be protected who die out as soon as they come into contact with European civilization [. . .] which led to the melancholy words of such a native: "we want to die out."[122]

In contrast, the Dutch van Tienhoven firmly positioned his vision of international conservationism within the colonial milieu of his day. Discussing the move from Brussels to Amsterdam of the organization he headed, the International Organization for the Protection of Nature (IOPN), established in 1928, van Tienhoven proposed as its new headquarters Amsterdam's Colonial Institute, "which is the real place for such an office to find its domicile." Responding to a Swiss proposal to move its offices to Switzerland instead, van Tienhoven remarked, "I don't think this practical, for Switzerland has no colonies."[123] Yet despite their polarized positions on colonialism, Sarasin and van Tienhoven shared a vision of an international conservation organization that ultimately materialized in 1948 as the IUCN.

Demonstrating the bonds with their British colleagues, both Sarasin and van Tienhoven were primarily concerned over the decimation of African fauna. Sarasin expressly wrote that one of the tasks of what would become the Advisory Commission for International Protection of Nature would be to "save the mammalian fauna of Africa."[124] Van Tienhoven's organization also focused on African fauna, issuing a series of publications on nature conservation legislation of African colonial territories.[125] Van Tienhoven argued that international cooperation stemmed from "[t]he menace of seeing certain large species of the African and Asiatic fauna disappear."[126]

Thematically wending its way throughout the narrative is threatened African fauna as the catalyst driving international conservation conventions. As noted by van Tienhoven, the threats to colonial African and Asian fauna drove international cooperation; and as argued by Sarasin, independent sovereign states could use their own national law to take care of their biodiversity. International law was for the "international" fauna of Africa. The shared beliefs of European conservationists in international law as the savior of African fauna converged in an updated and revised international convention, replacing the 1900 London Convention that never came into force.

A Second Elephant Treaty

> If you could call the animals of Africa into council and say to them, "My friends, do not go and eat the settlers' crops, because if you do you will be in for trouble," an agreement might be reached which would be all to the good, but of course you cannot do that [. . . .] But this proposal to set up National Parks is a measure of practical politics and can be carried out without interfering with the progress of a colony, the interests of the colonists, and not least, those of the indigenous natives.[127]
>
> — *C. W. Hobley*, Geographical Journal, *1931*

The earliest glimmers of the future London Convention Relative to the Preservation of Flora and Fauna in Their Natural State (the 1933 London Convention)[128] surface in a 1928 letter from the secretary of state for the colonies to the governor of Tanganyika. The secretary informed the governor that Captain K. F. Caldwell (member of the ubiquitous SPFE) would be part of a fact-finding mission on game conditions in the African colonies, in preparation for a new international agreement deemed to replace the 1900 London Convention.[129] In 1930, apparently in a separate project but also in anticipation of the new agreement, SPFE sent the respected physician, explorer, and naturalist Major R. W. G. Hingston to undertake a report on Africa's wildlife that would eventually bear his name.[130] Hingston visited Northern Rhodesia, Nyasaland, Tanganyika, Kenya, and Uganda, and held discussions with government officials and "representatives of public opinion." In his report, published in 1931 under the title *Proposed British National Parks for Africa*, Hingston isolated four threats to Africa's wildlife: farming, trade, hunting, and the "menace of disease" carried by the tsetse fly "that carries nagana to cattle and sleeping-sickness to human beings." Tsetse fly disease provoked demands for wholesale extermination of large mammals blamed as main carriers of the disease, resulting in the massive destruction of African wildlife.¹³¹ In response to these threats, Hingston called for the establishment of national parks as the critical element in saving Africa's endangered wildlife, operating as the separation mechanism between them and human populations. Reflecting the position of SPFE, Hingston was a firm believer in the role of parks in conservation efforts to "ensure the perpetual preservation of the fauna of these territories without undue interference with native rights or economic development."¹³²

Although the term *national park* appears contradictory to colonial rule in Africa, US national parks — acclaimed for their perceived success in preserving the country's wildlife and natural landscapes — were sources of inspiration for European conservationists. Yellowstone National Park became a global icon, serving as a model of US resourcefulness in protecting its unique nature, and duplicated in other lands. Yet these celebrated American experiences of nature had a darker and more menacing side, exposed by the US government's deployment of the army to evict indigenous populations from the parks. Banished from the vast landscapes of their homelands, they were herded into reservations. Signifying a global trend, the exclusion of indigenous populations from national parks was manifest in European conservation policy in Africa.

Hingston set out to impose the US model on colonial Africa. While upholding existing game reserves and their value as wildlife sanctuaries, he criticized their lack of legal status; accelerated development plus the demand for farming and grazing lands were making these reserves vulnerable to land-use changes. Aiming for a stronger institution, Hingston called for parks anchored by acts of Parliament.

The driving fear behind the momentum for national parks was species extinction: "[U]nless vigorous and adequate precautions be taken several of the largest mammals of Africa will within the next two or three decades become extinct." Echoing the scientist and early environmental activist Alfred Russel Wallace, who had urged action to prevent species extinctions almost a century earlier, Hingston argued that failure to prevent extinctions would represent abuse of a "trust and future generations will judge us accordingly."¹³³ Blaming humans for the decimation of African wildlife, Hingston argued that "the human life and the wild life must be separated permanently and completely [. . . .] [I]f the animal life is to be preserved, it must be segregated in a sanctuary."¹³⁴

Hingston was particularly alarmed about rapidly declining elephant populations. He proposed upgrading the Selous game reserve in present-day Tanzania to a national park, stating outright that the object in view in this proposal is the preservation of the African elephant. The elephant is the most harassed of all African mammals and its numbers, since the introduction of European firearms, have probably decreased more rapidly than those of any other species. The onslaught on the herds has been tremendous in the past, and there is little likelihood of diminution in the future. [. . .] It is obvious that some kind of action is necessary if the elephant is to be checked in that downward path along which trade drives all its victims to oblivion. The Selous Reserve of Tanganyika is at present a great stronghold of elephants.[135]

In contrast to other parks that were intended to sustain themselves by tourism, Hingston argued that because of the elephant's precarious status, "[t]hat intention does not apply to this proposal, which is made solely with a view to animal conservation. The site could never be a park for tourists."[136]

Hingston's proposal for establishing national parks reflected the broadly held consensus that preventing species extinctions demanded a policy of disengagement between humans and wildlife. Though they clearly contributed to protecting against extinctions of African wildlife, national parks kindled deep resentment among Africans because of the eviction of local populations from the areas enclosed. Despite the harsh consequences of this policy on local populations, and the anger and bitterness that it provoked, Hingston's report promoting "apartheid parks,"[137] for wildlife only, led directly to the 1933 Convention, crafted primarily for their establishment.

Discussions for a new convention were held at the July 1931 International Congress for the Protection of Nature in Paris, organized by the French Museum of Natural History.[138] Fourteen European countries participated, as well as representatives of "private societies." The British delegation was led by such a society—SPFE. Priding itself on professionalism and expertise in African wildlife, SPFE had sponsored Hingston's work in Africa and subsequently used his report to convince other European colonial powers to negotiate a new convention.[139] The Earl of Onslow, member of the House of Lords and president of SPFE, headed the British delegation. In his autobiography, Onslow recalls delivering the prime minister's personal message, launching with a testimony to the 1900 Convention.[140] Testifying to its powerful normative significance, Onslow noted that although the convention had never come into force, its provisions generally had been implemented by British colonial governments. He argued that a new convention was warranted, not only because technically the 1900 Convention had been valid for only fifteen years, but because of the need to extend its territorial coverage to the entire African continent. Moreover, more effective provisions were required "to control the traffic in ivory, rhino horn and other trophies, the use of motors and aeroplanes in hunting," while "provisions for the formation of permanent sanctuaries are desirable." Echoing colonial administrators who had tackled identical challenges thirty years earlier, Onslow articulated the British government's position that a new convention was the most effective means of securing international cooperation to halt the devastation of Africa's fauna. Recalling the ivory trade as the dominant issue driving the 1900 Convention, he reiterated this argument:

> It may be very difficult for a single Government to take effective steps to preserve this species in the territories under its control, if the inhabitants of neighbouring territories are not subject to similar restrictions. In these circumstances the co-operation of the Governments of all territories where the species is found, and in some cases the co-operation of the Governments of the countries where the product which is the cause of the undue destruction is principally consumed, may be an essential condition of really effective action. Thus international action is required to supplement the effects of individual Governments.[141]

Raising an argument remarkably evocative of present-day awareness of the critical role of ecosystem services and biodiversity for local populations, Onslow stressed the welfare of native populations as a key element in nature conservation. "The growth of knowledge has shown that in the less developed parts of the world the welfare of the native populations often largely depends on the maintenance of the delicate balance of Nature. For this reason also the protection of nature is a question in which Governments are deeply interested."[142]

Onslow's address was apparently well received, for the 1931 congress adopted a resolution calling on governments to negotiate a new convention.[143] The following year, Great Britain established the Preparatory Committee for the International Conference for the Protection of the Fauna and the Flora, chaired by Onslow and with representatives from the Foreign, Colonial, and Dominion Offices, the Economic Advisory Council, Kew Gardens, the London Zoo, the British Natural History Museum, and SPFE. The committee drafted proposals and texts for a new convention, drawing on Hingston's report and his recommendation of national parks as the key strategy for saving African wildlife. The *Report of the Preparatory Committee* was circulated to African colonial governments for their comments.[144] Reaping key benefits from an overlapping membership, Onslow was in an ideal position to promote SPFE policy and turn it into official government policy. Not only was he president of SPFE and a member of the House of Lords, he also held the powerful office of deputy speaker of the House and served as chair of various committees. He had family connections to the Colonial Office: his father had served as governor of New Zealand and undersecretary of state for India. His sister was married to Lord Halifax, Viceroy of India, who in 1938 became foreign secretary. Through Onslow's connections, SPFE continued to gain access to the highest levels of government, allowing it, as Roderick Neumann has argued, to "virtually write colonial park and wildlife policies."[145] The ramifications became clear at the plenipotentiary International Conference for the Protection of the Fauna and Flora of Africa, held in London in 1933. Onslow, once again head of the British delegation, served as chair of the conference. In his biography, as he describes the work surrounding the convention, it is not easily apparent which hat Onslow is wearing, and whether "we" refers to the government, to SPFE, or to both:

> We decided that we should confine our efforts to Africa as we did not wish to overload the work of the Conference. We then had to consult all the African Colonial Governments and they took a long time to answer. Then we drafted a convention to serve as a basis for discussion [. . . .] In due course all the delegates arrived. I became Chairman [. . .] we all worked hard for more than a week. [. . .] In due course the convention was ratified by all the Powers except Abyssinia, and serious efforts were made to carry it out.[146]

The text of the second elephant treaty, the 1933 London Convention, is distinct from the first in that it covered all of Africa. In addition, rather than focusing on hunting—and expressly reflecting SPFE policy of protected areas for African fauna—the treaty emphasized the establishment of national parks as an upgrade of the reserves of the 1900 Convention. Article 3 committed each contracting government to "exploring the possibility" of establishing national parks and strict nature reserves within two years of the convention coming into force. Article 4 required each "Contracting Government" to undertake measures for "[t]he control of all white or native settlements in national parks" so as not to disturb the fauna and flora. Each was also required to establish buffer zones around the parks and reserves within which hunting would be permitted "under the control of the authorities." Displaying the drafters' sense of urgency in establishing protected areas, a notoriously lengthy process, Article 7 obligated member states "as measures preliminary and supplementary to the establishment of national parks or strict natural reserves," to enclose land as reserves out of bounds for hunting.

Article 8 addressed listings of protected species. Instead of the five lists of fauna species annexed to the 1900 Convention, the 1933 Convention cut them down to two — species in Class A under total protection, and species in Class B "whilst not requiring such rigorous protection as those mentioned in Class A shall not be hunted, killed, or captured, even by natives, except under special license."[147] The African elephant was listed in Class A, but with a caveat: "Note: this species to be included in Class A only in respect of specimens of which the tusks do not exceed 5 kilograms in weight each." Article 9 required each contracting party to "control and regulate [. . .] the import and export [. . .] and the manufacture of articles from, trophies as defined in paragraph 8 of the present article." Ivory required special markings for identification, along with its weight, all of which were recorded in the "certificate of lawful export." Article 10 prohibited the use of "motor vehicles or aircraft" in hunting, the use of fire to surround animals, the use of poison or explosives, flares, "nets, pits, or enclosures, gins, traps or snares, or of set guns and missiles containing explosives for hunting animals." The convention came into force three years after its adoption.

The 1933 Convention and its bonds with SPFE become the leitmotif of the story. The society was the mastermind behind the second elephant treaty, capturing the government's traditional role in international law making. By mobilizing around the ruling elite and creating a power base, SPFE undertook a dominant role in its short and successful negotiation proceedings, and then went on to create an early model for implementation of an international convention by an NGO.[148] Yet its role in the narrative is that of a *colonialist* organization. It was actively dictating British colonial conservation policy in Africa, discriminatory of Africans. Identifying strongly with the civilizing mission, SPFE supported Great Britain's self-imposed role of world trustee for African fauna, which it also saw as an irreplaceable heritage.[149] The power to set the international agenda by initiating, drafting, and promoting the 1933 Convention cut through conventionally held definitions of actor identity. Although international agreements have traditionally served as the access point for NGOs to the international arena, SPFE's role in international law was unique because of its dominancy. More than a technical advisor, the society's identity merged with that of the government in executing what is deemed an exclusive government authority—the making of international law.

The society regarded the 1933 Convention as a source of power for diverse and seemingly contradictory objectives, which included ensuring ample numbers of African big game for its hunting members, protecting African fauna through the establishment of national parks, and particularly, nurturing its own reputation. By successfully drafting and negotiating the convention, SPFE became known as an *effective* organization. Moreover, it opened a window of opportunity to network with other international nature conservation organizations.[150] The convention became a hub of activity around which conservationists and conservation organizations congregated, both as a normative source of inspiration and an instrumental policy statement, and from which they launched further conventions. These organizations become enthusiastic supporters of SPFE's work in international law, their shared bond being the weight they gave international law as an instrumental component in their strategies.[151]

SPFE played a crucial part in promoting other international conventions subsequent to the 1933 London Convention. The society was in the midst of planning a conference for a regional convention for Asia in 1939 when World War II broke out.[152] SPFE was the inspiration behind the 1940 Convention on Nature Protection and Wild Life Preservation in the Western Hemisphere (Western Hemisphere Convention) and played a behind-the-scenes role in its design. It also developed a vision of a "world convention for nature" that captured the imagination of others and Harold Coolidge in particular, and became a core theme in the founding of IUCN.[153] Operating today under the name Fauna and Flora International (FFI), the organization rightly describes itself as "the world's first international conservation organization." Discarding its colonial roots, FFI's vision today is of "[a] sustainable future for the planet, where biodiversity is conserved by those who live closest to it, supported by the global community," a complete turnaround from its original policy of establishing protected areas to exclude the "natives."[154]

Coolidge and the American Committee

Shifting now from colonial Europe to the United States, in the parade of remarkable conservationists who march through this narrative, Harold Jefferson Coolidge stands out for the depth of his dedication to the nascent international conservation movement, the breadth of his accomplishments, and his endless energy for new and innovative enterprises in global conservation. Coolidge left a legacy of international organizations and conventions as well as groundbreaking projects that have become hallmarks of modern conservationism, exemplified by the establishment worldwide of national parks and other protected areas, and globally recognized lists of threatened and endangered species. He had a finger in every pie and accompanied the international conservation movement in its passage throughout most of the twentieth century.[155]

Coolidge came to international nature conservation through a fascination with African fauna. From 1926 to 1927, as a graduate student at Harvard in zoology, he participated in a Harvard Medical School expedition to central Africa. Allotted the task of bringing home a mountain gorilla as a specimen for the Harvard zoological museum, he did so successfully, writing a detailed account of an agonizingly cruel pursuit and killing of the terrorized gorilla.[156] In 1928 while studying at Cambridge University, and most likely inspired by T. Gilbert Pearson, president of the newly founded International Committee for Bird Protection (and perhaps by Sarasin and van Tienhoven as well), Coolidge came up with the an idea for an international organization for nature conservation. In a letter to Pearson, he proposed "an International Committee for the Protection of the Flora and Fauna of the World and for the Advancement of Science." Coolidge envisioned an organization composed of leading scientists concerned with species of flora and fauna, mandated as "an information clearinghouse, [to] fund fieldwork, [to] lobby for the creation of national parks around the world."[157]

The backdrop to Coolidge's idea was the wave of US international conservation activities during that period. In the first decades of the twentieth century, the US government entered into a series of international agreements to protect migratory species. To save the North Pacific fur seal from the verge of extinction, the United States, Canada, Japan, and Russia signed the 1911 Convention for the Preservation and Protection of Fur Seals, which banned the pursuit of seals on the high seas.[158] The 1916 Convention for the Protection of Migratory Birds, signed by the United States and Great Britain on behalf of Canada, was a response to escalating extinctions of migratory bird species of the Northern Hemisphere.[159] A more direct influence on Coolidge was the prevalence of African big-game hunters in the Boone and Crockett Club, of which he too was a member, the elite association made famous by the arch big-game hunter, President Theodore Roosevelt.[160] Mounting US interest in protecting African fauna was also generated by SPFE's growing contacts with American associations, for fund-raising purposes in particular. The British conservation organization naturally gravitated to the Boone and Crockett Club, a partner in the passion for African game hunting. In his oral history of the American Committee, Coolidge recalled that "many members of the Boone and Crockett and others who had hunted, photographed or made scientific collections in various parts of Africa [. . .] [were] crystallized into action by the visit of Mr. C. W. Hobley, secretary for the Society for the Preservation of the Fauna of the Empire who came to this country in 1930."[161]

During his visit, Hobley succeeded in raising 1,200 pounds sterling from the Boone and Crockett Club.[162] His visit must have been a memorable event for both the British and the Americans; the Earl of Onslow, the aristocratic president of SPFE, mentioned it in his 1944 biography, and Coolidge recalled it more than fifty years later.[163] Another visitor was Major John Burnham, who gave a talk to the club on the alarming decline in numbers of African fauna. A British explorer recently returned from Africa, Burnham deplored the ravages inflicted on African game animals by hunters, and urged Americans to become involved in African game preservation.[164] These British visitors sparked a fire in the belly of Boone and Crockett members for international activities and in Africa in particular, culminating in the founding of the American Committee for International Wild Life Protection (the American Committee).[165] Displaying the bonds between these early conservation organizations, Coolidge credits SPFE with the founding of the American Committee, noting that "this committee was greatly stimulated by the requests from the British Fauna Society because by geographical accident, some 70% of the important large surviving land mammals of the world were found [. . .] within British territory, and the Fauna Society fully realized that it was too big a problem to handle alone."[166]

Two members of the Boone and Crockett Club — Coolidge and John Phillips — were the creative force behind the new organization. They set it up as a coalition of US institutions and organizations concerned about the loss of species in lands beyond the United States, establishing a committee for "international wildlife protection."[167] The committee's founders were all familiar with African wildlife as hunters or scientists or both, and its work focused on the continent's fauna.[168] Links between the American Committee and SPFE were strong, and Sarasin's vision of international networking among national organizations was becoming a reality. Expanding its network beyond Great Britain, the American Committee became a member of IOPN, the Brussels-based international umbrella organization under the leadership of Peter van Tienhoven. Similar to the committee's relationships with the British organization, its relationships with IOPN were based on personal associations between Coolidge, Phillips, van Tienhoven, and other European conservationists.[169] The impact of the Europeans on their American colleagues was momentous. Phillips, exposed to key European conservationists as an observer to the 1933 London Convention negotiations, developed a theory of international cooperation for wildlife protection as a "world concern."[170] Speaking at the 1936 North American Wildlife Conference, Phillips explained the reasoning behind the establishment of the American Committee, displaying the influence of European conservation thought:

> At this point you may well ask why waste precious time and dollars on some forlorn hope in Africa or Asia, where the United States has no possessions, or vital interests of any sort [. . . .] As Paul Sarasin said so beautifully many years ago a species once gone can never be replaced and its loss is a crime against world civilization [. . . .] In some colonies belonging to European nations there are well-regulated game departments; in others almost no sentiment [. . .] curiously enough, there seems to be less resentment at a suggestion from an unprejudiced foreign source, like our American committee, than from the colonial home office which controls the destiny of distant colonial residents.[171]

Coolidge would enlarge upon Phillips's philosophy of international cooperation for nature. He developed the concept of international trusteeship imposed on "nations in the forefront of civilization" for all of humankind, swiftly leading him to a world convention for nature.

> The perpetuation of wild life of the world is a duty which nations in the forefront of civilization cannot ignore [. . . .] It is an international obligation [. . . .] The London Convention [. . .] has shown the importance of international cooperation for the protection of an international fauna [. . . .] We are trustees for the generations of the future.[172]

The 1933 London Convention would become a dominant influence on Coolidge's career, and it launched his lifelong fascination with international law as a mechanism for protecting nature. News of the convention's pending negotiations, spearheaded by SPFE, made Coolidge anxious to have the American Committee involved in this instance of international law making. He immediately plunged into the roiling activities surrounding the proposed convention by contributing scientific data: "Our studies on African wild life protection have contributed to the preparation of the important African treaty that is now being put into final form by an international conference at London."[173] Coolidge also made sure that Phillips attended the negotiations as a US observer and representative of the American Committee. Though he himself did not attend, Coolidge defined his role in the convention "as a briefing officer" for Phillips. Fifty years later, Coolidge still considered the 1933 London Convention "one of the most important international convention documents."[174]

John Phillips's participation in the negotiations, and particularly in the scientific-technical committees where he was charged with drawing up the lists of species, exposed him to the complexities of wildlife management. An outcome was a challenging new project for the American Committee promoted by Phillips and Coolidge — the vast, complex, and groundbreaking task of compiling a global inventory of species. The work was eventually published in the 1940s as the Harper-Allen Report, containing two volumes: Glover M. Allen's work *Extinct and Vanishing Mammals of the Western Hemisphere*, and Francis Harper's work *Extinct and Vanishing Mammals of the Old World*.[175] This landmark report became Coolidge's inspiration for the IUCN Survival Service Commission (today the Species Survival Commission) and the Red List of threatened species, globally recognized as international standards.[176] Another outcome of the American Committee's participation in the 1933 Convention was the beginning of its involvement in international conventions, under the direct influence of SPFE.[177] It was surely an intriguing experience for Phillips to observe the tactics of an organization similar to his own performing the extraordinary task of multilateral negotiations for an international convention, a role traditionally reserved for governments. A few years later, Coolidge would duplicate for the American Committee the role undertaken by SPFE in creating the 1933 London Convention, this time as the key architect for a convention for the Americas.

With the establishment of the American Committee in 1930 by Coolidge and other US conservationists, organized international conservationism expanded from Europe to the United States. The next step was to bring to the Americas an international convention for nature conservation based on the work of British colleagues.

An American Convention

> Do you remember you came to see me one day when you were in England a year or two ago and I mentioned the possibility of the American Government initiating the same kind of conference in Washington to deal with the subject in America, and I gathered you were not unfavourable to the idea. If, subsequent to the conference next year, there were European and American conferences, there would be a complete system of protection throughout the whole world.
> —*Earl of Onslow to John Phillips*[178]

Returning from a 1936 trip to Great Britain and talks with SPFE members on future conservation conventions, John Phillips eagerly set out to create an American version. He used his connection with his brother, a highly placed State Department official, to test the US position on a convention for the Americas.[179] Initial approval was tentatively given, and the result was State Department approval to launch what would formally be a US government initiative. The venue was the Eighth International Conference of American States, held in 1938 in Lima, Peru (the Lima Conference), under the auspices of the Pan-American Union (today the Organization of American States [OAS]). To obtain support of prominent scientists for the initiative, in October 1938 Coolidge turned to Alexander Wetmore, assistant secretary of the Smithsonian Institution, sharing his vision for the new convention. In a recurring theme, Coolidge raised the connection with the prestigious 1933 London Convention:

> Our Executive Committee [of the American Committee] has been most anxious to initiate international cooperation in the New World for the promotion of national parks and game reserves if possible, along somewhat the pattern of the London Convention for African Nature Protection.

Feeling compelled to persuade Wetmore, he added that

> Lord Onslow urged Dr. Phillips to have our Committee take the initiative for the International organization of future nature protection in the New World along those same lines that he has done for Africa and will shortly do for Asia. We certainly do not want the English to come over here and try and set up our convention for us![180]

Two months later, catalyzed by Coolidge and the American Committee, the Lima Conference adopted a resolution calling for a nature conservation convention for the Americas, the future 1940 Convention on Nature Protection and Wild Life Preservation in the Western Hemisphere.[181] Theodore Roosevelt Jr., the son of the former president and an avid if much-criticized conservationist, was a founding member of the American Committee and its representative at the conference. In his reports from the conference, Roosevelt described the underlying politics and the US delegation's warnings against lobbying Latin American delegations, enlarging on the United States' key fear of putting Latin American countries in "a poor light."[182] Roosevelt's wariness about impinging on Latin American sensitivities over the poor state of their own natural environments sprang from the American Committee's anxiety about antagonizing Latin American countries and endangering the convention negotiations. In a March 1939 letter from Coolidge to the director of the Pan-American Union, Coolidge discussed his article on international wildlife protection that he hoped to publish in the Pan-American bulletin. Ever the political animal, he wondered whether adding a quote by former president Theodore Roosevelt might be offensive to the United States' South American neighbors. Displaying NGO sensitivities to the political sensibilities of states, Coolidge feared ruffling the feathers of potential signatories to the proposed convention.[183]

T. Gilbert Pearson, chair of the International Committee for Bird Preservation, had been warned by Coolidge not to flaunt American dominance over the convention negotiations during a work trip to South America: "Regarding the Lima Conference and the proposed Convention, I shall certainly be carefully guarded to give out no impression that I am traveling in the interest of that undertaking."[184] Alexander Wetmore, who through Coolidge's persuasive lobbying had been appointed the official US representative for the negotiations, also displayed a heightened sense of political correctness. He objected to incorporating reporting obligations in the convention, wary that they might be construed as an insidious means of tracking Latin American implementation of the convention.[185] A major effort was made to prevent other countries from thinking that "this is one more case of a putup job by interests in the United States."[186] Coolidge went so far as to suggest to Wetmore that during the negotiations he "spin" criticism of the convention to create the impression that it was not a totally US maneuver.[187] Wetmore agreed to Coolidge's suggestion.[188] Coolidge did his utmost to avoid controversy, probably the reason for excluding the hotly controversial issue of fisheries from the coverage of the convention — as the sacrifice for peace.[189] By August 1939 Coolidge had sent the director of the Pan-American Union a preliminary draft of the convention for his comments, and by December an official draft had been distributed to governments.[190] Coolidge's connection with Wetmore bore fruit: in July 1940, Wetmore informed Coolidge that in response to the State Department's request for the Smithsonian Institution's official position on the issue, he heartily recommended that the United States sign the new Western Hemisphere Convention.[191]

The year 1938 marked a high point for international conventions for nature. A conference convened in London that year reviewed the implementation of the 1933 London Convention, which had come into force in 1936, and adopted a resolution to negotiate a similar convention for Asia and Australia in 1939.[192] The Lima Conference called for negotiating what would eventually become the 1940 Western Hemisphere Convention. In August 1938 Henry Maurice, secretary of SPFE, wrote to Coolidge that "we hope to have a conference next year to discuss the question of fauna preservation in the East, and in Australasia, and there is a general idea that these conferences — that is the African conference and the Asiatic one [. . .] may lead to what we may call a world convention."[193]

Yet European conservationists' plans were obliterated by World War II. The 1939 Asiatic Conference never materialized, and in a letter dated October 4, 1939, Maurice wrote to Coolidge expressing his disappointment at its cancelation. He further related that the executive committee of SPFE had decided to "formulate a programme for after the War, so as to be ready to take action at the first possible moment. That discussion naturally led to consideration of our relations with your Committee and with the USA."[194] With war in Europe, hopes for new conventions were pinned on the Americans. As noted by van Tienhoven, congratulating Coolidge for his work on the new Western Hemisphere Convention,

> It would be an important step forward if North and South America could accept a convention for protection on the base of the African convention which is working very satisfactorily. It is highly regrettable that the English government does not succeed in bringing forward a convention for Asia and Australia which was their intention for 1940, but the hopeless political situation in Europe prevents the working out of such a convention in this year.[195]

The "torch" for international nature conservation passed to the American Committee.[196] With the war bringing an effective halt to European-based activities, including the cancellation of the 1939 Asiatic Conference, Coolidge took the opportunity to ram forward the new convention for the Americas.[197] He wanted to achieve the prestigious and high-ranking international status enjoyed by SPFE by duplicating its work on the 1933 London Convention. Similar to the British organization's powerful links with the British government, the American Committee enjoyed influential connections with the US government, easing its entry into the process.[198] Coolidge made sure that the American Committee took the lead at all the critical stages of the Western Hemisphere Convention. He was not only involved in every facet of the process of this round of international law making, he was making the calls. He drafted the convention as head of a committee that he had himself manipulated into being. Recalling the 1933 Convention, which he greatly admired, he crafted the new convention for the Americas as the legal framework for the establishment of national parks and other protected areas. He drove the process forward by dealing with comments and other responses to the draft and making the necessary changes.[199]

Yet despite the fact that the war neutralized much of SPFE's work, the society still attempted to exert a measure of control over the new American convention. A turf war developed over the British organization's insistence on extending membership in the convention to European nations with territorial possessions in the Western Hemisphere. Coolidge firmly resisted.[200] He admitted that from "a faunistic point of view" it was preferable to include "the entire land area" in the convention. But justifying his refusal, he pointed out that as an exclusively American agreement, the Western Hemisphere Convention would be implemented by the Pan-American Union, implying that the inclusion of European nations as members would require new institutions. He also argued that adding European-held territories to the area of the convention would delay its coming into force.[201] Coolidge might have regarded the British organization as a competitor in the prestigious art of international law making, and may have wanted to ensure that credit for the new agreement would be awarded to the American Committee. He possibly feared an SPFE takeover of the convention by acquiring entry through British possessions in the Western Hemisphere, thus gaining a new power base for expansion of its own activities. Based on the British organization's greater experience in crafting and negotiating international conventions, Coolidge was conceivably worried that once SPFE had gained entry to drafting and negotiating the new convention, it would take control of the process, ousting the American Committee from the coveted role.

The Western Hemisphere Convention's territorial coverage became a hotly contested issue between Coolidge and European conservationists, particularly the British. Coolidge declined Onslow's suggestion to include Great Britain and Holland as member states in the convention.[202] European conservationists were annoyed by Coolidge's refusal, and the issue did not fade away.[203] Even after the convention's adoption, Onslow was still blaming Coolidge for the exclusion of European-held territories:

> [M]ay I express the regret which I share with a good many people on this side that all the American States are not included, and that some of them did not attend the Conference. Canada, Greenland (which, I suppose, we must reckon as part of America), Honduras, the West Indian islands, the Guianas and the Falkland Islands are omitted. I imagine that adherences to the Convention are possible, but [. . .] would [. . .] be more likely to materialise if representatives of the various countries I have mentioned were [. . .] included.[204]

In their pursuit of conservation conventions, both SPFE and the American Committee assumed government roles. Although international law making is traditionally recognized as an area of exclusive authority of sovereign states, the two organizations blithely ignored the problem, squabbling over the territories to be included in the convention. A reminder that they were *not* governments was Onslow's announcement of his intention to bring the issue of joining the new convention before the British government, in the "hope of our Society that it will be possible to adhere on behalf of the British Government and the British-American possessions to the Convention."[205] On the American side, apparently the US government *preferred* that the American Committee take the lead in promoting the Western Hemisphere Convention. In response to Wetmore's criticism that the initial resolution to promote the convention had been submitted by the American Committee instead of the government, Coolidge replied that "it was suggested to us that steps in this direction might be more acceptable if the original suggestion came from our committee rather than directly from an official source."[206]

The convention was finalized in 1940. Though a convention for the Americas, it was deeply rooted in colonial Europe. Despite the turf wars, the convention evolved from the close collaboration and cooperation between the American Committee and SPFE. Influenced by British colonialism under which he had developed as an international conservationist, Coolidge saw the American

Committee's role as part of the civilizing mission, imposing Western norms for nature protection on South America. In a letter attached to a copy of the draft convention that he had sent to Henry Maurice, Coolidge in a self-contradictory manner expressed his sensitivity to the feelings of Latin American countries regarding the United States, along with his conviction that the United States (and probably the American Committee in particular) "are the natural ones" to take a lead role in the new convention:

> It is most important that there should be no feeling among our neighbors to the South, that this is something which the [United States] is trying to put over on them [. . .]
> Your government has taken the lead in dealing with these problems in Africa, and you have plans for the same sort of convention for Asia. I think that we are the natural ones to take such a leadership as far as the New World is concerned.[207]

Drawing a parallel to the use of international law as a "civilizing mission" by colonial powers, Coolidge regarded Latin American countries—despite their independent and sovereign status—as quasi-colonial entities in need of US help to protect their nature. His approach to Latin American countries was strikingly familiar to the SPFE position regarding colonial African possessions. They shared a belief in their duty as Europeans and Americans to carry out the civilizing mission for non-Europeans, whether Africans or Latin Americans.[208] Using European colonial law to justify his self-imposed trusteeship over the fauna of other lands, Coolidge wrote, "The London Convention [. . .] has shown the importance of international cooperation for the protection of an international fauna [. . . .] We are trustees for the generations of the future."[209]

A World Convention for Nature

> Mr. H. G. Maurice, Secretary of the Society for the Preservation of the Fauna of the Empire [. . .] demonstrated the fact that the natural resources problems of our planet were common to all nations and emphasized their interdependence in that field. A world-wide Convention for Nature Protection was therefore the only way of avoiding ultimate defeat in the battle man had deliberately started against nature. —*International Technical Conference on the Protection of Nature*[210]

Interweaving throughout the narrative is the vision of a world convention for nature conceived by international conservation organizations as a union of regional conventions. Building on its success with the 1933 Convention Relative to the Preservation of Flora and Fauna in their Natural State, SPFE developed the concept of a global agreement for nature as a merger of this convention with planned future agreements for the Americas and Asia.[211] The idea captured the imagination of leading conservationists of the 1930s and 1940s, and became a ubiquitous topic of discussion. It was summarily and enthusiastically adopted by the indefatigable Coolidge. As early as 1935, in a letter to Julian Huxley, Coolidge wrote admiringly of Onslow's broad conservation vision and his call for an international convention for protecting Asian wildlife modeled on the 1933 London Convention.[212] Onslow and other SPFE officials envisioned a global conservation treaty as the framework for international cooperation for nature. With the spread of regional conventions, the vision was becoming a reality until World War II intervened and ended much international cooperation. In 1941 Onslow discussed the SPFE concept of a world convention with Coolidge:

> I hope that someday, although I fear it will be a long time ahead, there will be some sort of general agreement all over the World for the protection of Fauna and Flora.
>
> We had in our minds, when the Conference in regard to Southern Asia and Australasia was invited, to come to some general Convention which could include, also, the African Convention already signed.[213]

Coolidge, a firm believer in international law for nature, had been the force behind the Western Hemisphere Convention, which he viewed, as did Onslow, as a component of a future world agreement. With its adoption in 1940, Coolidge was ready to move on to his next challenge: a nature conservation convention on a global scale. Coolidge took the lead from Onslow, and with his immense energy pursued it relentlessly. In an article on the new "Convention on Nature Protection and Wild Life Preservation in the Western Hemisphere," Coolidge articulated the strategy:

> The American Committee for International Wildlife Protection believes that this Convention along with the London Convention for African Nature Protection [. . .] should serve as a basis for discussions which will lead to the establishment of a World Convention to further Nature Protection through international cooperation among Nations. Steps to accomplish these results should be carried out within the framework of the UNO.[214]

Colonial Beginnings 51

The beginning of the end of colonialism following World War II was itself a catalyst for a global convention. Leveraging the broad concern that nature conservation would become an even more critical challenge in the postcolonial period, Coolidge recognized that the newly created United Nations would assume a leading role.[215] In a 1946 letter to van Tienhoven, Coolidge suggested that "the Assembly next September should make provision for [. . .] a world convention on [. . .] nature protection pointing out the London-African Convention as terms of reference."[216]

And in answer to van Tienhoven's affirmative response to his idea,[217] Coolidge wrote that "with regard to an international convention for world nature protection [. . .] I hope that the Netherlands government and the Belgian Government will make such proposals at the forthcoming meeting of the United Nations assembly. It is best not to have all suggestions coming directly from the larger countries."[218]

Although the UN did not take up the challenge, the director of the Pan-American Union suggested to Coolidge the use of "the Pan American Convention as a possible pattern for a future world convention."[219] Pursuing this idea, Coolidge presented a paper titled "A World Approach to Nature Protection" at the Inter-American Conference on Conservation of Renewable Natural Resources in Denver, September 1948, floating the idea of a world convention. Ever the pragmatist, Coolidge had already developed a conceptual outline for the proposed convention, calling for parks and reserves to preserve threatened species. He suggested establishing

> an International Survival Office [. . .] where a watch list could be maintained of the vanishing species all over the world [. . .] This office would expect [. . .] governments to send them periodic reports on the status of their threatened species, and measures should be initiated to establish where possible parks or reserves to preserve [. .] the native habitat of each vanishing form to assure its preservation.[220]

Parallel to Coolidge's promotion of the visionary convention within the Pan-American Union, in Europe the Swiss League incorporated the concept as part of its unremitting efforts for an international conservation organization, the legacy of Paul Sarasin. The series of events that led to the founding of IUCN in 1948 began in Basle in 1946, at a small conference for nature conservation organized by the Swiss League. Its objective was to adopt a decision in favor of the new organization for nature. But it was unsuccessful, and the following year the Swiss League hosted another, larger conference in Brunnen that passed a resolution establishing the provisional IUPN (IUCN's original name). Beyond its formal mandate, the conference also became the testing ground for the exciting new idea of a world convention. Attending the Brunnen conference, the American Committee's representative argued that securing Earth's basic resources such as soil and forests "need to be dealt with eventually on a governmental level by world convention or treaty." He went on to declare that "the ultimate objective of the I.U.P.N will be to draft a world convention [. . .] after the model on a smaller scale of the London Convention or the Pan-American Convention."[221] The French representative agreed with the analysis and, in a sharp reminder that the political context was still colonialism, noted the immense environmental devastation in Africa, which, he claimed, was caused by native African populations. The only solution, he argued, was "[i]nternational rulings of a uniform character which every signatory state would undertake to respect."[222]

Having passed unscathed through the 1947 Brunnen conference and bearing the delegates' stamp of approval, the world convention for nature was heading for the October 1948 Fontainebleau conference, convened to establish the new international organization. The preparations provided opportunities to garner support for the proposal.[223] In an April 1948 letter to UNESCO, Coolidge drove home his strategy for consolidating existing regional conventions into a global convention, insisting that "the first point of discussion should be the question of international agreements for nature protection [. . .] with special emphasis on the London African Convention [. . .] and the Inter-American Convention [. . . .] The possible effectiveness of combining these conventions into a world convention is an important subject for consideration."[224]

Coolidge got his way. In the preparatory list of items for the conference agenda that UNESCO distributed in August 1948, the third (not first, as Coolidge had wanted) item on the agenda was "Fauna Conventions and International Legislation (discussion of the relation of regional Conventions to a possible World Convention)."[225]

International conferences were a sign of the times, signifying the post–World War II belief in international cooperation for world peace, embodied by the UN. International conservation conferences flourished. The 1948 Conference for the Establishment of the International Union for the Protection of Nature, held in Fontainebleau, France (the Fontainebleau conference), was not only the constitutional conference for the future IUCN, it was also the preparatory conference for the August 1949 UNESCO International Technical Conference on the Protection of Nature, held in Lake Success, New York (Lake Success conference).[226] The Lake Success conference, in turn, was the immediate follow-up to the UN Scientific Conference on the Conservation and Utilization of Resources (UNSCCUR), which addressed the role of resource conservation and utilization in postwar development. Decisive support for a world convention came from an individual in the right position at the right time. The eminent British biologist Julian Huxley had been appointed UNESCO's first director general, and as a firm believer in the use of law to protect the environment, and species in particular, he used his new position to support both the new IUCN and a world convention for nature.[227] He convened the Fontainebleau conference under the auspices of UNESCO and the French government, together with the Swiss League. He personally invited IUCN to take a lead role in UNESCO's conference at Lake Success the following year, displaying confidence in the technical and scientific abilities of the fledgling organization. Huxley intended the Lake Success conference to draft a world convention, and he invited Coolidge to chair the preparatory session at Fontainebleau.[228] Leveraging his powerful position as head of UNESCO, Huxley succeeded in tabling a world convention on the agenda of both these conferences.

Driven by the unrelenting energy and support of Huxley and Coolidge, the issue wound its way throughout the Fontainebleau conference proceedings, its ubiquity reflecting its centrality as a cutting-edge issue on the conservation agenda of that time. Charles Bernard, IUPN's newly elected president, framed the conference historically in his keynote address:

> The delegates assembled at Fontainebleau do not claim to have inaugurated International Nature Protection [. . .] I think I shall not be blamed if I mention here only the name of Paul Sarasin [. . .] a far-sighted scientist, he [. . .] saw how urgent it was to concentrate this by achieving an international agreement [. . .] to preserve fauna and flora menaced by man's so-called civilization.[229]

The task of considering a world convention was delegated to the European and African Technical Symposium at Fontainebleau. Emphasizing colonial concepts derived from an "imperial legacy," the symposium hammered home to participants that "anybody who abused natural resources for his personal ends should be held responsible by the rest of the human race for squandering a common legacy."[230] As a reminder that Africa was still under colonialist rule and hunting was still a major threat, the third session of the symposium addressed "Big Game Hunting in Africa." Its chair pointed out that the 1933 London Convention both defined big-game hunting and served as the basis for hunting regulations for Africa.[231] Evoking the important role assigned to protected areas in safeguarding African wildlife, a further session addressed the "Definition of National Parks and Nature Reserves." At the session on "Fauna Conventions and International Legislation," Henry Maurice of SPFE argued that a world convention for nature conservation was essential in "avoiding ultimate defeat in the battle man had deliberately started against nature." However, he also acknowledged that a world convention was a long-term goal. Jean Paul Harroy, who had just been appointed the first secretary general of the newly constituted IUPN, offered a pragmatic approach:

> Before forming any opinion as to [. . .] a World Convention for the preservation of fauna, the speaker thought an exact answer should be given to the following three questions:
>
> A. What fields did the authors of the London Convention (1933) and the Washington Convention (1940) consider it possible to cover in drafting an international agreement?
>
> B. What good results have sprung from the coming into force of the two conventions?
>
> C. What measures have been planned to make these agreements really effective?[232]

The outcome of the session was that except for Coolidge, other speakers displayed a general lack of zeal in promoting a world convention for nature.[233] But proving the extent of Coolidge's (and Huxley's) influence, the European and African Symposium issued a recommendation to include the topic on the agenda of the upcoming Lake Success conference.[234] Ironically and despite the unenthusiastic response to the proposal, as the constitutional conference for the new organization, the Fontainebleau conference did incorporate the concept as one of IUPN's "objects" in Article I of its founding constitution, "the preparation of international draft agreements and a world-wide convention for the '"Protection of Nature.'"[235] It could be rightfully said that IUCN was "born" into international law.

The fate of the world convention was determined the following year at Lake Success. Despite Huxley's initial intention that the Lake Success conference draft a text of the convention, the members of the commission appointed to study the issue decided that they must advise most strongly against attempting to organize such a convention at the moment [. . . .] It must be considered impossible to draw up in a reasonable space of time uniform rules for the protection of nature in all its aspects which would be acceptable to a great number of countries and at the same time be of any practical use [. . . .] An international convention on these subjects could do nothing except confine itself to vague recommendations.[236]

The commission further recommended focusing on specific and urgent issues such as "the protection of rare specimens of fauna and flora, the exchange of scientific collections, bird protection, and the establishment of international reserves."[237] IUCN was urged to first explore the effectiveness of existing conventions before launching initiatives for new agreements. Instead of a world convention, a resolution was adopted calling on IUCN to pursue conferences for the 1933 London Convention and the 1940 Western Hemisphere Convention, to discuss implementation and "progress reports."[238] Carrying out its mandate, IUCN approached the British government and the Pan-American authorities, requesting that they convene conferences for their respective conventions, but with no success. In face of governments' lack of interest, IUCN took another tack. Together with other organizations, it initiated the Third International Conference for the Protection of the Fauna and Flora of Africa, held in 1953 in Léopoldville (the Bukavu conference). The conference was officially sponsored by the Belgian government to convene the European signatories to the 1933 London Convention.[239]

Yet the vision of a world convention did not lose significance for IUCN. A proposal for a world convention reappeared on the agenda of IUCN's 1952 General Assembly, and was again rebuffed. As an alternative, the General Assembly called for a charter for nature inspired by the 1948 Universal Declaration of Human Rights. A draft "World Manifesto on the Protection of Nature" was summarily prepared but rejected by UNESCO on the grounds of lack of operability.[240] IUCN would have to wait another twenty years for its epic World Charter for Nature to be endorsed by UNGA. The elusive world convention was not actively pursued until the early 1970s and IUCN's work on major biodiversity agreements, its key role in the preparations for the Stockholm Conference.[241] Of all the conventions that IUCN has worked on over the past sixty years, the Convention on Biological Diversity[242] is ostensibly most similar to a *world* convention. Yet earlier biodiversity agreements—CITES in particular—were also the realization of this vision, especially because when they were drafted and negotiated, Coolidge as president of IUCN was personally involved in launching them on the agenda of the Stockholm Conference. By the time the original proposal for the CBD was raised in 1988, Coolidge was no longer part of the process, having died in 1985.

IUCN's Colonial Roots: The Elephant in the Room

Because IUCN is tirelessly at the forefront of conservation issues, it is tempting to frame the organization as coming into existence on the post–World War II wave of euphoric belief in international cooperation, symbolized by the birth of the United Nations. Intuitively, we identify IUCN with the fresh forces of light emerging from the darkness epitomized by the horrific wars of the first half of the twentieth century. Yet history shows us that IUCN was in planning for decades prior to its founding, and that without doubt, it emerged from colonialism. Its founders were primarily Europeans whose thinking about nature conservation had been shaped by the colonial milieu of the day and their experiences within it. IUCN's first secretary general was a high-ranking Belgian colonial official who eventually became governor of Rwanda-Burundi. IUCN was the continuation of earlier organizations that were part of the colonial establishment of the day, all sharing a firm belief in international law as a means for protecting nature generally and endangered fauna in particular. These organizations left behind a legacy of conservation conventions that have shaped today's global environmental governance.

The 1900 and 1933 London Conventions were designed to further the interests of European powers in the fauna of their African territories. As elephant treaties, they were primarily hunting and trade conventions, with the 1933 Convention institutionalizing national parks as a key conservation tool. Referring specifically to the 1900 Convention, Mark Cioc argues that despite its drawbacks, the convention meant the difference between extinction and survival for many species.[243] Yet these conventions succeeded to the extent that they did precisely because they *were* colonial conventions, imposed by foreign outsiders on rightless "natives" whose consent was not needed, who were not consulted during the conventions' drafting, and who did not participate in the negotiations. The colonial governance system was composed of centralized structures headquartered in Europe, enforcing these conventions through local administrators and regulations, against colonized populations lacking formal means of redress. Moreover, these early conventions were privileged in being able to focus on hunting as the overriding threat to biodiversity loss, in contrast to the myriad factors involved in biodiversity loss that international conventions face today. Another factor working in the early conventions' favor was their small number of contracting parties. Today, multilateral agreements can mean close to 200 contracting parties, but the 1900 Convention was designed for seven nations and the 1933 Convention for six. International institutions that might have worked for European colonial society are poorly suited to the needs of today's mega-diverse society.

The 1933 Convention closed a chapter in history. Colonialism would soon be coming to an end, and subsequent international agreements would be compelled to adapt to new political realities: the biological resources of colonial possessions would transform into the national resources of sovereign states. Even though the 1933 Convention had been drafted by biodiversity-poor Europeans in quest of Africa's natural riches, had provided for the establishment of national parks segregating Africans from wildlife, and had applied exclusively to lands ruled by colonizers, it would still serve as the model for postcolonial international biodiversity law.

Returning to the dilemma of scales as an underlying theme of this book, it should be noted that with the shift of Africa's biodiversity from an international-colonial scale to a national-local scale, states lost their brief and initial interest in international conservation law. Meanwhile, conservation organizations, agents for change relentlessly pursuing their own agendas, have persisted in developing and expanding international conservation law for their own purposes. The next two chapters focus on how they have done this.

CHAPTER THREE

Decolonialization

> I may say in conclusion that the real purpose of the Union is [...] to find norms and rules which are internationally valid for the defense of nature and the natural landscape, and then to draw up conventions necessary for their realization. —*M. Van der Goes van Naters, IUCN General Assembly, 2nd Session, 1950*[244]

The end of World War II sparked the beginning of decolonialization. Within the turmoil of the postwar years, faced with depleted treasuries and sharply declining public support for overseas possessions, European governments were rethinking colonial policies. Engaged in rebuilding their countries and their economies while confronting domestic hardships and unrest, governments lacked both the political will and the resources to maintain expensive global empires. The German Nazi devastation of Europe, and the perpetration of genocide against Jews and other minorities, reframed concepts of imperialism and colonialism that had once connoted national power and pride. Europeans were becoming uncomfortable with their colonies. The new global power configurations were another spur to decolonialization: although the war had greatly weakened European colonial nations, it had catapulted the United States and USSR as the two superpowers. Both opposed European colonialism, each for its own reasons.

Meanwhile the newly established United Nations, with its institutional structures for international cooperation, was challenging the prevailing colonial reality of the 1940s. Galvanized into creation by the dreadful war and perpetration of previously unimaginable acts of depravity and cruelty, the UN swiftly launched the 1948 Universal Declaration of Human Rights. As an expression of its anticolonial stance and as the base for the transformation of colonies into independent states, the UN General Assembly (UNGA) incorporated the right of self-determination into the UN Charter (Article 1.2). UNGA served as the international forum for contesting colonial rule and promptly linked the doctrine of self-determination to the sovereign rights of countries over their natural resources, expressed as the Permanent Sovereignty over National Resources (PSNR) principle.

IUCN's founding in 1948 coincided with the postwar era and European recovery; the beginnings of decolonialization, which would shape the young organization's identity in its early years; and the newly created United Nations, which would become a key IUCN partner and source of support. Only in 1972 did the UN officially launch international cooperation for the environment, yet by 1946 Coolidge had already recognized that the UN would ultimately assume a leadership role for nature protection.[245]

A Focus on Africa

Like SPFE and the American Committee before it, IUCN lived and breathed Africa. Its work in international law ensued primarily from its anxiety over the taking back of African biological resources by newly independent nations that resented European colonialism.[246] With the approaching end of colonialism, saving Africa's nature from the Africans was a hotly debated issue at the 1949 Lake Success conference. Its participants "stressed the urgency of directing attention towards Africa [. . .] [T]he great error made by European governments is in deluding themselves about African resources — a delusion that may bring destruction to the continent."[247] IUCN's first secretary general, Jean Paul Harroy, presented Africa as incapable of protecting what was in 1949 still considered a common legacy:

> Africa is perhaps the more greatly menaced when its biological equilibrium is disrupted [. . . .] Elsewhere the situation is different; the U.S.A. has been able to contend with its problems to a great extent because it possesses the necessary brain-power and material means. In Africa however, available material is at a minimum, and there is not yet a sufficient body of public opinion to protect the common heritage of natural resources.[248]

The fate of Africa's national parks under independent African rule struck deep fear among conservationists. Despite his sensitive position as secretary general of an international conservation organization at the dawn of decolonialization, Harroy didn't hesitate to openly express his despair over the fate of the "African reserves established by the colonists":

> Is there reason to believe that if the people of the Congo become self-governing at some time, they will be wise enough to perpetuate the strict nature reserves with the same interest as the Europeans who set them up?

[. . .] [W]ould not the habitat of the mountain gorilla and, as a result, the animal itself be rapidly endangered?[249]

Continuing the eternal debate over African hunters versus European hunters, Harroy publicly declared that African hunters were a primary threat to local fauna.[250] But worry over the impact of decolonialization was not limited to Africa. Asia was also a source of concern, as portrayed by the proceedings of IUCN's second General Assembly in Brussels in 1950:

[The] Netherlands Government has given the Government of the Indonesian Republic complete sovereignty over Indonesia, where there are treasures of such great beauty that no imagination can picture them [. . .] exceptional vigilance should be exercised on behalf of the threatened fauna of Indonesia.[251]

International conventions for Africa's nature continued to hold sway. Reiterating the historical link between protection of African fauna and international law, the 1950 IUCN General Assembly, "being aware of the grave dangers which threaten [. . .] the natural life and the very fertility of tropical Africa," proposed that the authorities draw up agreements on "Nature Protection" as a means of entrenching a measure of control before the end of colonialism.[252] Africa became the core of IUCN's work. Worry increased with accelerating decolonialization in the early 1960s. IUCN fretted that new African governments were unprepared to protect their parks, reserves, and fauna species, which European and US conservationists had, it argued, labored so arduously to protect throughout the colonial period. By 1960 Coolidge was lamenting that "[t]he immediate problems which will have to be faced by the newly emerging African nations with regard to safeguarding the heritage of national parks and reserves is a matter of grave concern, particularly in the Belgian Congo, Tanganyika, and in the French Territories."[253]

The "grave concern" of IUCN members is sharply reflected in the first three resolutions of its 7th General Assembly, held in Warsaw in 1960. These resolutions focused on Africa and launched the African Special Project (ASP) that would be recognized as one of IUCN's outstanding achievements. Resolution 1 called for "an African project[254] [. . .] to inform and influence public opinion [. . .] that [. . .] conservation practices [are] [. . .] in the best interests of all African countries." Resolution 2 focused on education. It determined that "in view of the extremely rapid changes threatening the future of wildlife and natural habitats in Africa, the IUCN General Assembly welcomed the educational initiatives of UNESCO and FAO."[255] Resolution 3 summed up by declaring that "in view of the emergence of Africa [. . .] the Union give special attention during the immediate future to African problems."[256]

Decolonialization and Africa affected even the location of IUCN headquarters, another issue on the 1960 agenda. IUCN's Kenyan members argued that locating IUCN headquarters in a country that had no colonial possessions in Africa, would portray the union as a truly international body and "enhance its standing in Africa." The Sudanese representative concurred. He thought it "wise to move the headquarters to a completely neutral country, such as Switzerland, and hoped that such a move would bring in more independent African countries as members."[257] Africa continued as the dominant issue at the 8th IUCN General Assembly, held in Nairobi in 1963. A proposal was raised titled "Ultimate Responsibility for the Preservation of African Species," specifically aimed at African countries to make them internationally responsible "for the preservation of individual species."[258] Ostensibly IUCN's expectation was to create a new principle of international law as a counterforce to the PSNR principle approved in a 1962 UNGA resolution. Although the proposal did not reappear at later IUCN General Assemblies, it signified IUCN's concerns about the fate of African nature under independent African nations.

Worry over the impact of African independence on African nature was not limited to IUCN European venues. In a 1963 speech in which Coolidge introduced the US conservationist Russell Train, a loyal aide to President Nixon who would later become the first chairman of the president's Council on Environmental Quality and the second EPA administrator, Coolidge displayed the colonial mindset that characterized him throughout his long and extraordinary career. Displaying his chronic concern for Africa's national parks, he told his audience that "the best hope of saving parks and wild game that had been safeguarded by the colonial administrations of the Belgians, French, and British [. . .] was to train Africans to look after and develop their own wildlife assets."[259] Coolidge's enduring conviction, which guided him as IUCN president, steadfastly remained that Africa's nature, protected under colonialism, was now endangered by African independence and required IUCN's help. The elusive but persistent civilizing mission continued to manifest itself throughout IUCN's work after the formal end of colonialism, detectable through policy decisions, international conventions, and simply the day-to-day correspondence of an international organization. The mission is primarily seen in hotly contested issues of national parks. In 1963 Coolidge urged the chair of a committee, which had been set up by the US interior secretary to reconsider the hunting ban in US national parks, to leave the ban in place because of the potential impact on developing countries:

> I would consider that it would be disastrous if this country, which is looked upon as a model when it comes to national parks, should in any way change the standard we have established about not allowing public hunting in our National Parks. You are as well aware as I am of the effect this would have on countries in Africa, Latin American and Asia [. . . .] While we might carefully screen a group of chosen hunters in this country, this would in no way be possible in the countries referred to.[260]

In the 1960s IUCN found itself becoming deeply involved in the politics of Africa, both colonial and postcolonial. Equatorial Guinea remained under Spanish rule until 1968. Charges were brought that in anticipation of decolonialization, Spanish administrators were speeding up exploitation of the region's natural resources. The Spanish were accused of being "opposed to conservation in any form," and criticism was voiced that "[t]he Spanish will want to exploit the country as much as they can during the last two years."[261] IUCN under the leadership of Coolidge was drawn into the politics of the approaching end of Spanish rule. In a 1966 incident, IUCN attempted to use its reputation as an eminent international conservation organization to persuade the colonial administration to protect a highly valuable nature reserve.[262] Faced with the intransigence of the local Spanish government, Coolidge deliberated using his connections with the US ambassador in Spain to persuade Franco himself to intervene and override the interests of the local administration.[263]

Harder choices and dilemmas were yet to confront IUCN. The conviction that postcolonial Africa was unprepared to assume responsibility for what IUCN still considered a global heritage was a key factor driving IUCN policy. Faced with uncertainty about the future of Africa's parks and reserves, IUCN countered by increasing its operations in Africa. Under colonialism, the lobbying efforts of conservationists had been expedited by the small number of powerful European nations that had ultimately decided African conservation policy. The overlapping relationships between governments and NGOs had made for close personal connections, strengthened and extended by vast conservation networks that spanned continents. But with the end of colonialism and the carving up of colonial Africa into independent states, new African governments became the "other,"²⁶⁴ outsiders, not part of the networks of conservation organizations and individuals based in the United States and Europe. How would IUCN engage with the new governments? The colonial civilizing mission had marginalized and denigrated Africans to justify their exclusion from their own lands and biological resources, but in postcolonialism the "natives" could no longer be evicted or excluded, at least not openly and directly. More subtle methods were needed to protect the megafauna and their habitats in former colonial possessions, taking into consideration that the victims of colonialism were now local populations marginalized by governments of new African countries.²⁶⁵

The ongoing violence in the Congo during the 1960s dragged IUCN into harsh and deeply disturbing political forays. In a step evocative of colonial land enclosure policies, Coolidge strongly advised the Congolese government against reestablishing a fishing village in Albert National Park, warning that "[w]e would regret any change of government policy which would re-establish this village." Coolidge mustered the power of the European organization he represented, and urged that the military throw out "all illegal settlers and poachers" from the area of the park.²⁶⁶ Yet Coolidge and other IUCN officials fretted about what they themselves saw as abusive political meddling. In a 1968 executive board meeting discussion on "Congo-Kinshasa," Coolidge

> stressed that this was a strictly confidential document and asked those present to return their copies [. . .] it had already produced some results [. . . .] and in fact a hundred and fifty guns had been sent to the national parks [. . . .] A long debate followed on the propriety of IUCN recommending the killing of cattle which had entered the park from Rwanda. It was agreed that letters to be sent to the Conga and Rwanda calling the attention of Governments to the problem but not instructing them what to do. R. E. Train asked whether there was any mechanism in Africa itself which could deal with problems of this sort, so that pressure from outside was not necessary. D. P. S. Wasawo said that no such mechanism existed [. . .] IUCN was the only body which could . . . .²⁶⁷

IUCN was framed as "the only body which could" protect African nature, invoking the civilizing mission to justify intervention in internal African problems. Only IUCN could "bear the burden" of protecting the national parks, the precious heritage of the imperial legacy. If no other body could address these issues, and action was necessary to protect the national parks, then IUCN intervention was both right and reasonable.²⁶⁸

IUCN's most primal fears were materializing. Ill at ease and troubled by its involvement in these violent and chaotic re-creations of "colonial confrontations," IUCN sought solutions to avoid them in the future, triggering its work on the African Convention on the Conservation of Nature and Natural Resources (the 1968 African Convention). These and other incidents also generated the Stockholm conventions—CITES and the World Heritage Convention—and perhaps the CBD as well. Harking back to the 1900 London Convention and demonstrating the bonds linking these conventions, IUCN's objective was to prevent the reoccurrence of such incidents by deploying another "international arrangement." As more pieces of the puzzle fall into place, in its early years IUCN saw the significance of international conventions in general, and of a world convention in particular, as a means to contend with the challenges of nature conservation in Africa. Facing the perceived powerlessness of new African governments, IUCN's historical emphasis on international agreements became even more pronounced, to counter exclusive African control of the continent's biodiversity. The chains of colonialism were hard to shake off.

A Postcolonial African Convention

The transformation of Africa into independent states meant that the colonial 1933 London Convention had become obsolete and by 1968 would be replaced by the African Convention on the Conservation of Nature and Natural Resources.[269] Its origins trace to the resolution of the 1953 Bukavu conference calling for a new agreement to replace the existing one that focused on fauna and largely ignored soil, water, and vegetation.[270] But the timing of that resolution was inopportune. Africa in 1953 was still under colonialist rule, a delaying factor in launching negotiations for the new agreement.[271] A window of opportunity opened with the 1961 Symposium on the Conservation of Nature and Natural Resources in Modern African States, known as the Arusha Conference. It was a key component of IUCN's African Special Project for promoting modern conservation in Africa; and discussions of new conservation tools for postcolonialism were pivotal to its proceedings.[272] Although the Arusha Conference did not expressly address a new convention, it did adopt a more general resolution endorsing a "Declaration of Principle on the Conservation of Nature in Africa."[273] Ensuing African conferences went further, and explicitly recommended revising the 1933 London Convention to bring forth a uniquely African convention, calling on IUCN to take the lead.[274]

Throughout 1962 and 1963, IUCN's executive board debated the revision of the 1933 Convention as well as the appropriateness and value of IUCN's role in the process. Despite initial hesitation, the board did set up a working group to examine the feasibility of a new African convention.²⁷⁵ After lobbying African leaders, the working group reported back in September 1963 that there was "considerable interest on the part of the African participants in the possibility of a new Convention." It strongly recommended that "the advice of interested African groups should be sought during preparations," and most significant, that "IUCN is the appropriate body [. . .] to undertake the preparatory work."²⁷⁶ In light of the encouraging report, the executive board established a committee under the newly formed Commission on Legislation and Administration (Commission on Legislation) to prepare an initial draft.²⁷⁷ But it still harbored grave reservations about whether the organization was right to undertake a convention for sovereign African countries. Reiterating the working group's message, the executive board clarified that it was "essential [. . .] that the final initiative should come from governments themselves."²⁷⁸ In the political reality of the 1960s, IUCN's undertaking of a new convention for Africa was extremely sensitive. Formally at least, foreigners could no longer dictate conservation policy for Africa or negotiate among themselves international agreements to tackle its conservation problems. IUCN feared charges that in undertaking the task of convention making for Africa, the organization was furtively recycling colonial policies, and thus stressed that the decision to launch a new convention had to be that of African nations. These concerns were expressed in a September 1963 meeting of IUCN's executive board:

> Several members emphasized that this was a matter to be approached with caution [. . .] and that it was important that the Bukavu recommendations (1953) for the revision of the Convention [. . .] might tend to be associated with the colonial era, [and] should on no account be allowed to obtrude on the consideration of the matter.²⁷⁹

After a preliminary three-day session in Morges, Switzerland, with representatives of African countries, work on the new convention shifted to Africa and to a committee under the Organization of African Unity (OAU; today African Union [AU]) assisted by IUCN.²⁸⁰ IUCN served as the key architect of the new convention, coordinating a review process to achieve consensus on a final draft, and undertaking a general consultancy position to assist governments during the negotiations. IUCN's political sensitivities to drafting an agreement for African nations was not the only challenge that the new project presented.

IUCN was competing in drafting the new convention with FAO, a major player in Africa. FAO argued that because it had more experience than IUCN in drafting international conventions, it should take the lead role. It charged IUCN with ignoring wildlife as a resource consumed by poor local populations. It relied on its formal status as a UN agency to lay claim to a more authoritative base for action than IUCN.[281] And, clinching the argument, FAO had been asked first.[282]

By 1965 both IUCN and FAO were immersed in drafting their own texts of a new convention. Reflecting its focus on nature protection, IUCN's draft was titled the "African Convention for the Protection of Nature and Natural Resources." FAO emphasized the links between nature protection and resource management, labeling its own draft the "African Convention for the Conservation and Management of Wildlife." Attempts to reconcile the differences between the two organizations by combining their drafts were rejected by OAU.[283] And although both enjoyed the support of significant numbers of African nations, OAU ultimately adopted the IUCN text for the new convention and submitted it to its Council of Ministers for approval. In a letter of gratitude that rankled sorely with FAO, OAU thanked IUCN for its help in the convention's adoption.[284] Coolidge as IUCN president reported on the letter at the executive board meeting in May 1968, the protocol of which discloses the bitterness between the two organizations as well as the general sentiment that the convention was too much of a compromise, resulting in a disappointing document.

> He [Coolidge] considered that IUCN had been well served by its delegation at Addis Ababa which had worked to draw up the best Convention it could in the circumstances. Dr. G. Budowski [UNESCO] appreciated the difficulties, but was not happy about the compromises reached [. . . .] Mr. T. Riney, on behalf of FAO, also expressed disappointment, and explained the extent to which FAO was obliged to satisfy the specific request of its member countries [. . . .] D. P. S. Wasawo considered that IUCN had been asked to do a particular job and had now done it. Political emotions in Africa were running high, and OAU had accordingly dealt with the draft Convention in its own way. Attempts to salvage the Convention had been made too late [. . .] Mr. T. Riney stressed that the African Convention for the Conservation and Management of Wildlife came from Africa and [FAO] had been requested well before OAU had asked IUCN for the Natural Resources document.[285]

The 1968 African Convention brought to a formal close the 1933 London Convention, created by Europeans both to legitimize their exploitation of African fauna and to counter the devastation triggered by European conquest and rule. Its completion signified IUCN's fulfillment of its founding mandate to create international conventions for nature. Yet the quarrel with FAO disrupted the relationships between the two organizations and became a source of mistrust and even animosity. The core problem remained that although recognizing the need for full involvement of African countries in all stages of convention making, the initial decision to draft an agreement had been manipulated by foreign organizations.[286] Recalling the making of conservation conventions under colonialism, both IUCN and FAO had their own political interests to promote in Africa. Both had pursued and received formal requests from African countries to draft the 1968 African Convention.[287] Similar to the rivalry between the American Committee and SPFE over the territorial coverage of the Western Hemisphere Convention, the competition between IUCN and FAO over the 1968 African Convention discloses the processes by which nongovernmental actors manipulate international conventions for reputational concerns. This recurring theme is displayed vividly in the competition between IUCN and UNESCO over the World Heritage Convention, a round that this time IUCN lost.

The World Heritage Convention

A key international convention that emerged from IUCN's focus on Africa is the Convention Concerning the Protection of the World Cultural and Natural Heritage (the World Heritage Convention, or WHC).[288] Counteracting African policies perceived as threats to protected areas established under colonialism, IUCN crafted the convention as a protective mechanism that operated by "internationalizing" them. The convention's origins and links can be traced to Africa: at the 1949 Lake Success conference, Jean Paul Harroy stressed the difficulties facing Africa in protecting the "common heritage of natural resources."[289] Shifting to postcolonialism, it is significant that both Russell Train and Harold Coolidge have been credited with coining the phrase *world heritage* at the 1965 White House Conference on International Cooperation.[290] Interest in the concept swiftly expanded to Europe. Not only had US conservationist Joseph Fisher chaired the 1965 conference, but the following year as keynote speaker at the IUCN General Assembly in Lucerne, he proposed a "Trust for the World Heritage":

> Certain scenic, historic and natural resources are part of man's heritage [....] Some of the resources, however, are in danger of being damaged or destroyed [...] some lie within states that may find it difficult to bear the costs of preservation [....] I now propose that there be established a Trust for the World Heritage that would be responsible to the world community [....] Here is another magnificent opportunity for IUCN to lead the way.[291]

Influenced by Coolidge as IUCN president and Train as a board member, a few months later the IUCN executive board responded to Fisher's proposal by calling for a "World Heritage Trust."[292] As a top Nixon aide, Train continued to promote the concept in the United States. He leveraged the remarkable environmental achievements of the Nixon administration starring the EPA, and exciting new laws such as the National Environmental Policy Act (NEPA) and the Endangered Species Act (ESA), to thrust the United States into a leadership role in promoting a world heritage trust.

> Our government has given dramatic new leadership to conservation programs in the US [...] I submit that there is now a tremendous opportunity for the US to exercise similar leadership, probably through the UN, on a world scale [...] I suggest that the trust be established [...] in close association with [...] IUCN.[293]

Prophetically, Train foresaw that simply classifying an area "as part of the World Heritage will carry with it such prestige that the classification will be eagerly sought."[294] Yet he also rightly predicted that sovereignty would undoubtedly prove an obstacle to implementing the concept. "Nations would reject interference with their sovereign right to manage their own national territory free of outside interference."[295]

THE NGORONGORO INCIDENT

The flurry of conferences, activities, and speeches during the mid-1960s did not by themselves launch an institutional structure for a world heritage. The crisis that ultimately triggered the World Heritage Convention was tied directly to Africa and specifically to the Tanzanian government's 1969 decision to convert vast areas of the Ngorongoro Conservation Area into farming and grazing lands. An article in the Nairobi *East African Standard* from August 29, 1969, "Serengeti May Have to Die," issued a call to protect this "world treasure," which "should be under international care and not the pawn of politicians." The author urged, "If we are to leave anything for our unlucky descendants it is time that there should be a United Nations Charter for the protection of places of unique beauty or historical importance."[296] The warning was supported by a report prepared by Bernard Grzimek, a German zoologist internationally recognized for his remarkable conservation work in Africa, while criticized for his colonial approach to Africans.[297] He reported that the Tanzanian minister for agriculture (Derek Bryceson, "the only European Minister in the Tanzanian Cabinet"), on a visit to local politicians of the Serengeti and Ngorongoro District, announced that the 3.200 square miles of the Ngorongoro Conservation Area would be turned over to farming and cattle, and only the 140-square-mile crater and the 20-square-mile Empakaai Crater would be preserved. Fearing the end of the work of a lifetime in protecting the Serengeti, Grzimek accused the minister of endangering the unique Ngorongoro area for political reasons.[298]

The incident spurred IUCN to transform the concept of a world heritage trust into a concrete proposal. Grzimek's report triggered Coolidge's immediate reaction, a letter to Prime Minister Nyerere of Tanzania urging him to reconsider his government's decision. Coolidge reminded Nyerere that the proposed project "appears to be contrary to the firm declaration embodied in the Arusha Manifesto and signed by Your Excellency at the time of the Pan-African Symposium on the Conservation of Nature and Natural Resources [. . .] in 1961."[299] Several days later Coolidge forwarded the letter he had sent Nyerere to Noel Simon of IUCN, who was already at work on a preliminary draft of a world heritage project. He requested from Simon a "list of key areas as well as your thoughts on the criteria that should be, as you have said, carefully and stringently defined."[300] Coolidge's request elicited prompt action, and by October 1969 Simon had completed a draft of a "World Heritage Trust." In its introduction he expressly linked the new project to the Tanzanian government's development plans.

> Within the last weeks the Government of Tanzania has announced proposals for the development of the Crater Highlands Conservation Area which, if implemented, could have far reaching repercussions on the Serengeti National Park and the Ngorongoro Crater.[301]

Echoing the organization's deeply entrenched belief that "IUCN was the only body which could," Simon believed that the severity of the threat warranted IUCN intervention. He noted in a letter to a colleague that the "situation serves to underline the importance of Russ Train's proposal for a World Heritage Trust. In my opinion the time has come for IUCN to act on Russ's idea."[302]

The World Heritage Trust was intended to provide "long term security of status at least for those areas that are regarded as of superlative importance from the international standpoint."[303] Simon, echoing the 1963 IUCN General Assembly proposal to impose international responsibility on African nations for their nature, concluded his draft with the welcome, if unrealistic, suggestion that governments should be "requested to make an unequivocal declaration to the effect that they will guarantee the status of each area in perpetuity."[304]

The Ngorongoro incident sparked IUCN's deepest fears, validating its foreboding about the impact of African independence on colonial parks. The organization responded by proposing an international level of decision making for these sites by declaring each one a world heritage. Illustrating the inherently local-national scale of the issue, rather than calling for a multilateral convention, the original design for a world heritage institution called for bilateral relations between the country concerned and an international trust. IUCN did not set out to create a convention. Instead, it envisioned a "trust" that would "[b]y virtue of its immense prestige [. . .] impress upon governments the notion that each natural area selected comprises part of the world's patrimony," and that each "has a solemn responsibility to hold it in trust for all mankind." The trust was also intended to bring "moral pressure to bears on wayward governments in emergency situations." A further function was advisory, to help governments manage their trust areas. The proposed trust would not be part of the UN system. Instead, trusteeship would be vested in the leading academies of science.[305]

WORLD HERITAGE AND UNCHE

By October 1970 a world heritage trust had become an official IUCN project. The objective was to open it for signing at the upcoming Stockholm Conference (UNCHE), with IUCN taking the lead role in its subsequent implementation.[306] Meanwhile, the United States had regained interest in the idea. In a January 1971 meeting between Robert Cahn of CEQ and Frank Nicholls, IUCN deputy director general, Cahn asked for an update on the world heritage proposal. He noted that the United States was considering its submission for the agenda of the Stockholm Conference. In response, Nichols suggested that the United States remain low-key so as not to alienate other states. The historical-political setting was the Vietnam War, and the United States was at a low point in international popularity.[307] IUCN preferred that the UN itself take the lead in tabling the world heritage trust on the UNCHE agenda, and UN staff members promised to raise the issue with Maurice Strong, the Stockholm Conference director general.[308] Yet the US government continued to promote a world heritage trust as a US project under the Department of the Interior. A month later, in February 1971, President Nixon unveiled his proposal for a "World Heritage Trust" in his message to Congress:

> As the US approaches the centennial celebration in 1972 of the establishment of Yellowstone National Park, it would be appropriate to mark this historic event by a new international initiative in the general field of parks [. . . .] [T]here are certain areas of such unique worldwide value that they should be treated as part of the heritage of all mankind [. . .] part of a World Heritage Trust. Such an arrangement would impose no limitations on the sovereignty of those nations which choose to participate but [. . .] would make available technical and other assistance [. . . .] I am directing the Secretary of the Interior [. . .] to [. . .] further [. . .] a World Heritage Trust.[309]

By the second session of UNCHE's Preparatory Committee (Prep Comm), which also took place in February 1971, the proposal for a "World Heritage Foundation" had become part of the conference's agenda. The Prep Comm recommended drafting a constitution "to define its objectives and mode of action, to settle the criteria for the selection of natural areas and sites, and to outline the measures to be adopted by States for the conservation of trust areas."[310]

UNESCO VERSUS IUCN

With negotiations forging ahead, by April 1971 the original world heritage foundation had metamorphosed into a convention under the leadership of IUCN.[311] But as in previous interorganizational conflicts, a major stumbling block for completion of the future World Heritage Convention was a turf war between IUCN and UNESCO. Both organizations sought international agreements for world heritage. Each defined the term in accordance with the aims and objectives of its own organization. Each had been spurred into action by different factors. IUCN's steely determination to bring forth an international convention sprang from threats to the Serengeti and the Ngorongoro Conservation Area in Tanzania. While IUCN aimed for a few carefully selected natural sites of outstanding "universal" value,[312] UNESCO was concerned about protecting cultural sites. UNESCO's interest in the convention stemmed from its campaign to save the Abu Simbel temples in the Nile Valley, under threat from the Aswan Dam project. In 1959 Egypt and Sudan had formally requested UNESCO's help in saving these unique archaeological monuments, and the ensuing successful campaign is considered an example of international cooperation at its best. Through an operation orchestrated by UNESCO, the archaeological sites were dismantled and relocated at a cost of $80 million donated by the international community.[313]

The conflict came to a head at the meeting of UNCHE's Intergovernmental Working Group on Conservation (IWGC) held at UN headquarters in September 1971. The session was "opened by the Secretary-General of the Conference, who [. . .] stressed the importance of the establishment of a world heritage, as a new concept that recognized that there were certain areas of outstanding natural, scientific and cultural values which could be accepted by all nations as part of the common heritage of mankind."[314] Strikingly reminiscent of the IUCN-FAO battle over the 1968 African Convention, in fierce competition IUCN and UNESCO had both tabled their own texts: the IUCN "draft Convention on Conservation of the World Heritage," and the UNESCO "draft Convention on the International Protection of Monuments, Groups of Buildings and Sites of Universal value."[315] IWGC diplomatically decided "that it was beyond [. . .] [its] competence to examine in detail the UNESCO draft [. . .] which was in the course of being considered through the usual UNESCO machinery." Although the IUCN draft was chosen as the basis for its work, the working group did note the importance of taking the UNESCO draft into consideration to avoid duplication.[316]

Beyond the turf war, two major challenges faced IWGC. One was defining the concept *world heritage*, regarding which the working group decided that "the draft convention should stress the conservation of natural areas, without excluding cultural sites."[317] The second challenge concerned the decision-making process, and primarily the identity of the decision makers in selecting world heritage sites.[318] Some delegates insisted that the role belonged exclusively to states guided and advised by an expert panel, while others argued that the decision-making body should be a foundation or board elected by representatives of contracting states.[319] In the final outcome, states rejected the original IUCN proposal for an independent international body authorized to decide on world heritage sites.[320] They replaced the proposal with the current procedure, through which each state nominates candidate sites, while a World Heritage Committee composed of twenty-one state members decides which sites reach the coveted World Heritage List.[321]

US LEADERSHIP

Concluding the session, IWGC charged IUCN with the preparation of a revised text to be sent out to governments for their comments. But UNESCO continued to work on its own draft, and the two parallel drafting processes were impeding the completion of a final, approved convention text for tabling on the UNCHE agenda.[322] The United States decided to intervene. It undertook to combine the two drafts, achieved through a working group composed of the key organizations that merged the IUCN articles on natural sites into the UNESCO draft.[323] Continuing its leadership role, the United States swiftly made the decisions regarding which organization would administer the new convention. On the one hand, the US government decided that UNESCO should house the convention because of its influence with the USSR and developing countries. On the other, the United States wanted IUCN to assume a lead role for world heritage natural sites.[324] The upshot was that UNESCO was chosen to administer the convention, and IUCN became the scientific advisory expert. So despite IUCN's key role in creating the World Heritage Convention, and despite its knowledge, expertise, and proven track record of achievements in conservation issues, the bottom line remained that IUCN was excluded from positions of power that might have prompted the changes it sought.

The process leading to the World Heritage Convention sharply illustrates the largely unrecognized role of the United States in promoting international conservation conventions. The United States had sponsored the 1965 White House Conference on International Cooperation where the concept *world heritage* was initially raised and discussed. It had contributed considerable expertise to the drafting of the WHC and promoted its inclusion on the UNCHE agenda. When the completion of the convention was held up by organizational squabbles over the draft, the United States had decisively stepped in. Through its critical role in the creation of the WHC, the United States was *re*assuming its role from the early part of the twentieth century as an international leader for conservation conventions.

As predicted by Russell Train, sovereignty remained a key obstacle in finalizing the new World Heritage Convention. To overcome it, Article III clarifies that "[r]ecognition of an area as part of the World Heritage shall not prejudice the sovereignty of the CS [contracting party] concerned over that area." Adapted to the postcolonial reality of sovereign states, the WHC was a quasi-exclusionary device. Though the convention would not intervene in the sovereignty of states over their territorial possessions, IUCN had designed it as a monitoring system for national activities, and specifically to counter decisions and actions of African governments that clashed with IUCN interests. IUCN's response to Tanzania's decision to develop conservation areas in the Serengeti plains, one of the world's most unique ecosystems and critical habitat of endangered African fauna, was to create an international level of decision making that would preempt the Tanzanian government's decisions.

Yet this intrusion into the realm of national policy making would have its price. In an early manifestation of the principle of "common but differentiated responsibilities," the developing countries succeeded in adding to the preamble "that the responsibility of those countries in which areas forming part of the World Heritage are situated should have its counterpart in a responsibility of the international community to give assistance," shaping the WHC into a North-South funding channel. Countries with world heritage sites in their territorial jurisdiction would commit to ensuring their protection, while richer countries would recognize their "international responsibility" by committing to financial aid.[325] The convention was not completed in time for signing at the Stockholm Conference, and to improve its chances of eventually coming into force, Recommendation 98 of the UNCHE Action Plan called on governments to continue working on the draft "with a view to its adoption."[326] The WHC was finally adopted at the UNESCO General Conference in November 1972 and entered into force on July 1, 1975.

The Making of CITES

The Convention on International Trade in Endangered Species[327] is considered one of IUCN's most remarkable accomplishments, launching the organization onto the world stage of international law making and international environmental politics in particular.[328] Despite inherent constrictions deriving from biodiversity's national scale, trade in endangered species has historically been recognized as dictating international cooperation, institutionalized as international conventions. British concern—and initially German concern as well—about trade in African species, and the elephant in particular, led directly to the 1900 and 1933 elephant treaties. Moving on from regional conventions, conservationists alarmed over the impact of trade on fauna species envisioned a global convention that would impose unified trade rules. By the late 1930s, the first faint traces of CITES can be detected in discussions of a "world convention for nature" to "secure uniformity of practice, throughout the World" and specifically "custom regulations in all countries [. . .] to support all measures for preservation which each country makes in respect of its own fauna."[329] Yet the much sought after convention did not materialize, and the task of tackling international trade in endangered species was handed over to the newly created IUCN in the early 1950s.

The historical focus of CITES is Africa. Its roots are planted firmly in these early conventions for African fauna and—regarding the 1933 Convention—flora as well. International trade in fauna species was an element of colonialism that has remained entrenched in postcolonial international conventions. The trade in species, from African possessions to metropolitan Europe and wealthy countries elsewhere, continued after decolonialization through the traditional South-North route. Tracing its origins to Africa of the early 1960s, and similar to the World Heritage Convention regarding natural and cultural sites, CITES monitors the trading activities of developing countries in endangered species. Just as the earliest agreements operated to guard European trade interests in African mammals, IUCN designed CITES as part of its African strategy of the early 1960s, addressing its own concerns about and interests in Africa's unique species of fauna and flora, and its large mammals in particular.

A review of IUCN General Assembly resolutions throughout the 1950s and early 1960s bears out IUCN's focus on trade as a key factor in species extinctions. These resolutions disclose that IUCN's ultimately critical role in promoting an international trade convention originated in its more modest call for national laws to restrict imports of endangered species. Its 1952 General Assembly issued a resolution urging countries to ban the importation of species prohibited for export by their country of origin.[330] A 1960 IUCN resolution on trade in endangered species continued to call for national legislation to stop the import of species banned for export.³³¹ But resolutions and national legislation alone could not counter the devastating impact of trade on wildlife. African conservationists from newly independent nations were complaining about ineffective enforcement and calling for strong international regulation.³³² These issues featured prominently on the agenda of the September 1961 Arusha Conference, which African delegations leveraged to protest the inadequacies of existing regulatory structures. The turning point was IUCN's 8th General Assembly, held in Nairobi in 1963, which adopted Resolution 5 on "Illegal Traffic in Wildlife Species" calling for an international convention to tackle illegal trade in endangered species, and signaling the launch of CITES:

> [W]hereas many rare and vanishing species of wildlife are threatened with early extinction through illegal export from their native land and whereas such illegal export would be much less frequent if import into other countries were prohibited [. . .] [the 8th General Assembly] recommends [. . .] that an international convention [. . .] be drafted and submitted for the approval of governments.³³³

The backdrop to this key resolution was the work undertaken by IUCN's Commission on Legislation and Administration. Today the World Commission on Environmental Law, it had been formally established by Resolution 307 of IUCN's 8th General Assembly to gather information on national trade legislation in species. Mindful of colonial administrator Harry Sharpe's analysis of an "international arrangement" regulating the ivory trade, in the *Report of the Committee on Legislation and Administration* from August 1, 1963, the commission's chairman noted that "[e]xperience has shown that the strongest measures will prove ineffective, unless ALL Governments come to an agreement."³³⁴ The 1963 resolution became IUCN's constitutional authority for "[t]he study of practical and political problems involved in controlling the traffic in wild animals, leading to the drafting and sponsorship of an international Convention." But the convention's progress was being held up because the "problems involved are so far-reaching or intractable that only a major operation or campaign, with matching personnel and finance, could be expected to make a break-through."³³⁵ Despite these setbacks extending over several years, by September 1967 the Commission on Legislation had distributed a first draft to ninety governments for their comments.³³⁶ Proceeding slowly, consultations with countries stretched out until 1971, when a final IUCN draft was completed.³³⁷ Thus IUCN's work on a trade agreement in endangered species, in progress from the early 1960s, reached its height amid preparations for the Stockholm Conference and would become part of the UNCHE process.

THE UNITED STATES AND CITES

Parallel to IUCN's work on the future CITES, the US Congress was strengthening US wildlife legislation (the Lacey Act of 1900) to protect species threatened by international trade. Because of IUCN's expertise on wildlife issues, and specifically its work on an international convention, the organization's officials were invited to Washington to give expert testimony and contribute data in support of the new legislation.[338] Participating in the 1967 hearings, Wolfgang Burhenne, chair of IUCN's Commission on Legislation, gave a submission emphasizing the need for international cooperation to which was attached the IUCN draft convention. He subsequently took credit for the 1969 amendments to the Lacey Act endorsing an international convention on trade in endangered species.[339] Yet the United States harbored several reservations regarding the IUCN draft. Similar to the controversy over the decision-making authority for world heritage sites that marked the WHC negotiations, a key obstacle to reaching a final CITES draft was determining the identity of the decision maker for listing species.[340] The IUCN draft called for an international committee of experts to decide on the contents of the lists. But developing countries rejected this concept, and instead insisted on the right of each country of origin to have a say in imposing trade restrictions on its own species.

Kenya led the objections and distributed an alternative draft, which the United States supported over the IUCN draft, particularly because the United States also exported several of its own endangered species.[341] Moreover, both the United States and Kenya insisted on strengthening the new convention's enforcement mechanisms to clamp down on violations, in line with US wildlife trade legislation. Pursuing its role of breaking deadlocks in convention negotiations, the United States distributed a discussion document comparing the IUCN draft, the Kenyan draft, and the US compromise text. The solution to Kenya's insistence on a stronger role for governments in determining the species to be listed emerged as Appendix III to CITES, which allows countries to restrict trade in species other than those appearing in Appendixes I and II.

The final and amalgamated draft was distributed in March 1971 to all 130 UN member nations.[342] Objections were not forthcoming, so moving ahead, the US government declared its intention to host a plenipotentiary conference to adopt the convention. "It had a mandate from its Congress to convene such a meeting at the earliest possible date [...] the month of April 1972 was agreed to be the earliest practical date."[343] But although US support was a major contribution to the convention negotiations, it also had its drawbacks. The Stockholm Conference was impacted not only by North-South conflicts but by East-West ones as well.[344] In his history of IUCN, Martin Holdgate relates that the United States postponed the plenipotentiary conference pursuant to the People's Republic of China's joining the UN and the subsequent implications for Taiwan, until then the US-backed UN representative for China. The United States would not convene an intergovernmental conference until the issue of China's representation in the UN was resolved.[345]

Despite these drawbacks IUCN recognized the power of US support, and to reap its benefits, it tightened its associations with the US State Department. Moreover, lacking any formal governance role, IUCN needed the United States to convene a plenipotentiary conference to adopt CITES. Richard Gardner, professor of law and international organizations at Columbia Law School, had been brought on by IUCN to represent its interests at the UN in the run-up to the Stockholm Conference. In a letter dated February 8, 1972, Frank Nicholls, deputy director general of IUCN, thanked Gardner "for the splendid work that you and Hal [Coolidge] have done with the State Department in regard to the two conventions," referring to US support for both the future WHC and CITES.[346]

Gardner's and Coolidge's successful lobbying of the US State Department on CITES brings to mind the relations between SPFE and the British government regarding the 1933 London Convention, and the American Committee and the US government concerning the 1940 Western Hemisphere Convention. CITES was to a great extent a result of the network of relations between US government officials and IUCN. The highest-ranking US government official to support the IUCN draft convention was Stewart Udall, secretary of the interior and an IUCN supporter for many years.[347] The well-connected Russell Train, who had reached the highest echelons of the US government under the Nixon administration, was actively involved in IUCN's work. Parallel to serving during the late 1960s and early 1970s as undersecretary of state in the US Department of the Interior, chair of the president's Council on Environmental Quality, and EPA administrator, Train was a member of IUCN's executive board and extremely supportive of the IUCN draft of the future convention. Lee Talbot was another example of overlapping relationships between IUCN and US government officials. Though he eventually became IUCN director general

(1980–1982), from 1969 he was also a member of the IUCN executive board, as well as field representative for the Smithsonian Institution, and in 1970 was appointed chief scientist to CEQ. Talbot was well positioned to give testimony at the congressional hearings in support of IUCN's draft convention.[348]

A similar process was going on in Europe. IUCN was influencing the preparations for the Stockholm Conference through the International Parliamentary Conference on the Environment (IPCE). The purpose of the conference was to prepare parliamentarians for UNCHE, including drafting recommendations on issues of environmental law. IPCE had been organized by the Interparliamentary Working Center, whose secretary general was Wolfgang Burhenne, also head of the IUCN Commission on Legislation. As technical advisors to IPCE, IUCN legal experts were the force behind resolutions promoted by European parliamentarians calling for international conventions, including the future CITES.[349] Thus IUCN, through its Commission on Legislation, successfully influenced international decision making without a formal role in the process. By advantageous use of its international network, composed not only of NGOs but of government agencies as well, IUCN promoted this new generation of conservation conventions, continuing a legacy of overlapping relations between governments and nongovernmental organizations.

The US-sponsored plenipotentiary conference adopting CITES finally took place in Washington, DC, in February 1973, and CITES came into force in July 1975. IUCN continued its association with CITES by administering the convention for UNEP at IUCN headquarters in Switzerland, from 1973 until 1984, at which point UNEP itself took over the task. During this period, IUCN's Environmental Law Programme served as the legal advisor to the convention and assisted developing countries in implementing CITES. IUCN continues to be a major force in its implementation.[350]

THE FUTILITY OF CITES

Despite the hope and expectation that its adoption had created, looking back from the vantage point of forty years and using trade in ivory as an indicator, CITES has been judged a failure. According to environmental writer Alex Shoumatoff in a 2011 article in *Vanity Fair*,

> Dr. Richard Leakey [. . .] was the only critic to go on the record—"CITES is now anachronistic and a sham. It's funded and controlled by the ivory

trade—and should be put away. The very concept of trade in high value wildlife species as a tool for conservation is completely untenable."[351]

And,

> A man deeply involved in elephant poaching and smuggling interdiction compared CITES to the U.S. Securities and Exchange Commission: It was created to become a regulator and became a facilitator, and the victim is not millions of people, but nature.[352]

The innate predicament facing CITES lies in the use of international law to legitimize a trade that cannot be monitored, and to protect species not for the sake of the species, but for their economic worth.[353] A trade convention in endangered species is a contradiction in terms. Endangered species require absolute protection. Trade in these species should be outlawed rather than regulated by a convention under the guise of a global biodiversity convention. By differentiating between legal trade and illegal trade through a complex regulatory structure, CITES encourages and facilitates the illicit international trade in wildlife.

CITES is an extension of colonial hunting and trade agreements designed in particular to ensure an abundance of African elephants for the ivory trade. These elephant treaties were designed by and for a band of fairly homogeneous European countries that shared beliefs, values, and norms. They were able to bind themselves together by international treaties because the rules of the game were known to all. Moreover, they had only themselves to deal with, did not negotiate with independent African nations, and for the most part ignored local populations. Yet the dangers elephants faced under colonialism appear mild in comparison to the horrific onslaught they face today—driven by criminal rebel gangs and terrorist groups, including groups identifying with Al-Qaeda. The lucrative profits made from selling ivory to newly rich Chinese and other Asian populations hankering for ivory finance their criminal and terrorist activities.

The financial incentives are too attractive to give up,[354] as demonstrated by the alleged participation of African governments and their armies in the poaching as well.[355] An estimated 100 elephants are being slaughtered each day in Africa to feed the ivory trade. CITES reports that "China remains the paramount destination for [. . .] illegal ivory leaving Africa,"[356] yet the convention remains powerless to stop the smuggling. In an example of the complexities brought on by a legal ivory trade, ivory eventually finds its way not only to state-owned "legal" factories, but to China's illegal factories as well. State-approved facilities supposedly use only ivory supplied from the sales of old stock that CITES allowed South Africa, Botswana, Namibia, and Zimbabwe to sell in 2008, an exception (along with another one-off sale in 1999) to the ban CITES imposed on trade in elephant ivory in 1989.[357] Although the intention was "that China and Japan would be happy with so much ivory, and the poaching would be reduced,"[358] poaching is escalating and illegal ivory is being sold as old stock approved for sale by CITES. Shoumatoff argues for a total ban on trade in ivory:

> [N]o ivory should be sold, legally or illegally, it has to be taken off the table completely, you can't keep feeding the demand and providing incentives to poor Africans to continue killing their elephants. That — and educating the Chinese — is the only hope for the remaining ones in the wild.[359]

But China does not want to control its consumption of ivory. Nor does it want to take responsibility for its nationals, employed by Chinese companies building roads in Africa, who make lucrative profits by smuggling ivory. Although CITES has "requested" that China monitor its internal ivory trade and submit reports, and has "invited" the country to reassess this trade, CITES's soft approach is outrageously inappropriate to the devastation wrought by China's greed for ivory. An entry on the CITES website optimistically titled "CITES acts to curb smuggling of elephant ivory and rhino horn"[360] is shamefully misleading. Displaying the culture of conferences that pivot around empty rhetoric, the entry declares that the CITES Standing Committee "decided unanimously to take urgent measures to tackle the current poaching and smuggling crisis threatening elephant and rhino populations." Yet these "urgent measures" boiled down to polite requests to combat smuggling. Saving the African elephant means that China has to completely shut down its domestic ivory trade and production, harnessing the extensive authorities of its formidably powerful centralized government to firmly enforce these prohibitions.[361]

At best, CITES is irrelevant for the African elephant. The severity and dimensions of elephant poaching have gone far beyond its resources and capabilities, and it remains a helpless bystander as the elephant approaches extinction in the wild. More worrying are charges that CITES is a driver behind the elephant crisis, by approving the sale of old ivory stocks and hence creating a legal cover for poached ivory. CITES must admit that it is powerless to protect the elephant; and as a UN convention, CITES should bring the elephant crisis before UNGA for debate and the adoption of resolutions, among others, condemning

China and other countries identified as key players in the ongoing disaster. Moreover, the international criminal and terrorist aspects of elephant poaching call for referring the elephant crisis to the UN Security Council, to consider use of its authorities in countering elephant poaching for the "maintenance of international peace and security."

Experiences of the past century raise doubts about the efficacy of cooperative action in protecting nature generally and about the role of the UN in particular. But accepting the fate of the elephant as sealed and inescapable portends a menacingly dangerous mindset that extinctions are the unavoidable price of human development. Once the extinction of the elephant is believed to be inevitable, it will be swiftly followed by a rethinking of other species extinctions, with profoundly frightening consequences. The elephant crisis is bringing the human relationship with other species to a head. Whether governments are capable of summoning the political will and the resources to prevent the elephant's extinction will determine the future of the human relationship with the biosphere.

International trade in species, as institutionalized by CITES, stubbornly remains a colonial concept, and the shift from colonialism to postcolonialism has made no difference to long-persecuted African elephants. Just as they were tradable objects under the elephant treaties and any protection these treaties extended was determined by the size of their tusks, international law today assigns elephants value reflecting only their worth in international trade. Elephants continue to be victims of a human thirst for ivory that does not abate. Whether by colonial Europeans lusting after ivory billiard balls, or by contemporary Asians craving ivory knickknacks, the greedy pursuit of Africa's biological resources viciously and violently escalates. Meanwhile, "legal" trade in ivory relentlessly continues, stamped with the seal of approval of a so-called biodiversity convention.

A Convention for Islands

Among IUCN's repertoire of international conventions under preparation for the 1972 Stockholm Conference, in retrospect the most intriguing was the elusive Convention on Conservation of Certain Islands for Science, or the Islands Convention. Its narrative does not have an ending; the convention simply disappeared from view, leaving an unfinished story. The origins of the draft Islands Convention can be traced to a flurry of activity in 1952 over islands in the Western Hemisphere.³⁶² Beyond this isolated surge of activity, the issue appears to have remained dormant until 1966. At that time, in face of mounting concern that human development would ultimately reach uninhabited islands, IUCN drafted a "checklist of important uninhabited or relatively undisturbed islands"³⁶³ The project was spurred by IUCN members, alarmed that new water technologies along with escalating development would mean ecological devastation for islands. Expressing these fears, an IUCN member noted that "the threat to islands would shortly become greater when desalinization on a small scale became economic. Many islands at present uninhabitable, within twenty years would become desirable residential areas."³⁶⁴

Harold Coolidge was IUCN president at that time. Harnessing his unflagging enthusiasm for international conventions, he was determined to create a new one to confront the double threat of development and technology that faced uninhabited islands. Coolidge got his way, and IUCN undertook the preparation of a draft convention.³⁶⁵ By January 1971 the draft had become an official IUCN project, the scope of which was defined as "action to [. . .] safeguard a number of Pacific Islands as "Islands for Science" through [. . .] a suitable treaty."³⁶⁶ The draft convention was submitted to the secretariat of the Stockholm Conference, bundled together with the World Heritage Convention and the Ramsar Convention on Wetlands of International Importance.³⁶⁷ The Islands Convention was to be included, along with WHC, as a proposal for Level III of the Stockholm Conference, meaning that it was slotted for immediate action.³⁶⁸

The final draft of the Islands Convention called for a 'List of Islands of International Importance to Science," to which a contracting party could elect suitable islands "under its sovereignty." Inclusion on the international list would not impinge on the sovereignty of the state concerned. However, contracting states would "be deemed to have given their consent to the principle that the conservation of the islands [. . .] included in the List shall be a matter of joint concern." States were obliged to protect listed islands, and in the case of any "environmental disturbance," they were required to take steps to mitigate it outright. More problematic, a state that became aware of an environmental disturbance on *another* state's listed island was required to inform the convention's secretariat of the disturbance. Listed islands were to be "used for peaceful purposes only." The convention prohibited their use for the testing of nuclear explosions or disposal of nuclear or toxic waste, as well as for military purposes including the construction of military bases.

By September 1971 the draft convention was on its way to be opened for signature at UNCHE.[369]

While WHC and CITES smoothly shift from colonialism to postcolonialism, continuing anthropocentric approaches to nature conservation, the draft Islands Convention remains tantalizingly aloof. Its origins lie in the catastrophic impact of European colonialism on island ecological systems. In contrast to the other conventions discussed in this chapter, which were designed to balance the needs of humans with those of nature, the Islands Convention was specifically geared to *prevent* human habitation. This was probably the reason for its downfall, as countries perceived it as too audacious an interference in their territorial sovereignty. Yet the Islands Convention is a significant link in the chain of conventions that weaves throughout the story, displaying two recurring themes: international lists—in this case, lists of islands—and the authority to determine the contents of those lists.

So what happened to the Islands Convention? Though initially marked for immediate action, why did it disappear from view, while the other conventions went on to become major international biodiversity agreements? Distinct from WHC, the Ramsar Convention, and CITES, the Stockholm Conference ultimately did not call on governments to negotiate an international convention for islands. It sufficed with a recommendation for a study "of all possible procedures for protecting certain islands for science."[370] Yet IUCN did not give up on its initiative despite the rejection by states. With the close of the conference in June 1972, Gerardo Budowski, director general of IUCN, wrote to Maurice Strong, "We will also look forward to further discussions with you in the follow up of the proposed Convention on Conservation of Certain Islands for Science."[371] And at IUCN's 11th General Assembly held in Banff, Canada, in September 1972, CEPLA (Commission on Environmental Policy, Law and Administration) reported that "discussions are in hand with the UN on the further elaboration of this draft."[372]

The Islands Convention demonstrates the limits of international law in protecting biodiversity. It has gone the way of global conventions for forests, both succumbing to the stubborn resistance of countries to perceived threats to core sovereignty issues. Committing states to forego development of their own territories for the sake of science was simply too radical an idea, and states rejected the convention. As long as international conventions are limited to compiling lists of wetlands, world heritage sites, or endangered species without forcing governments into conflicts of interests covering a broad political spectrum, countries will put up with these conventions. But international law cannot tackle the major underlying factors in biodiversity loss, simply because this would mean changing the behavior of states and their populations regarding how they live, eat, work, commute, play, travel, and more—all politically fraught issues.

The Stockholm Conference

The origins of the World Heritage Convention, CITES, and the Islands Convention trace to IUCN's beginnings in the 1950s and early 1960s, and in particular, to its constitutional mandate for crafting international conventions. Yet the catalyst that drove WHC and CITES to completion and adoption was the 1972 Stockholm Conference. Branded as an environmental megaconference—the harbinger of the 1992 UNCED in Rio de Janeiro (the Rio Summit), the 2002 World Summit on Sustainable Development (WSSD) in Johannesburg, and the 2012 UNCSD (Rio+20)—the Stockholm Conference was an initiative by the UN and developed countries to address global environmental and conservation issues. Initiated by Sweden, which suffered from acid rain, the conference was meant to address escalating industrial pollution and its impact on the environment.[373] It was not the *first* UN environmental conference. As pointed out in Chapter 2, UNESCO had sponsored the 1948 Fontainebleau conference and the 1949 Lake Success conference. It had also organized the 1968 Intergovernmental Conference of Experts on the Scientific Basis for Rational Use and Conservation of the Resources of the Biosphere, known as the Biosphere Conference; IUCN had been a major contributor to the Biosphere Conference, and was even credited as its initiator. Distinguishing between the Lake Success and Stockholm conferences, a 1978 UNEP report noted that

> Lake Success in 1949 was attended almost exclusively by scientists. Scientists were present in even greater numbers at the 1972 Stockholm conference, but they were far outnumbered by politicians and administrators—and the politicians and administrators did the work. Some scientists may lament the rapid rise of the conservation bureaucrat, but it is one of the many signs of the fact that conservation in 1978 is firmly established—which it was not 30 years ago.[374]

The Stockholm Conference can be further distinguished from previous UN conferences in that it was the first major postcolonial environmental conference, a description made all the more accurate by the acrimonious North-South conflict that characterized it.

Under the leadership of Coolidge, IUCN devised its strategy for the Stockholm Conference based on heightened visibility, the promotion of international conservation conventions, and the preparation of conference documents.[375] By the time of the conference, in June 1972, four conservation conventions were on the agenda. The Convention on Wetlands of International Importance had been adopted in Ramsar, Iran, the previous year, and was tabled at the conference to collect more signatures of contracting states. CITES was awaiting a conference of plenipotentiaries undertaken by the United States that had been delayed for political reasons and rescheduled for April 1973. The other two conventions, dealing respectively with world heritage sites and islands for science, were still in draft form. How did these conventions, the work primarily of IUCN, an NGO, make their way onto the international governmental agenda?

A CONTRIBUTION OF INTERNATIONAL CONVENTIONS

The official entry of IUCN into the Stockholm Conference process began with a letter dated February 6, 1969, from Philippe de Seynes, UN undersecretary for economic and social affairs, to Coolidge as president of IUCN. In accordance with the UNGA resolution convening the Stockholm Conference, de Seynes requested "contributions from appropriate intergovernmental and non-governmental organizations" toward its preparation.[376] Coolidge forwarded de Seynes's letter to IUCN officials and requested their response. The tone was set by IUCN's Robert Standish, who replied that "this seems to me to be a fine opportunity for additional exposure of IUCN's work before the world community."[377]

Joe Berwick, IUCN secretary general at the time, suggested that the Stockholm Conference focus on policy and legislation issues. Regarding legislation, Berwick noted that "IUCN is deeply concerned in this [legislation]" and submitted an update of IUCN activities. Referring to the future CITES, "Research done in compiling the Red Data Book leads directly to the Draft Convention on the Import, Export and Transit of Certain Species which could (if it has to wait as long as this) be signed at the Conference."[378] Raising a recurrent IUCN theme, Berwick also suggested an agreement on the "ultimate responsibility of survival of species to be signed by all countries."[379] Echoing the vision of the Earl of Onslow and other SPFE members of an Asian regional convention (and apparently unaware of the Western Hemisphere Convention), Berwick noted, "Our work in South East Asia and Latin America could lead to Conventions on conservation of natural resources for these regions in the same way as the African Special Project led to the African Convention." Moreover, "The investigation on relatively undisturbed islands now being conducted [. . .] might lead to a Convention for limited international sovereignty of the Antarctic Treaty type. Other areas where international conventions might be useful would include migratory birds, international animals such as whales, turtles, seals, polar bears, pollution both air and water, ocean deeps."[380]

Wolfgang Burhenne, chair of the IUCN Commission on Legislation, also argued for international conventions as IUCN's contribution to the Stockholm Conference, to counter the effects of increased "communication and the greater mobility which have greater impact on, among other things, natural resources." In analyzing the use of international law, Burhenne's argument makes the case for unified international environmental standards to avoid unfair competition in light of growing international trade. Countries that do not adhere to minimum legislation for pollution are not only misusing their own natural resources, but are causing unfair competition in the world market because they can produce at lower prices.[381]

Coolidge collected these comments and others, and on April 5, 1969, he replied to de Seynes.[382] He incorporated Berwick's position that the conference agenda should focus on government policy and legislation, and their implementation.[383] Coolidge further proposed the adoption of a "Universal Declaration on the Protection and Betterment of the Human Environment," offering IUCN services in its preparation. Coolidge then turned to international conventions, drawing on his rich experience from the 1930s and 1940s to bring forth a new generation. He suggested "designing new conventions to deal with such environments as relatively undisturbed island areas and undersea marine areas that should be left in their natural state for scientific study." Coolidge made a point of emphasizing IUCN's law-making expertise:

> We have had considerable experience in the field of legislation. Our African Special Project and deep concern over African environmental problems enabled us to play an advisory role in the preparation of the [. . .] Convention that has replaced the effective London Convention [. . .] which originated in 1933. [. . .] In Latin America the Convention on Nature Protection and Wild Life Preservation in the Western Hemisphere [. . .] was designed to assist member countries in environmental matters . . .

Turning from past and existing conventions to future conventions, Coolidge proceeded to market the future CITES. He explained,

> The lists compiled for the Red Data Books of our Survival Service Commission on endangered and vanishing species [. . .] indicated the necessity of developing a Convention [. . .] requiring protection in trade between countries. A draft of such a convention is now under study by 40 countries.[384]

Strengthening his argument for international conventions, Coolidge noted IUCN's work on listing endangered marine species, arguing that they "can only be safeguarded through enforced international agreements." He stressed the need for a further convention to counter the effects of pollution of the marine environment and its exploitation. And finally, Coolidge did not miss the opportunity to further his lasting quest for a world convention. He emphasized "the need for more worldwide international agreements and regulations" leading to "a coordinated system of world environmental policy." Describing IUCN's work on national parks, Coolidge proposed "a world convention [. . .] to reinforce existing conventions and to enable governments not included in the Americas or Africa to benefit from such a convention."[385]

Thus IUCN's major input to the Stockholm Conference was to be its extraordinary work on international conventions. IUCN aimed to persuade the UN to adopt its own agenda for international conventions, and it succeeded. Tracing IUCN's path of success indicates that its influence on the Stockholm Conference began prior to de Seynes's formal letter to Coolidge in February 1969. Its own mention in the 1968 UNGA resolution on Problems of the Human Environment hints that IUCN was probably involved in the drafting of the resolution itself. Further, the highly respected scientist Raymond Dasmann—key architect of the joint 1968 UNESCO and FAO report for the UN Economic and Social Council (ECOSOC), *Conservation and Rational Use of the Environment*, which became a guiding precept of the UNCHE process—was appointed IUCN's senior ecologist in 1970.[386] IUCN had also been carrying out a UN project on listings of national parks, affording another opportunity for the organizations to forge a relationship.[387] From the beginning, the secretariat of the Stockholm Conference expressed interest in cooperating with IUCN.[388] The start of the 1970s was viewed as a new era of "international governmental cooperation in the field of conservation, in which IUCN could and should play a leading role."[389] Institutional changes were in the air, led by the UN and its organizations.

But the winds of change could also threaten IUCN. In January 1970 the

Swedish zoologist Kai Curry-Lindahl, member of the IUCN executive board, worriedly wrote to Coolidge about an initiative for a new UN conservation organization (the future UNEP) launched by his own government. He warned Coolidge that a new institution could threaten IUCN's position as the leading international conservation organization with government agencies as members, and could relegate it to peripheral matters and private conservation organizations. Curry-Lindahl argued that a new institutional structure could mean a loss of power for IUCN. To counter these threats, wrote Curry-Lindahl, IUCN must strengthen its relations with UN organizations and governments, defeating Sweden's proposal for a new organization by showing "that such an organization already exists, although in non-governmental form."[390] In reply, Coolidge thanked Curry-Lindahl for the warning, but maintained that IUCN did not have much to worry about as long as it continued to excel professionally (dependent also on successful fund-raising), pointing out its current cooperative efforts with the UN and, in particular, with the Swedish mission at the UN.[391]

So the Stockholm Conference not only presented opportunities for IUCN; it also presented challenges and threats. To counter them, and to maintain its role as a key international conservation organization and a dynamic and influential force shaping the agenda of the conference, IUCN early on became directly involved in the conference's preparations. First, IUCN had to be visible. Moreover, it had to be professional and effective. Competition among organizations, familiar from SPFE and the American Committee and from IUCN's own turf wars with FAO and UNESCO, was a consideration in IUCN's strategy leading up to the Stockholm Conference. In a February 1970 letter, Gerardo Budowski suggested to Coolidge that "to strengthen and justify IUCN's presence in the UN, it might be worthwhile to prepare a draft declaration of policy as a basis for an universal declaration [. . . .] This was of course your own idea but I feel that time is getting short and I am of course also afraid that some other organization will switch the initiative. Therefore the sooner we get to it [. . .] the better."[392]

By June 1970 IUCN had prepared a contact paper on environmental law depicting IUCN's tactics for promoting international conventions at the Stockholm Conference. Its Environmental Law Center (ELC) would serve an advisory role for the Declaration on the Human Environment (as suggested by Budowski), as well as for the draft text of the future World Heritage Convention. The organization did not assume that it had a monopoly in drafting international conventions: IUCN'a deputy director general took it upon himself to "attempt to find out about any other conventions [. . .] being submitted to the Stockholm Conference by groups outside of IUCN which may be of interest to IUCN." The contact paper noted that it would not be possible to conclude "a Pacific Island Convention" in time for the 1972 conference. Regarding the future CITES, work was far enough advanced in June 1970 to be able to commit to a final draft for the conference. The future Ramsar Convention was also addressed, as well as international regulation of sealing and a draft convention on pollution.[393] In the surge of activities leading up to the conference, international conventions were an entry point for IUCN involvement in the Stockholm Conference preparations, "justifying its presence"—as strategized by Budowski regarding IUCN's work on a "universal declaration."[394] By mid-1970 IUCN had progressed sufficiently in its work on international agreements to submit final drafts of WHC, CITES, and the Islands Convention to the Stockholm Conference secretariat.

Together with international agreements, another element in IUCN's strategy for the Stockholm Conference was *visibility*. Coolidge made sure that IUCN was well represented at the conference secretariat in UN headquarters in New York. IUCN had been invited by the UN "to strengthen its organization in New York to ensure active co-operation."[395] IUCN employed a liaison officer at UN headquarters who reported to Coolidge on a bimonthly basis. She had been given an information desk, which—bearing in mind that she represented an NGO—was considered exceptional, and was interpreted by IUCN officials as displaying a high degree of integration in preparations for Stockholm.[396] Besides its administrative staff, in 1971 Professor Richard Gardner of Columbia University was appointed IUCN's high-level representative to the UN. The organization's preparations for the Stockholm Conference were marked by an overlapping of roles between its own and UN officials. Gardner, along with Professor Lynton K. Caldwell, chair of the IUCN Commission on Environmental Policy, Law and Administration, had been asked by the secretary general of the Stockholm Conference to prepare documents for "the international administrative framework" as a possible outcome of the Stockholm meeting, leading to the future UNEP.[397]

The result of all this activity was a strong relationship between IUCN and the UNCHE secretariat, and Maurice Strong in particular.[398] The relationship strengthened when the secretariat moved to Geneva, not far from IUCN headquarters in Morges. In September 1970 Strong visited IUCN as part of a series of visits to NGOs involved in preparations for the Stockholm Conference. They discussed projects for cooperation that included the World Heritage

Trust as well as a "police force" to deal with wayward and recalcitrant countries.[399] Tracing the path by which IUCN's work on international conventions reached the UNCHE agenda shows that although the short contact note of the September 1970 meeting did not mention international conventions, they were in all likelihood discussed by its participants: at an informal meeting of the UNCHE Preparatory Committee two months later, Strong announced a three-level process for the Stockholm Conference preparations. The first level was "intellectual-conceptual"—gathering and compiling the required knowledge to address the "relationship man-environment and the development of a comprehensive approach to the environmental management." The second level was the action plan to be adopted at Stockholm and which would consist of the work to be undertaken following the conference. The third level was "[a]ction which can be completed at the Conference, for example adoption of conventions."[400] If conventions were IUCN's contribution to UNCHE, and if Strong announced in November 1970, after meeting with IUCN, that a goal of the conference was to adopt a number of conventions, then IUCN's fingerprints are all over the decision.

IUCN apparently did not query or contest Strong's three-level strategy. In retrospect, it seems obvious that completing negotiations on scientifically complex and politically sensitive issues, and adopting a multiple number of conventions within eighteen months, was manifestly unreasonable. Yet throwing caution to the winds, IUCN was bent on fostering a lead role in UNCHE. By December 1970 Coolidge was able to write, "I am happy to say that our Union is working ever more closely with Maurice Strong and his preparatory office for the Stockholm Congress."[401] Further, beyond reputational concerns as well as normative interests in promoting international conventions, the Stockholm process was a source of funding, if a modest one. Money problems were a chronic IUCN concern, and UNCHE offered an opportunity for funded projects.[402]

An October 1971 memo from Budowski to IUCN's executive board, on "IUCN participation in preparations for the UN conference on the Human environment," displayed the myriad interests and considerations working beneath the surface and shaping IUCN strategy. Budowski began by pointing out that "IUCN has been closely involved, since the very beginning, in different matters connected with the conference."[403] The relationship between IUCN and the secretariat was strengthened following its relocation to Geneva, and "relationships were established with practically all staff members." In implementing its strategy for a high-visibility role for Stockholm and a strong and cooperative relationship with the secretariat, Budowski offered suggestions as well as some telling caveats: "IUCN should always be regarded as a centre of excellence in world conservation," yet money was a primary consideration. Although IUCN wanted to take a leading role in the preparations for the conference and strengthen its ties with the secretariat, Budowski pointed out that without financial resources, IUCN would not be able to carry out the work requested by the secretariat.[404] But along with these overriding financial considerations, and depicting the eternal dilemma, Budowski urged that

> IUCN should do its utmost to preserve its unique non-governmental position [. . . .] This implies that IUCN should resist pressure—or maybe it should be called "temptation" since it may solve part of IUCN's financial problems—to have close governmental ties, and therefore obligations that would restrict the freedom and the role it has and will continue to play as the world's "conscience for conservation."

In the same memo, Budowski also gave an update regarding IUCN's progress on international conventions:

> During the PC [Prep Comm] meetings [. . .] it has been agreed that different conventions prepared by IUCN be included as part of the proposals to be submitted for Level III at the SC, namely for immediate action. These include the draft convention on World Heritage and a Convention on the conservation of Certain Islands for Science. They may be open for signature at the time of the Stockholm Conference. Two other conventions, namely the convention on Export, Import and Transit of Certain Species of Wild Animals and Plants, and the Convention on Wetlands [. . .] could gather additional signatures during the Stockholm Conference provided they are open for signature [. . . .] Much discussion has been devoted to the drafts of these conventions during the meetings of the PC.[405]

AN ONGOING COLONIAL CONFRONTATION

Yet beyond IUCN's work on international conventions and the official image of UNCHE projected by the UN, developing countries' unhappiness and mistrust of the Stockholm Conference dominated the entire process. Because of its Western backing and its focus on industrial pollution associated with developed countries, UNCHE generated deep suspicion among developing countries. They saw it as a plot of developed countries to solve their own environmental problems—created by their high standard of living, fed by their ravenous consumption of natural resources—by denying developing countries the same standard of living. Leveraging the confrontation, Brazil initiated the UNGA resolution titled "Environment and Development" that sharply articulated the polarized positions of the developed and developing countries. The resolution set the background for the negotiations of the "Declaration of the United Nations Conference on the Human Environment" (the Stockholm Declaration), composed of a preamble of seven proclamations and twenty-six principles "to inspire and guide the peoples of the world in the preservation and enhancement of the human environment."[406] Together with its Action Plan, the Stockholm Declaration would be the major outcome of UNCHE.

To release mounting tension and resolve the bitterness that threatened a successful outcome for the Stockholm Conference, Strong convened a meeting on environment and development in Founex, Switzerland, that has become legendary in the annals of sustainable development. The meeting's findings determined that the environmental problems of developing countries—in pointed contrast to that of developed countries, linked to high standards of living—derive from poverty and lack of development. Resolving the environmental problems of developing countries meant economic development to be paid for by the developed countries. Hammering the message home, the meeting determined that protecting the environment of developed countries must not curtail the right of the developing countries to develop.[407]

Despite these attempts to bridge the wide gaps between the developed and developing countries, the atmosphere surrounding the UNCHE preparations was marked by discord, and sensitive sovereignty issues remained a critical obstacle to furthering international cooperation. Sharply depicted in the third session of the Prep Comm, IUCN liaison officer Robert Gruszka's report on the session illuminates the intensity and contentiousness of the sovereignty factor in developing countries' opposition to the UNCHE process. In another example of the theme of scales of governance underlying this book, Gruszka identified a key element in the debate as deciding on "[t]he most appropriate level for environmental action (national, regional, international)."[408] He observed the marked preference of states for national and regional approaches rather than international approaches to environmental problems.[409] Although the Stockholm Conference was intended to "concentrate on problems requiring international cooperation for their solutions; at the same time the Conference and the preparations for it [. . .] identify and draw attention to problems that are best dealt with at the national or regional levels." Gruszka explained that the preference for activities at the national or regional level stemmed from

> the character of the international system; its fragmentation into sovereign units and the heterogeneity among these units. The theme of sovereignty expectedly was implicit and very often explicit at the 3rd Session of the Preparatory Committee, as is the case in other contexts. More revealing however, was the extent to which delegates cited the diversity of conditions from nation to nation and region to region as the reason for the appropriateness of locating executive decision and implementory action at the national or regional levels.[410]

The colonial confrontation, which had forged European internationalization of African biodiversity, ultimately transformed into the ubiquitous North-South conflict over sovereignty. It hovered persistently and threateningly over the Stockholm Conference and determined its outcome. Yet the conflict did not occur *because* of the conference. It had been angrily simmering for decades, and flared up when given the world stage by UNCHE. Tracking the conflict beyond the narrow context of the Stockholm Conference reveals it as a replay of the conflict between European powers and "native" populations, in 1972 still a very recent event. The Stockholm Conference, overwhelmingly shaped by IUCN's powerful work on international conventions under the tutelage of Coolidge, was continuing conservation strategies that had originated under European colonialism. Yet distinct from previous conferences, by 1972 former colonial possessions had transformed into sovereign states. Instead of the 32 countries that had participated in the Lake Success conference, 134 countries participated in the Stockholm Conference. Developing countries now had the numbers to determine the outcome.

With the end of colonialism, developing countries *re*-created international law by forging the Permanent Sovereignty over Natural Resources principle. This new principle of international law contested the conceptualization of natural resources as the common heritage of humankind. It decreed them instead the exclusive property of the state in which they were located, to be used and exploited as the state saw fit with minimal restrictions. Leveraging the Stockholm Conference to promote an alternative international law, developing countries entrenched the PSNR principle within the Stockholm

Declaration as Principle 21, which became the paradigm for future international environmental law.

The principle of PSNR developed initially as a political statement of newly independent states emerging from colonialist rule, to assert and strengthen their political and economic status. It was the creation of a long line of UNGA resolutions, enabling new states to gain control of their natural resources exploited in pre-state rule by colonialist powers and foreign companies.[411] Control of natural resources was a prerequisite for the development of new national economies, so the exclusive rights of the state to its natural resources have been defined as a corollary of the right to self-determination, and a basic component of the principle of state sovereignty, the foundation of international law.[412]

The PSNR principle also evolved as a tool for developing countries to counter what they perceived as a new threat: the emerging Western concern over environmental pollution and devastation, spearheaded by their former colonial masters. Early uses of the PSNR principle to block international environmental cooperation pivoted around events surrounding the Stockholm Conference. Working on the first draft of the Stockholm Declaration, the Prep Comm proposed a principle subjecting state sovereignty over natural resources to the duty of the state to protect the environment while exercising its sovereignty.[413] The proposal was thrown out by countries that objected to any restriction on their use of their natural resources or impingement of their sovereignty. The end result was that instead of juxtaposing a state's exclusive right to its national resources with the duty to refrain from harming them or the environment in general, the right was juxtaposed with the responsibility to refrain from causing harm to the environment of *other* states or to areas beyond territorial jurisdiction. Principle 21 of the Stockholm Declaration proclaims,

> States have, in accordance with the Charter of the United Nations and the principles of international law, the sovereign right to exploit their own resources pursuant to their own environmental policies, and the responsibility to ensure that activities within their jurisdiction or control do not cause damage to the environment of other States or of areas beyond the limits of national jurisdiction.

Despite its origins as a compromise text reflecting postcolonial politics rather than ecological necessity, and although that its first part originated as a corollary economic right to the right to self-determination, Principle 21 is today considered an international principle of customary law. As such, and despite the inherent contradiction, it has been consistently incorporated into subsequent international environmental instruments.[414]

Constructing International Law

With the end of colonialism, two opposing but parallel developments were taking place. IUCN had launched an extraordinary labor of international convention making, mobilized around its deep anxiety over the fate of reserves, parks, and species of former African colonies. As IUCN was configuring international law to address its own concerns about decolonialization, developing countries were attempting to *re-create* international law as a tool for self-determination and economic development. They established the New International Economic Order (NIEO), a set of proposals incorporating the PSNR principle as an alternative international law distinct from colonial law. Each group of actors was stretching, pulling, and shaping international law to fit its own strategy and to implement its own unique objectives. While developing countries were building new international legal structures to meet their demands for development, IUCN, the UN, and a powerful nation—the United States—continued to promote international conventions based on earlier colonial ones, imposing European-American norms for nature conservation on peoples of different cultures. By the time of the 1972 Stockholm Conference, the "civilized-uncivilized," European–non-European conflict had transformed into the now familiar North-South quarrel.

The Stockholm Conference not only offered IUCN a powerful platform for self-promotion; the conference was primarily a platform for the UN, signaling its entry as a world environmental leader. With the mounting awareness of the dangers of environmental pollution to human health, public concern was swiftly escalating, and governments took note. Strong global leadership was in demand, and the UN recognized the opportunity and stepped in to fill the vacuum. The Stockholm Conference would launch the UN's new role. It had been years in the planning and preparation, requiring immense scientific and professional input on issues that had not yet been addressed on so broad a scale, as well as substantial financial resources. Maurice Strong and the UN had to show results, and the adoption of environmental conventions symbolizing international consensus would signal success of the Stockholm Conference to the international community. These conventions would demonstrate the UN's power and capacity to successfully tackle complex environmental issues, justifying the vast resources invested in UNCHE as well as countering criticism leveled at it by developing countries. Without detracting from its sincere interest in making these conventions work, the UN promoted them primarily as symbols of its successful leadership for the global environment; hence the hurry to complete them and sign them at the conference itself. In doing so, the UN was using international law, as did IUCN, UNESCO, and FAO, to promote its influence, ambitions, and reputation.

Among the multiple actors involved in these conventions and the range of incentives that motivated them, the ultimate actor was IUCN, and its key motivation was Africa. A passion for African fauna had not only launched the international conservation movement but fueled it for decades afterward. International biodiversity law was born in Africa. Beyond the obvious example of the 1968 African Convention, IUCN created the Stockholm conventions expressly for postcolonial Africa. They were based on the premise that international law would overcome the challenges of conservation in the postcolonial reality of independent African nations by establishing rules and norms that would be internationally recognized and implemented. This premise was IUCN's guiding principle throughout its early years. Yet at some point this conviction passed, with the dawning realization that international conventions were not achieving IUCN's goals. By disclosing the colonial roots of each convention, more pieces of the puzzles that triggered this study fall into place. Completing them, the next chapter addresses the last in this continuum of biodiversity conventions — the Convention on Biodiversity (CBD).

CHAPTER FOUR

Disillusionment

> The main focus of wildlife conservationists at the Rio Conference was the Convention on Biological Diversity. In a sense this was unfinished business arising from the World Conservation Strategy in 1980. Its roots went back long before [. . .] indeed, in a sense its roots go back to the 1933 Conference and the 1900 Convention. — *William Adams,* Against Extinction[415]

A Biodiversity Decade

Pursuing its mandate of international law making, by the 1970s IUCN had succeeded in creating a remarkable body of biodiversity conventions. Yet as attempts were made to implement them, doubts set in about their efficaciousness and criticism of these conventions was surfacing. The challenges of halting biodiversity loss were becoming evident, and the conventions were accused of being weak, issue-specific, and fragmentary.[416] Worriedly tracking escalating biodiversity loss, by 1975 IUCN had launched an international policy for nature that became the *World Conservation Strategy* (WCS), both an intellectual framework and the practical guidebook on how to conserve biological resources.[417] Its publication in 1980 triggered IUCN's "biodiversity decade" of the 1980s, a period dedicated to defining the concept of biodiversity and culminating in IUCN's early drafts of the CBD. WCS devoted a great deal of attention to international conventions, stressing their critical role in a conservation strategy. Yet signaling IUCN's growing recognition of the conventions' inadequacies, WCS also issued a prophetic warning that "weak conventions, however, are dangerous and to be avoided, because they permit the illusion that problems are being tackled when in fact they are not."[418]

Seeking explanations for worsening biodiversity loss despite these conventions, WCS reviewed existing biodiversity agreements, identifying the drawbacks of each. It was inconclusive about the need for a new convention, however, generally recommending the "development of new law to remedy any deficiencies."[419] Despite its role as lead visionary and architect of these treaties, and the labor it had invested in each, the determined IUCN acknowledged their limitations, and so saying, doggedly set out to craft the future Convention on Biological Diversity.[420] The novel and tantalizing (perhaps because it was simply not well understood) idea of biodiversity was making its way onto the world scene, and the Stockholm conventions, together with the 1979 Convention on the Conservation of Migratory Species and the new CED, would soon be referred to as the *biodiversity conventions*.

In yet a further step toward the future CBD—and evoking the proposal raised by Britain and Germany that led to the 1900 London Convention—the following year IUCN's 1981 General Assembly called for an "international arrangement" for the conservation of genetic resources.

> RECOGNIZING that genetic resources form part of the natural heritage of mankind and should therefore remain available to all nations [. . .] CONSIDERING that States have a duty of stewardship towards the conservation of genetic resources [. . .] INSTRUCTS the IUCN Secretariat to undertake an analysis [. . .] providing a basis for an international arrangement and for rules to implement it.[421]

Defining *genetic resources* as a "natural heritage of mankind" that should be "available to all nations," and imposing a duty of stewardship on states regarding their genetic resources, the 1981 resolution reflected concepts that had rationalized the exploitation of non-European lands in the dark colonial past. The first in a series of operative measures leading directly to the CBD, the resolution was spearheaded by Cyrille de Klemm.[422] If the Earl of Onslow, Julian Huxley, and Harold Coolidge were visionaries for a world convention for nature, the Belgian environmental lawyer Cyrille de Klemm, a legal expert in wildlife and biodiversity issues and a member of CEPLA, upgraded the vision to the protection of biodiversity and played a key role in making it happen. Indications of IUCN's growing disillusionment with international conventions are evident in de Klemm's work starting in the early 1980s.

Attempting to analyze the problem, de Klemm asked whether "the most serious shortcoming of conservation-conventions stands in the fact that they are de facto if not in law, the sum of a number of unilateral commitments the non-performance of which is of no consequence, economically or legal, for the other parties." And in a full circle back to Onslow in the 1930s and 1940s, in 1982 de Klemm lamented that "there is no world convention for the conservation of species and natural habitats." He emphasized that "in the last analysis, the fate of species rests with states since it is states and only states, which by their direct action carry out, encourage, authorize or subsidize the destruction of natural ecosystems, and hence of species [. . .] [W]ithout an enforceable commitment to conservation on the part of the states of the world, millions of species will be doomed."[423]

The policy that de Klemm advocated for governing genetic resources was reminiscent of European colonial policy for governing non-European natural resources. De Klemm urged that "the property of species should be vested in the world community."[424] He framed genetic resources as the common heritage of humankind. He envisioned a new world convention based on principles of global ownership of species, unrestricted access to genetic resources, and the duty of all states to conserve species under their jurisdiction, while also advocating monetary compensation for states that fulfill this duty. Seeking further international forums to stamp their seal of approval on the new convention, de Klemm and other IUCN lawyers succeeded the following year in persuading the World Congress on National Parks, a forum under the sponsorship of IUCN, to adopt a resolution for a world treaty to protect wild genetic resources.[425]

IUCN also promoted soft law as part of a global biodiversity strategy; the best known example is the 1982 World Charter for Nature.[426] The charter dates from IUCN's 12th General Assembly, in Kinshasa, Zaire, in 1975. President Mobutu of Zaire raised the idea in his opening speech at the General Assembly. He pointedly blamed the developed countries for global environmental problems, reminding his listeners of Zaire's very recent colonial past:

> Industrialized countries put the blame on those who have not yet reached that stage, for not controlling the growth of their populations [. . . .]
> At the same time, however, they forget that their populations, although representing one-third of mankind, consume ninety percent of the planet's resources [. . . .] We, who have been colonized, were taught that the civilization of our former masters was the best one [. . . .] [T]he crisis is one of civilization [. . . .] Thanks to zairianisation, we have become the owners of our lands [. . . .] If I had any advice for you, I would suggest the establishment of a Charter of Nature [. . . .] [I]nsofar as Zaire is concerned, we are ready to help you succeed [. . . .] The jungle of liberal capitalism is finished. Every citizen in this world must defend his heritage, the area in which he lives, against those modern savages, the killers of Nature who do not hesitate to slaughter her to swell their wallets.[427]

Following Mobutu's proposal, the same IUCN General Assembly adopted a resolution recommending a World Charter for Nature.[428] The charter was drafted by IUCN through a process lasting several years. It was first debated at the 35th session of UNGA in October 1980. True to its traditional role as the redoubtable advocate for the G77 nations (the coalition of developing nations within the UN system, with 77 founding members and currently numbering 132 members) and vigilant guardian of their sovereignty, the Brazilian delegate reminded other delegations "of the paramount importance of [the principle of] the permanent sovereignty of States over their natural resources and the inalienable responsibility of States to ensure the development of their own countries [. . . .] Poverty and underdevelopment are major causes of the deterioration of the human environment."[429]

The course of the charter's adoption was marked by the persistent objections of the developing countries. While African countries were more supportive of the initiative in light of Zaire's leading role, South American countries charged that the charter favored conservation over social and economic needs. Brazil framed the debate on the World Charter for Nature as the ubiquitous conflict of Northern exploitation of Southern natural resources. During the final session, Brazil raised an issue that cut to the core of IUCN's role in the process, an ominous harbinger for the CBD negotiations. Brazil questioned "why the drafting of the world charter for nature was conducted entirely outside any intergovernmental process [. . .] the text was primarily the result of the work, worthy though it may be, of a non-governmental body."[430]

Brazil further argued that "throughout history the developed countries have been not only the main polluters of our world but also the main contributors to the damage done to nature. This is a fact that the Amazonian countries feel has not been taken into account at all in the text of the Draft World Charter for Nature."[431] The making of the World Charter for Nature was a replay of the acrimonious North-South disputes of the Stockholm Conference and an omen of the future CBD negotiations, which would also be marked by the hostility of developing countries in general and Brazil in particular. The battle lines were being drawn, the arguments honed, and the themes developed. Arguments that would become classics were being skillfully crafted, such as the *common heritage* concept as a violation of the sovereignty of developing countries, and NGO (specifically, IUCN) usurpation of the exclusive authority of states in the area of international law.

Milestones

Parallel to work on policy documents and soft-law instruments, IUCN officials began to promote a new convention in earnest. Pursuing his vision for a convention on genetic resources, de Klemm continued to drive the idea deeper within IUCN's own institutional structure. In November 1984 IUCN's 16th General Assembly in Madrid adopted a resolution requesting IUCN to promote "a preliminary draft for a global agreement on the conservation of the wild genetic resources [. . .] by late 1985." The "international arrangement" of 1981 had by 1984 become a "global agreement." Continuing to reflect traces of colonial concepts, this milestone resolution noted "that these processes by their very nature cannot be the subject of exclusive or proprietary rights on the part of any state or individual," and that they "form part of the common heritage of mankind."[432]

After the IUCN General Assembly signed off on a global agreement for genetic resources, the next step was to achieve IGO support for the initiative, namely UNEP. Because UNEP was the lead UN agency for environmental issues, gaining the approval of its member countries was essential in launching the actual negotiations. With UNEP's backing, a proposal was tabled for the agenda of the 14th session of UNEP's Governing Council (GC) in 1987, officially submitted by the US government. Yet behind the scenes and at this early stage in June 1987, the concept of a biodiversity convention was very much an IGO/NGO-controlled process, a result of cooperative efforts between UNEP and IUCN. The two organizations drew justification and support for a biodiversity convention from the 1987 landmark Brundtland Report, *Our Common Future: Report of the World Commission on Environment and Development* (WCED), which had proposed a "Species Convention, such as a draft prepared by IUCN, which should articulate the concept of species and genetic variability as a common heritage [. . .] individual nations would no longer be left to rely on their own isolated efforts to protect species within their borders."[433]

Thus IUCN leveraged intergovernmental and other UN-sponsored forums as a medium for promoting its own initiatives, and the reverse — IGOs used IUCN to advance their own. Besides the United States, governments were not yet part of the process.[434] They were not particularly receptive to the proposal for a biodiversity convention at the 1987 UNEP GC session. This agenda item was outshone by the Brundtland Report and the WCED chair, Norwegian prime minister Gro Brundtland, who addressed the Governing Council.[435] Reflecting states' initial disinterest in a biodiversity convention, the GC adopted a low-key decision that went no further than requesting UNEP's executive director to establish a working group of experts on biological diversity "to investigate the desirability and possible form of an umbrella convention."[436] Nevertheless, decision 14/26, "Rationalization of international conventions on biological diversity," is a further milestone in the evolution of the CBD, opening the way for UNEP to convene intergovernmental meetings. Significantly, demonstrating the cooperation between UNEP and IUCN, the decision specifically makes note of IUCN's work on a biodiversity convention.

IUCN's efforts to promote a new convention for biodiversity were producing results. It had succeeded in achieving a favorable decision from UNEP's GC. The prestigious WCED was calling for a species convention based on IUCN's own draft. The organization had the support of the global superpower, the United States, which was itself vigorously promoting an international agreement for biodiversity conservation. Recalling US leadership in drafting and bringing to adoption the World Heritage Convention and CITES, IUCN in all likelihood viewed US involvement as a guarantee that a biodiversity convention would also be successfully negotiated. The future CBD was envisioned along the lines of traditional nature conservation treaties, emphasizing in situ conservation to protect species and habitats. IUCN and UNEP still firmly held that biodiversity was a global and common heritage, and still advocated unrestricted access to genetic resources. Development, sustainable or otherwise, and ownership of biodiversity were not yet issues for the new convention.[437] As a portent of what lay in store for the CBD negotiations, at the same GC session UNEP, arguably intent on expanding its role in international conventions and perhaps in consultation with IUCN, proposed an international agreement for forest conservation that "was fiercely rejected by a number of developing countries."[438] But otherwise, there is no hint of what would become the all-pervasive North-South split, of the issues that were to hold center stage during the negotiations, including biotechnology, access to genetic resources, benefit sharing, ownership of genetic resources and property rights, financial compensation, and transfer of technologies.

In support of its long-term objective of a global biodiversity convention, IUCN continued to publish policy papers and to pursue resolutions of its General Assembly. Responding to the Brundtland Report, IUCN determined that "[t]he world's environment is getting worse at a faster rate," and recommended that "a new international convention [. . .] would help encourage nations to meet their responsibilities to the world community."[439] Moving forward in promoting the future CBD, in February 1988 IUCN's 17th General Assembly, held in San Jose, Costa Rica—referring to its own resolution 16/24 from its previous GA, UNEP's GC decision 14/26, as well as the Brundtland Report—recognized IUCN's success in promoting the new agreement, and adopted a recommendation calling for "the draft convention on the conservation of wild genetic resources [. . .] [to] be widely circulated for comment by governments and NGOs."[440] IUCN's vision of a global agreement for protecting genetic resources appeared to be swiftly becoming a reality.

A US Initiative

> [I]n a rare demonstration of confidence in UNEP, the United States came to the GC with an initiative calling for work on a global convention on biological diversity [. . .] with a view to bringing everything together under an "umbrella" convention [. . . .] Some delegations liked the US idea; others preferred to give their support to efforts being made by IUCN [. . .] to draft a global convention on in situ conservation of flora and fauna. —*Fiona McConnell*, The Biodiversity Convention: A Negotiating History, *1996*[441]

Corresponding to the IUCN initiative and continuing its traditional leadership role in international conservation issues, the US government had reached the decision to "strongly support efforts to convene an international convention for preservation of the Earth's biological diversity." President Reagan signed a Joint Resolution of Congress in 1988 calling on the United States to initiate discussions for a biodiversity agreement.[442] A year earlier, the United States had submitted its proposal to the UNEP Governing Council. Similar to IUCN's position, the United States advocated a convention along the lines of a traditional nature conservation convention committing nations to protect "habitat, species and ecosystems" and "to conserve as much biological diversity as possible."[443] The United States had by now accumulated significant expertise in the area of international conservation policy and law, starting from its early twentieth-century initiatives for migratory birds and marine mammals conventions, and through its work on the Stockholm conventions in the 1960s and early 1970s. It was reassuming its earlier leadership position in promoting earlier conservation conventions and the 1940 Western Hemisphere Convention in particular.

But under attack by developing countries fiercely opposed to its proposal, and because of their dogged insistence on including biotechnology issues, the United States ultimately decided that its own interests would not be served by such a treaty.⁴⁴⁴ By the final CBD negotiating sessions, the US delegation was instructed to undertake delaying tactics to *not* meet the June 1992 deadline for the upcoming UNCED in Rio, in total conflict with UNEP's desperate efforts to secure this deadline.⁴⁴⁵ Similar to the United States, other developed countries also feared the impact of an international convention on their domestic biotechnology industries. The genetic resources on which these industries depended were located in developing countries, so developed countries became actively involved in the negotiations once they sensed a threat to their own national interests.⁴⁴⁶ Nevertheless, excluding the United States, within two years of the convention's coming into force in 1993, virtually all developed countries had ratified the CBD. Veit Koester points out that "[b]y May 1995 the Convention had been ratified or otherwise adhered to by the EC and by one hundred and seventeen states, among them all the Nordic Countries and most of the EU Member States (by November 1996 the figure is 162)."⁴⁴⁷ Arguably, countries' reputational concerns overrode their interests in *not* having a biodiversity agreement; even those that objected to elements in the text, and attached declarations as such to the Final Act, speedily ratified the convention.⁴⁴⁸

Ironically, although the United States has been habitually vilified for not ratifying the CBD, it not only formally submitted the proposal for the future convention to UNEP, but it has a long tradition of promoting international conservation conventions generally, a history that has been largely ignored.

Launching the Negotiations

> The negotiations on the Biodiversity Convention spanned a period of five years. During this time, while no one disputed the fact that the loss of genetic resources, ecosystems, and species was accelerating at an alarming rate through human actions, when it came to adopting measures for halting this acceleration and trying to reverse the trend, negotiations centered on political, financial and economic gains. —*Mustapha Tolba and Iwona Rummel-Bulska,* Global Environmental Diplomacy⁴⁴⁹

Implementing its Governing Council's 1987 decision to explore the idea of a new biodiversity convention, in August 1988 UNEP convened a meeting of scientists in Nairobi. The meeting's objective was to prepare a "report on the conservation of biological diversity" for the first session of the Ad Hoc Working Group of Experts (the Working Group), scheduled for November 1988 in Geneva.⁴⁵⁰ Accounting for the influence of IUCN's work on the August 1988 meeting, of its nine participants, four were or had been IUCN officials;

and of these four, three had been, were then, or would be, director generals.[451] Reinforcing IUCN's position, the scientists agreed that "biodiversity must be viewed as a common resource, like the atmosphere or the oceans, in which all nations have a common interest and towards which all have a common responsibility."[452]

UNEP circulated the scientists' report as an information document for the November meeting, including "Draft Articles for [. . .] a Proposed Convention on the Conservation of Biodiversity." A key element was the establishment of a "World List," conjuring up the lists of species annexed to the 1900 and 1933 London Conventions. Evoking European policy of enclosing sensitive habitat as protection, the scientists emphasized "a worldwide network of ecosystems adequate in size and distribution to conserve the greatest feasible proportion of the earth's biodiversity." Another article was an updated rendition of the "imperial legacy" narrative, declaring, "States have a duty to conserve biodiversity for the benefit of present and future generations of mankind."[453] Yet the scientists also emphasized that the key to a successful convention was support of developing countries, and stressed the need for "transfer of resources" from wealthy countries to countries containing "much of the world's biological diversity" but lacking "adequate resources for its conservation." The group of scientists concluded their report with the following caveat:

> We consider that a global Convention would be a powerful catalyst [. . . .] But [. . .] it must be more than a series of noble aspirations. It must do more than state on paper needs for action which cannot be fulfilled for want of resources, or will not be fulfilled for lack of political will among Governments. A convention must not be adopted as a substitute for action, or it will blunt and deflect the efforts the world needs.[454]

Drawing from the scientists' report, UNEP prepared a working paper titled "'Rationalization of International Conventions on Biological Diversity,' Note by the Executive Director." It adopted verbatim the scientists' view of biodiversity as a common resource, endorsing the precept of the "incorporation of the maximum amount of biological diversity in protected areas," and referring to states as "stewards of biological diversity." It emphasized "guaranteed access to genetic resources both in situ and ex situ," and finally, it determined the need "for a new global convention on the conservation of biological diversity." UNEP had adopted the IUCN model of a traditional conservation convention, to protect habitats and "engage action to conserve as much of the world's biological diversity as possible."[455] There was still no mention of intellectual property rights, access and benefit sharing, or biotechnologies. Nevertheless, echoing the proposals of the group of scientists, UNEP also adopted their view that committing developed countries to contribute financially to developing countries was the key to successful implementation. Taking a further lead from IUCN, by 1988 UNEP was also noting the drawbacks of the Stockholm conventions in reversing biodiversity loss.[456]

Although the UNEP document "Note by the Executive Director" signaled IUCN's success as an NGO in gaining the support of an IGO for a new biodiversity convention, the enthusiasm was limited to non-state actors. As depicted by the proceedings of the Working Group's first session in November 1988, considered by Veit Koester as the launch of the negotiation process,[457] the key actors in international law—states—were initially disinterested in the future CBD. As an IGO representing sovereign states, did UNEP have the required support of governments to launch a new convention on biodiversity? Apparently the question had initially troubled UNEP's executive director, who in September 1987 had sent a questionnaire to governments seeking their position on a new biodiversity convention. After receiving and reviewing responses from fifty-two governments, UNEP came to what appears an obvious conclusion, as noted by the executive director: "that the majority of the world community wants to see the biological diversity of the planet protected."

> The Executive Director is encouraged in this belief by the response of 52 governments to his letter of 10 September 1987, written pursuant to Governing Council decision 14/26. Ten of those Governments recorded that the conservation of biological diversity would form part of their national conservation strategies, 15 supported the examination of the desirability of an umbrella convention on biological diversity and 23 positively supported the development of an international agreement on the conservation of biological diversity.[458]

Despite UNEP's apparent confidence in the support of governments for the new convention, the proceedings of the early working group sessions disclose a lukewarm response. They reflect the cautious concern of many governments regarding a new convention, developed and developing countries alike. A biodiversity convention originally raised little interest among states, and only twenty-five countries sent representatives to the first session of the Ad Hoc Working Group of Experts, in November 1988.[459] The caution and disinclination displayed toward a new biodiversity convention crossed the North-South divide. Drawing from the proceedings of this session, neither developed nor developing countries were convinced by IUCN's and UNEP's arguments about the need for a new convention. The developing countries viewed such a convention with distrust, as a tool of the developed countries to gain control of their genetic resources. They refused to be lectured that it was their duty to conserve their biological resources for the rest of the world. Neither did they want the threat of a global list hanging over their heads, coupled with an international advisory committee to determine its contents.[460] As for the developed countries, they displayed "treaty fatigue," were wary of restrictions on access to genetic resources, and worried that the new convention would cost them dearly. The only participating country strongly in favor of a new convention was the United States. Despite its efforts, the US delegation did not succeed in persuading other delegations that the key to reversing biodiversity loss was an umbrella convention, geared for habitat and species protection. As the negotiations got under way, the United States did not back down from this position, and consequently became the target of heated attacks by the G77.[461]

The November 1988 Meeting

The G77 could undoubtedly claim to have set the agenda and shaped the content of the convention. They were quickly successful in seeing off the idea of biological diversity as the common heritage of mankind with its components freely available for exploitation. It took only a little longer for the developed countries to realize that their ambitions for saving the diversity of life on earth would have to be paid for—by themselves—in the form of money, technology, training, benefit sharing, and so on. The G77 negotiating line was in effect: "We've got most of it: you want it; you'll have to pay for it."
—*Fiona McConnell*, The Biodiversity Convention[462]

Drawing on its strong reputation as an authoritative scientific organization together with its expertise in convention drafting, IUCN's goal at the first session of the Ad Hoc Working Group of Experts was to convince governments of the need for a new convention. Yet the European Community (EC) made the valid point that prior to a decision on a new convention, "it was necessary to examine whether existing mechanisms were sufficient to maintain genetic variability." Its representative then proceeded to review EC wildlife directives, pointedly suggesting that the EC did not need another international convention to protect Europe's biodiversity.[463] France also did not initially support a new convention. Its representative opined that the problem was not the lack of a specific convention on biodiversity, but rather "an obvious problem of co-ordination among the existing conventions," later questioning "whether a new instrument was needed."[464]

True to form, Brazil's representative argued that "the need of a convention remained to be proved [. . . .] Under any circumstances, action should not be based on the concept of a common heritage."[465] Other countries also queried the need for a new convention. The Netherlands argued that before a decision could be made, the meeting "should try to identify the gaps in world-wide conservation of biological diversity."[466] Egypt's representative reminded other participants of the harsh reality of life in developing countries, where the "conservation of biodiversity in developing countries was competing with the livelihood of the populations [. . . .] Convincing the policy makers of these countries of the importance of biodiversity might be difficult."[467] The delegate from Switzerland also responded coolly to the proposal for a new convention, questioning "whether there were not already enough conventions." Raising an argument that has since become ubiquitous, he reminded the other participants that "the workload involved in making the mechanism of a convention function is very heavy, quite apart from the funding problems connected with financing a secretariat." Similar arguments were raised by Malaysia and Haiti, both claiming that there were already too many conventions making it difficult for them to join and burdensome to implement.[468] Norway, which would ultimately become a major supporter of a new convention, was still equivocal in November 1988; the Norwegian delegation emphasized using existing conventions and other mechanisms for protecting biological diversity.[469] The United Kingdom's delegate noncommittally noted "that the existing conservation conventions functioned quite well in their specific fields."[470] As for the United States, in sharp contrast to the positions of other countries, it stressed the need for a *new* convention to address worsening biodiversity loss.[471]

States were not the only participants questioning the need for a new convention. Both FAO and UNESCO opposed the initiative outright, raising arguments redolent of the turf wars over preceding conventions. FAO played an active role in the Working Group session, and fought valiantly to avoid a new biodiversity treaty. In contrast to the United States' and IUCN's support of a traditional nature conservation agreement, FAO stressed that "conservation and development had to be discussed in the same forum." Reversing biodiversity loss demanded resources that many governments lacked outright, "as they sought survival for their growing populations."⁴⁷² Noting that the Working Group had to deal not only with biodiversity but with sustainable development as well, the FAO observer pointed out that biodiversity loss was a result of *un*sustainable development.⁴⁷³ FAO displayed a deeper and more perceptive understanding of the underlying factors in biodiversity loss than either IUCN or the United States, or UNEP, its fellow IGO. But the United States and IUCN lost no opportunity in pointing out that FAO dealt with ex situ rather than in situ conservation, and in any case, FAO was not the lead agency for biodiversity issues.⁴⁷⁴ UNESCO took FAO's side in the quarrel. Evoking the NGO-IGO tensions of previous conventions, UNESCO reminded the Working Group that nonlegal tools such as biosphere reserves can also contribute to the conservation of biodiversity.⁴⁷⁵ Yet when a new convention became a certainty as the negotiations progressed, FAO took a dynamic role in the process.⁴⁷⁶

Meanwhile Brazil, bringing to mind the internationalization of Africa's biodiversity by European colonial powers, consistently and defiantly objected to any hint of "internationalization" of biological resources. Unflagging in his defense of the sovereignty of developing countries, its delegate voiced such countries' mistrust of a convention that not only was perceived as a threat to national sovereignty, but had been initiated and drafted by an NGO.⁴⁷⁷ While the UNEP representative noted that IUCN's draft might be used as the basis for the group's work in the future, to soothe the fears of the developing countries he also added that "any further session should be deferred until after the meeting of the UNEP Governing Council in May 1989."⁴⁷⁸ Brazil was repeating its position from the UNGA World Charter for Nature debates, objecting to an NGO taking the lead, and insisting "that priorities must be set by governments, not by experts."⁴⁷⁹ Maintaining this line, the US representative suggested that the UNEP secretariat "might explore the text of a draft convention" (that is, instead of IUCN), to which the chair replied that "a bridge should be built between work within the UNEP framework and work within the IUCN framework." Brazil's delegate took up the challenge, and retorted that he "would have difficulty in discussing the matter in the IUCN framework since Brazil was not a member of IUCN." A subdued IUCN replied that it "entirely agreed that its initiative should be co-ordinated with any UNEP GC decision, and would be very willing to discuss the modalities with the ED, since IUCN had no authority to convene formal plenipotentiary meetings."⁴⁸⁰

The November 1988 session marked a critical juncture for IUCN's meteoric rise in promoting its vision of a biodiversity agreement and its equally swift decline. IUCN had responded to criticism raised during the meeting that there were already enough international conventions, by pointing out that although no one doubted the worth of existing conventions, these treaties were disadvantaged by not addressing biodiversity in its entirety. Unwittingly endorsing colonial conservation norms, IUCN's observer was keen on explaining to sovereign countries why their natural resources were a global resource requiring a new agreement that would both recognize their global nature and support countries "who were the custodians of biodiversity" in their conservation.[481]

Although the meeting had started as an IGO/NGO-controlled initiative, by its close, the process was starting the inevitable shift to states. Yet even with the marked lack of enthusiasm for a new convention, some sort of consensus *had* been reached, indicating the combined power of NGOs and IGOs to promote the future CBD. Despite the record of the proceedings, which show the lukewarm reception of states to the idea, UNEP officials summarized that "the working group concluded that existing conservation conventions [. . .] did not cover the full range of biological diversity [. . .] [and] there was an urgent need for a new international legal instrument."[482]

The 1988 session presented an opportunity to define the issues and construct and test arguments in anticipation of the heated battles of the actual negotiations. The developing countries were coordinating their positions as the G77, a formidable and enviably well-coordinated negotiating bloc. The Working Group insisted that the links between development and conservation must be incorporated in any new convention, and that the transfer of technical and financial resources from developed to developing countries was critical to successful negotiations. Other issues addressed were framework conventions versus substantive conventions, and the question of free access to genetic resources. Evoking an "imperial heritage," common heritage continued to be a contentious and unresolved issue. The session began with the firm declaration of UNEP's executive director that biodiversity represented a global resource, but it limped to the finish line with the vague statement that "the Working Group did not reach a consensus on the notion of biodiversity as a common resource of mankind, some delegations stressing the principle of the sovereignty of states over their natural resources."[483]

So did IUCN get what it wanted, or was this a pyrrhic victory? On one hand, general consensus was achieved about a new global agreement for biodiversity. But on the other, the IUCN draft had been cast aside, and states were taking over the process with UNEP — after it humbly and summarily changed its mind on the common heritage concept — replacing IUCN as key drafter. IUCN went from a leadership role in drafting and promoting a biodiversity convention, to a begrudgingly bestowed advisory role in a convention that focused on funding, biotechnologies, technology transfers, and access and benefit sharing, and was on its way to becoming a development convention.[484]

The Turning Point

IUCN's initial success in promoting a comprehensive agreement for in situ biodiversity conservation by states was fizzling out. The watershed was UNEP Decision GC 15/34, titled "Preparation of an International Legal Instrument on the Biological Diversity of the Planet," adopted by UNEP's Governing Council at its 15th session, in May 1989. It was a complete turnaround from the previous 1987 decision, GC 14/26, which simply referred to protecting biological diversity. GC 15/34 introduced socioeconomic considerations and biotechnology issues, and threw out the concept of common heritage of humankind along with unrestricted access to genetic resources. The developing countries succeeded in incorporating in the decision's preamble the clause "aware that the full implications of the new biotechnologies should be taken into account," as well as the following decisive declaration:

> [T]he economic dimension, including [. . .] financial transfers from those who benefit from the exploitation of biological diversity, [. . .] to the owners and managers of biological resources [. . .] will need to be properly considered in the negotiations of any future legal instrument for the conservation of biological diversity.[485]

The November 1988 session of the Working Group had surely contributed to the sharp clash between these two decisions. The session had raised developing countries' suspicions that IUCN and UNEP were floating an international convention as a ploy to turn biodiversity into a global common heritage, restricting countries' right to "exploit" their own resources by compelling them to protect these resources for the rest of the planet. UNEP Decision GC 15/34 would set the tone for the rest of the process. Fiona McConnell, head of the British delegation, recounts in her negotiating history of the CBD that government delegations to the 1989 Governing Council session displayed caution regarding a new convention. Echoing the concerns of many participants in the Working Group, the United Kingdom and other countries were worried about duplication of agreements. The United States continued to promote an umbrella agreement, but its resistance to the inclusion of biotechnology in the convention was countered by the ultimatum of developing countries that there would be no biodiversity convention without biotechnologies. Developing countries opposed any new convention that did not acknowledge that most of the world's genetic resources had been and were being taken from them without fair compensation. Colonialism was still fresh in their minds, and their message was that "those who claimed that the planet's living resources should be regarded as global commons were preaching a new form of colonialism: the resources belonged to the countries where they were found."[486]

The 15th GC session also became the scene for the proverbial IGO-NGO controversy about which organization would run the new convention. Several delegations proposed UNESCO as the administrator because it was already running the World Heritage Convention, reminiscent of the UNESCO and IUCN competition for the job. As vividly described by McConnell, a few even dared to suggest that IUCN should receive the mandate in light of its work on a draft text, a proposal that

> infuriated a number of diplomats who pointed out that a[n] NGO, however eminent or well-supported, could not be permitted to usurp the functions of governments [. . .] [T]he representative of IUCN [. . .] tactfully proposed [. . .] that the text that they were preparing could be offered to UNEP without any strings attached whenever the Governing Council decided to go ahead with a convention. The UNEP secretariat in turn promised to take full account of proposals from IUCN and any other competent NGO.[487]

Although the bottom line was that the GC authorized UNEP to start work on "an international legal instrument,"[488] the rules of the game had changed. The draft convention was sent back to the Ad Hoc Working Group of Experts on Biological Diversity "to consider the technical content within a broad socio-economic context."[489] The developing countries would swiftly take control of the negotiations by using their almost total monopoly over Earth's remaining biological and genetic resources as leverage over the developed countries. Sustainable development had come on board, as had the socioeconomic perspective. The heated debate over sovereignty, which had become pivotal to the negotiations process juxtaposed to the common heritage concept, was resolved at this session of the GC, as noted in a UNEP report from September 1989:

> Since GC 15/34 imports the concept of ownership into the law on biological diversity, it follows that the concept of free access and common ownership of biological diversity is rejected. Biological diversity becomes a national resource subject to the normal rules of national jurisdiction.[490]

By virtue of expanding its scope from biodiversity protection exclusively to financial and technology transfers, biotechnology, and other concerns of the developing countries, the 1989 GC session succeeded in drawing attention to the new convention's potential impact. Forty-one countries, twenty-three of them developing, participated in the second session of the Ad Hoc Working Group of Experts, held in Geneva in February 1990, a substantial increase over the twenty-five delegations to the November 1988 meeting.[491] Countries were starting to take the negotiations more seriously. Faithfully conveying UNEP's reconstructed position as dictated by states, UNEP's executive director unequivocally declared that any new agreement "should not infringe upon the sovereignty of nation states [...] and [should] provide incentives for conservation of biodiversity without inhibiting growth or sustainable development."[492]

By the time of the Working Group's third session, in July 1990, the North's biotechnologies linked to the South's genetic resources had been bundled with access and technology transfers. The conservation of biodiversity was held hostage to the demands of the South for development, left to the mercies of the hard negotiations over how much the North was willing to pay the South for conserving its biological resources.[493] Mustapha Tolba, executive director of UNEP at that time and a critical player in the CBD negotiation process, noted that "[t]he third meeting was attended by 78 countries, more than three times the number that attended the first meeting and almost double the number at the second, a clear indication of the interest governments were beginning to give to the subject."[494] The number of states participating in the negotiations increased from session to session, as it became evident that this was not another nature conservation convention, but rather a convention concerning intellectual property rights including patents claimed by Northern biotechnology industries for technologies based on Southern biological diversity; access to genetic resources as raw material for biotechnologies; and control and ownership of genetic resources. Tolba urged "gene-rich developing countries to work in tandem with technology-rich developed countries as the basis for an arrangement that would benefit both North and South."[495] The negotiations were heavily weighed down by never-ending quarrels over ownership of genetic resources. As succinctly stated by G. Kristin Rosendal in her article on the CBD and biotechnologies, "The story begins with the principle of a common heritage of mankind and ends with patents and state sovereignty."[496]

Subsequent meetings continued to be tense. The ongoing North-South confrontations had implications for IUCN as well, as depicted by McConnell in her description of the fourth session of the Working Group, held in November 1990:

> Many delegations had brought with them [. .] the text of a draft convention drawn up by the IUCN [. . . .] It contained good ideas but was generally considered naïve because it concentrated on *in situ* conservation measures and the obligation of developed countries to pay for nature protection in the poorer countries. Perhaps because it was both idealistic and mandatory in its approach it managed to offend practically everyone: the G77 who objected to being told that they had a moral duty to protect their wildlife as the common heritage of mankind; the major industrialized countries who were resistant to anything that looked like a blank cheque [. . . .] Consequently the IUCN text formally disappeared from the process of negotiating [. . .] although it was drawn on quietly [. . . .] IUCN did however make an important contribution throughout the negotiations by providing scientific and legal expertise to the Secretariat.[497]

IUCN's disappointment over its displacement from a leadership role in drafting the new convention is portrayed in a recommendation adopted a month later, in December 1990, at the 18th IUCN General Assembly in Perth, Australia. The almost mournful recommendation, titled "Convention on the Conservation of Biological Diversity," recognizes "the valuable work carried out for over 40 years by IUCN in promoting the conservation of the world's biological diversity [. . .] [and] the substantial progress [. .] made [. . .] by the IUCN Law Programme in promoting [. . .] a Convention on the Conservation of Biological Diversity." Critical of the pressure put on delegations to complete the negotiations by the 1992 UNCED Rio Summit, the recommendation remonstrates that "the process of negotiating a practical and effective legal instrument should not be compromised by the imposition of unrealistic timetables for conclusion." The recommendation further "REQUESTS UNEP, the other members of the Ecosystem Conservation Group, and the negotiating parties to utilize IUCN expertise fully during the negotiation process and to use the draft Articles prepared by IUCN to the maximum extent possible."[498]

Gone is the enthusiasm of the 1988 IUCN General Assembly. IUCN's biodiversity decade was drawing to a close, leaving the organization no choice but to abandon conservation norms and values rooted in its colonial past.

Manipulating Interests and Reconstructing Norms

In retrospect, IUCN's victory in getting the CBD onto the international agenda and launching its negotiations was remarkable. With the end of colonialism, the free-for-all exploitation of colonial natural resources came to an end with their transformation into *national* resources. As an example of the new political configurations, IUCN's success in launching the CBD negotiations was probably due in no small part to the general indifference of governments to a new convention. Yet by pushing the right buttons, by inadvertently playing developed and developing countries against each other through "manipulation" of states' interests, IUCN triggered a process that left governments no choice but to join the negotiations.

Drawing on its colonial legacy, IUCN had designed the CBD as a traditional conservation convention, incorporating elements such as the top-down approach, protected areas, global lists of species, and the common heritage principle. Developing countries saw these elements as threatening their newfound sovereignty, and in response tossed them out, even defiantly deleting the term *global* from the text of the convention.[499] They had already attempted to re-create international law as a tool for self-determination and economic development, establishing the New International Economic Order as the initiative of the developing countries "to remedy colonial inequities,"[500] incorporating the PSNR principle. By the time of the CBD negotiations, developing countries had harnessed these principles to scrap the "international arrangement" based on common heritage and unlimited access to genetic resources. Bent on recompense for the injustices committed against them, the developing countries turned the convention into a strategy for restorative justice; developed countries would have to compensate them for colonial wrongs by technology transfer, intellectual property rights — and of course, by substantial funding.

As for the developed countries, although they had been initially fairly indifferent about a biodiversity convention, they viewed the fundamental changes proposed by the developing countries as threats. Worried about developing countries' demands for what they framed as restitution for the ills of colonialism, the developed countries joined the fray. Once the CBD negotiations were launched, developed countries had no choice but to participate—not so much because they *wanted* to achieve certain objectives, but rather to prevent *un*wanted consequences. They did not need the CBD to protect their own biodiversity, because they possessed national and regional legislation as well as implementation and compliance systems. They were also not particularly concerned about biodiversity in other countries except as it affected them directly, either as raw material for their biotechnologies or as concerns escalating climate change associated with the loss of tropical forests. They *were* worried about the imposition of restrictions on access to biological resources; until the adoption of the CBD, access had been unrestricted. And most of all, the developed countries feared the demands of developing countries for unlimited funding.

Beyond portraying how states negotiated an international convention for issues other than substantive ones of the convention itself, the CBD negotiations demonstrate that although IUCN had set out to change states' norms of behavior for the biosphere, by 1992 states had successfully challenged some of the organization's own most fundamental norms. As reflected in the resolution of its 1981 General Assembly, IUCN had originally advocated that natural "processes by their very nature cannot be the subject of exclusive or proprietary rights on the part of any state or individual," being "part of the common heritage of mankind."[501] States were considered "stewards" or "custodians" of their genetic resources, a duty they owed to the rest of the world.[502] By 1992, after IUCN's trial by fire in the CBD negotiations, its norms had undergone drastic changes. "Genetic resources have traditionally been treated as [. . .] a common heritage of humankind—free to all who could use them." Yet, "The growing importance of biotechnology has forced a reassessment of the ownership issue [. . .] and [. . .] of treating them as free goods."[503] In recognition of states' sovereign rights over their biological resources, the hallmark IUCN norm of "common heritage" was transformed into the milder "common concern." As a result, access to genetic resources is now "contingent upon prior informed consent of the country concerned."[504]

The restructuring of IUCN norms by states contests widespread views of the transformative power of experts in shaping states' norms.[505] Kal Raustiala has argued that IUCN did not have much influence over the CBD once the negotiations started. Rather, using the United Kingdom and United States as examples, Raustiala asserts that domestic "regulatory politics" played the central role in the decision-making process for both countries:

Environmental experts failed to extend their influence very far into the actual national and international decision-making processes. Although conservation issues provided the impetus for the treaty, they did not, despite the efforts of the epistemic community, fundamentally shape the policy responses of either the US or the UK. Indeed, as one negotiator stated, for many important issues "much of the IUCN language was discarded as the negotiations got down to business."

Raustiala notes that the IUCN contribution was as "a shaper of international agendas rather than of state interests." He concludes,

[T]he epistemic community was unable to significantly shape the debate around the most contentious issues of the convention [. . . .] [and] was most influential during the pre-negotiation and post-negotiation phases, rather than during the negotiations themselves.[506]

So although IUCN succeeded in framing biodiversity and a biodiversity convention as cutting-edge issues, and in getting these issues onto the international agenda, it has been less successful in using international law to change states' behavior regarding their biodiversity. Moreover, in a complete reversal of roles, developing countries, once the rightless objects of an international colonial law, successfully reconstructed IUCN's own norms and rejected its attempts to re-create elephant treaties.

The Race for Rio

The hostility and mistrust displayed in the early Working Group sessions became even more nerve-wracking when confronted with Tolba's steely determination to finish the negotiations by June 1992. A theme marking the negotiations throughout was the "race for the Rio Summit," evoking the Stockholm Conference and Maurice Strong's strategy in defining international conventions as "third-level" activities to expedite their adoption. By the November 1990 Working Group meeting, Tolba was urging reluctant states to start negotiating the convention, claiming that their unwillingness only increased the already tense atmosphere. Tolba blamed the hostile and bitter relations between the developed and developing countries for the slow progress of the meetings.[507] The deep North-South schism, and the intensity of developing countries' distrust of the process in general, led to the general feeling among participants that they would not meet UNEP's target for completion.[508] The acrimonious negotiating atmosphere steadily became more heated as the date of the UNCED Rio Summit approached. The tension reaching unprecedented heights during the meeting in Madrid in June 1991, which Tolba in his book *Global Environmental Diplomacy* claimed "was the real start of negotiations and saw the unfolding of deep differences between negotiators from North and South."[509] McConnell recounts the bitter attacks of the South on the North at the Madrid meeting:

> The Nordics were patronizing, the EC was trying to throw its weight about. The US was determined to wreck the convention. Intellectual property was theft. Multinational enterprises were making exorbitant profits at the expense of the poor. Biotechnologists were conducting secret experiments which threatened the whole of the Third World.[510]

The next negotiation session, in Nairobi, September 1991, was marked by similar vitriolic attacks. McConnell has described the "savage interventions" and "explosions of rage" during the negotiations. Access to and transfer of technologies was a particularly contentious issue, as was G77 insistence on "'new and additional' financial resources [. . .] repeated [. . .] for virtually every Article." Another subject that raised the ire of the developing countries—and India and Malaysia in particular—was that the Global Environmental Facility (GEF) served as the financial mechanism.[511]

In answering the question he himself had posed, "Why was the last meeting successfully concluded at all?" Veit Koester—a key player throughout the CBD negotiations, head of the Danish delegation, and chair of one of its two working groups—answered, "One interpretation is that the meeting would never have been able to finish in time without the Rio-deadline."[512] The US delegation desperately tried to prevent the conclusion of the negotiations, arguing that the many issues still open made it impossible to finish the convention by the Rio Summit.[513] Some developing countries were also unhappy with the speeded-up negotiations, particularly the Malaysian delegation, which was angry at losing its battle to replace GEF as the financial mechanism.

Yet in spite of strong opposition from lead countries, the negotiations *were* finished by the June 1992 Rio Summit, due in no small part to the concerns of governments that not completing them in time would harm the governments' reputations in the international community. Insistent on completing negotiations by the Rio Summit, Tolba succeeded in persuading negotiating countries—except for the United States—that missing this target would be interpreted as failure. Individual countries had their own unique reputational concerns. France was under pressure from its environmental groups to incorporate global lists into the convention. Similar anxiety over the reactions of domestic environmental groups to the negotiating results was shared by the United Kingdom and others, as McConnell notes:

> [T]he UK [negotiating] team shared much of Chairman's gloom about the prospect of completing work [. . . .] They wondered where blame for failure would be attributed. The US would no doubt be accused of consistent obduracy but Japan would escape censure because it had kept a horizontal profile. The UK however could not expect to win plaudits for its continuing hard line on finance and British Environmental Groups would be especially critical [. . . .] On the other hand if the convention was ready for Rio the UK might get a grudging pat on the back [. . . .] Even so there was little chance that the UK would be hailed as the driving force of the convention, and nor would the EC.[514]

In sharp contrast, the US negotiating team stubbornly refused to be drawn into the race against the clock, apparently unconcerned about the impact on its reputation of not meeting the deadline.[515] Beyond states' reputational concerns, Tolba and UNEP had, of course, their own reputations to consider; hence their determination to complete their task on schedule.

The Kenya-Brazil controversy is a notable display of reputational concerns as an impetus in promoting international law. Nairobi served as the venue for a large part of the CBD negotiations. Rio de Janeiro had been chosen to host the 1992 UNCED. Consequently, both Kenya and Brazil wanted the CBD to be called by the name of their particular city. To resolve the dispute, it was decided that the final act conference would be held in Nairobi (the "Nairobi final act") while the convention would be opened for signing in Rio (one of the "Rio conventions"). Motivated by these incentives, Kenya and Brazil, as crucial countries in the negotiations, assumed the roles of mediators to ensure completion of the negotiations in time.[516]

By incentivizing key states to finish the negotiations in time for the 1992 UNCED, UNEP succeeded in completing the convention according to schedule. The most ironic outcome of these incentives was their impact on Brazil, which progressed from intransigent opponent of a new convention and fierce protector of the sovereignty of the G77, to an equally eager supporter once the decision was made to hold the summit in Rio.[517] Brazil had resisted a biodiversity convention. Yet the bait that UNEP dangled—a reputation as a world leader hosting a global megaconference—was irresistible. From a formidable foe, Brazil metamorphosed into an enthusiastic, strong supporter.[518] Harnessing international law for reputational concerns aided in overcoming states' objections. Though most delegations sensed that the negotiations should not be rushed, and even assumed that they would extend beyond 1992, no country (except the United States) was willing to take the blame for not meeting the June 1992 deadline.[519]

Not only were states using the CBD to promote their reputations. The negotiations for the CBD illustrate how NGOs and IGOs used international law for their own reputational concerns and empowerment. Turf wars between conservation organizations intertwine throughout the narrative. Newly independent states played organizations against the other, as illustrated by the FAO-IUCN feud over the 1968 African Convention and Coolidge's efforts not to disclose the quarrel to the African countries concerned, stressing the importance of a united front. The FAO-IUCN dispute over the CBD played out against the background of FAO's work on legal instruments—both soft and hard—for genetic resources, progressing simultaneously with the CBD negotiations. FAO objected not necessarily to a new convention, but to the fact that the convention would be credited to IUCN. FAO did not want IUCN to have another international convention under its belt, increasing its power in areas in which FAO worked as well. FAO held out against a new convention until, faced with IUCN and UNEP competition, it eventually felt that it had no choice but to give in.[520]

A Closing

The 1980s biodiversity decade had been a prolific phase for IUCN, marked by a series of notable policy documents. Crafted as guidelines for protecting Earth's biosphere, they also divulge IUCN's growing disillusionment with international biodiversity conventions. The grace period for the Stockholm conventions was over, and with each new strategy that IUCN issued throughout the 1980s and early 1990s, starting with the *World Conservation Strategy*, its disappointment with existing conventions became more perceptible. The 1990 *Conserving the World's Biodiversity* frames the dilemma: "Most governments have joined international conservation conventions [. . . .] but still the devastation continues, and even accelerates. Why?"[521] Yet true to the vision of its founders, IUCN was still seeking the ultimate convention that would craft new norms for states, change their behavior, and halt biodiversity loss. The CBD was meant to make up for the mistakes of the earlier agreements. IUCN marketed it as "the primary means of establishing accepted international norms for biodiversity conservation."[522] The 1992 *Global Biodiversity Strategy*, completed during the CBD negotiations, was designed as a "base for the practical action [. . .] while the Convention is ratified and entering into force." IUCN used its newest policy document to appeal to polarized state interests:

> For developing countries, the attraction of the convention is that it [. . .] recognizes their sovereignty over biological resources within their territories. For industrialized countries, the convention will help ensure their continued access to genetic resources albeit at a higher cost than before."[523]

IUCN was detaching itself from its colonial past and discarding the beliefs and values of its founders, a transformation reflected in the *Global Biodiversity Strategy*'s list of "Essential Elements of a Convention on Biodiversity." Most significantly, in recognition of states' sovereign rights over their biological resources, the common heritage concept had been tossed out along with unrestricted access to genetic resources.[524] By restructuring IUCN beliefs, developing countries had successfully challenged its historic mission in transforming norms and values through international law, a continuation of the work of earlier colonial organizations.

Burrowing into the past discloses the remarkable—almost symbiotic—entwinement of international conservation law and organizations. SPFE was founded in the wake of the 1900 London Convention forged by two colonial powers, and it assumed a critical role in the convention's implementation. In an ongoing cycle with conservation organizations in the lead, further conventions were drafted, negotiated, adopted, and finally, judged ineffective, triggering a new convention. The 1933 Convention replaced the 1900 Convention, and the 1968 African Convention replaced the 1933 Convention. The American Committee, the creation of which had been inspired by SPFE, duplicated SPFE's work on the 1933 London Convention with the 1940 Western Hemisphere Convention. Both SPFE and the American Committee were actively involved in the founding of IUCN in 1948, leaving their trademark of international convention making in its founding statutes. By the early 1950s, IUCN was chasing after governments to tackle the perceived ineffectiveness of both the 1933 London Convention and the 1940 Western Hemisphere Convention. The Stockholm conventions were optimistically designed for postcolonialism, yet they too proved disappointing, as was repeatedly pointed out by IUCN policy documents of the 1980s. The CBD was meant to replace *them* after IUCN determined that a more forceful convention was needed. The cyclical making of biodiversity conventions by conservation organizations in pursuit of the ultimate convention came to an end with the CBD.

These organizations had historically seen themselves as agents of change and international treaties as their tools. Thrust forward by their extensive knowledge and expertise, they assumed quasi-governmental roles. With increasing NGO power and influence, fortified by the founding of the United Nations along with the emergence of IGOs such as UNESCO and FAO, for a short time IUCN assumed the role of world crafter of biodiversity treaties. It was filling a vacuum: except for the United States, which promoted both CITES and the World Heritage Convention, and Kenya, which played a key role in CITES, governments on the whole did not display notable interest in the Stockholm conventions. The Stockholm Conference secretariat noted, at the fourth session of the Prep Comm in March 1972, that only five governments had responded to the draft of the Islands Convention sent out to all UN member states.[525] Regarding the draft of the World Heritage Convention—undeniably a much higher-profile issue—only six governments had responded.[526] Twenty years later, reviewing the number of governments participating in the CBD negotiations shows that the first meeting was attended by only twenty-five state delegations. But despite its initial success, IUCN eventually became a victim of its own legacy. It was identified with the camp of the colonial rulers, the wealthy "civilized" countries, or even worse, was considered an interloper trespassing on sovereign state turf. In a throwback to the exclusion of Liberia and Ethiopia from the 1900 Convention, IUCN became the "other," and as such was denied a formal status in the convention-making process.

Recalling Richard Sandbrook's observations on the disease he called "conventionitis,"[527] although IUCN and earlier conservation organizations shared a resolute and profound belief in the ultimate normative force of law to bring about change, the narrative offers a more instrumental explanation of their use of international conventions. By a careful crafting of these treaties and a subtle restructuring of the colonial confrontation, IUCN's intent was to hoard the last vestiges of control over Africa's biodiversity, locking in its own influential role under colonialism. The theme of international law as empowerment for NGOs winds its way through the narrative. These treaties often became contentious issues over which IGOs and NGOs wrangled in competition for lead roles in their drafting, negotiations, and administration. Moreover, conservation conventions became issues of controversy between states and NGOs, as revealed by states tossing out IUCN as lead architect for the CBD, and the opposite: by IUCN's suspicions over the negotiations of the future Convention on the Conservation of Antarctic Marine Living Resources, adopted in 1980. IUCN claimed that governments were negotiating this convention secretly, to divide among themselves the unique resources of the Antarctic zone.[528]

But IUCN is not only compromised by its colonial legacy. It is enslaved by an oversized and hungry budget, forging complex allegiances and hidden agendas, and sparking allegations of undue influence of corporate donors and governments. In discussions of international institutional reform, NGOs emerge as candidates for formal governance roles in failing structures.[529] Formerly recognized as the "conscience of the world," respected for "her complete freedom of expression," IUCN's operations today challenge once prevalent thinking of the organization, and of other NGOs, as environmental heroes.[530] Care should be taken to avoid a misplaced faith in these organizations as a reserve governance force, for they too—and not just states—assume roles of colonizers.

Despite the efforts of IUCN and earlier organizations, international law has not succeeded in transforming human society's relationship with the biosphere. Wrought originally as a tool for European governance of African nature, international law was stripped of elements evocative of colonialism by the developing countries, as they rebuffed attempts by UNEP and IUCN to recycle colonial law during the CBD negotiations. Developing countries ousted IUCN from its dominant role in the making of the CBD and handed the task over to UNEP, a more docile IGO mandated to take orders from its member states. Heeding the adage "Beware of what you wish for," and in a sharp turnabout from its historical role, IUCN became openly critical of biodiversity conventions. It cautioned against adopting an international agreement as a red herring, noting hidden dangers lurking within these agreements. Therefore, beware of weak biodiversity conventions, for they are liable of doing more harm than good, by creating the illusion that something *international*—that beguiling, seductive term connoting prestige and power—will save the planet, while formidable forces, far beyond the conventions' limited power and authority, rip up Earth's surface unchallenged.

A profoundly disturbing aspect of these weak conventions is the accusations they silently invoke, testifying to the abandonment of Earth's endangered biodiversity by those entrusted to protect it. Governments are the ultimate hypocrites. Hiding within a cloak of fine rhetoric, they are collaborators in a conspiracy of deafening silence that surrounds these treaties. Contrasting biodiversity agreements with human rights agreements keenly underscores the handicaps of the former, tightly woven within their origins. With all their drawbacks, human rights agreements still mark a major milestone in international legal history. Biodiversity agreements do not. Broad consensus holds that abuse of humans by their own governments is morally and ethically wrong, and constitutes an international crime. Governments do not argue anymore that mistreatment of people living within their borders is their own business, and that national sovereignty allows them to do as they please. Yet the human rights paradigm does not easily transpose onto a state's abuse of its own biodiversity, and countries continue to shun international attempts to regulate exploitation of their share of the biosphere, as violations of sovereignty.

Today's governance of biodiversity draws directly from colonial engagement with nature. Legitimizing the slaughter of elephants for trade in their tusks, elephant treaties were contrived to both exploit the elephant and protect it so as to continue exploiting it—a way of thinking entrenched in current governance regimes as "sustainable development." Whether elephant treaties that applied exclusively to Africa or modern biodiversity agreements intended for developing countries, these international conventions represent powerful forces dictating conservation policy for "others." Transforming international law into a tool for protecting the poor, the weak, and the voiceless means transcending its colonial legacy. As noted by William Adams in *Decolonizing Nature*, "Conservationists have much to learn about their past, and much of it will be painful [. . . .] The challenge of decolonizing the mind is urgent and of huge significance to the future of conservation."[531]

Biodiversity conventions are frozen in a time warp, shackled to elephant treaties and unequipped to brave the ongoing devastation of the biosphere. In an attempt to protect nature and yet maintain a human dominance over the biosphere, marked by class and race, they have failed nature. Disillusioned by the failure of international law to achieve the changes it sought, IUCN has abandoned its historical mission of biodiversity convention making. Its post-1992 strategy demonstrates new directions, as it leaves behind its role as global law maker for the biosphere. In retrospect, the CBD was the conclusion of a series of colonial conservation conventions, a genre of international law finally rejected by developing countries approximately thirty years after the formal end of colonialism.

CHAPTER FIVE

Epilogue and Renewal

> It would be comforting to think that all the international negotiations, summit and conference agreements, conventions and protocols have at least got us to the point where we are now prepared to act decisively—comforting but wrong.
> —*James Gustave Speth,* Red Sky at Morning[532]

Retreat

As James Speth has rightly observed, "My generation is a generation, I fear, of great talkers, overly fond of conferences. On action, however, we have fallen far short."[533] Proving his point, this book is a history of conferences and organizations, referred to by bewildering acronyms that mystify the uninitiated. Global environmental governance is conducted through these conferences, as well as diverse other forums, that convene participants who are there to talk. International conventions too are drafted, negotiated, adopted, and implemented through work carried out at these global gatherings, part of the international institutional establishment unquestionably accepted as the norm for carrying on the business of the biosphere.

Within these governance structures, multilateral biodiversity treaty making has come to a halt. The CBD—at least for now—is the last of the major biodiversity agreements, not because all relevant issues have been addressed by international law, but because of the growing awareness of its limits as a tool for change. By November 1992, just half a year after the CBD's adoption at Rio, IUCN was publicly rethinking its use of international law. At again another conference, The Future of IUCN, participants suggested that instead of developing new international instruments, IUCN should shift to national-level initiatives, helping countries with implementation and enforcement of their own national laws. A call went out to "simplify international law" by crafting a single legal instrument that would consolidate "the principles of the different treaties."[534] The allusion was to the draft Covenant on Environment and Development initially based on the 1987 report *Our Common Future*, which recommended a convention "setting out the sovereign rights and reciprocal responsibilities of all states on environmental protection and sustainable development."535

The covenant was endorsed in 1988 by IUCN's 17th General Assembly in San Jose, Costa Rica, by the same recommendation that had endorsed IUCN's draft of the future CBD.536 By 1995 IUCN had published the covenant's first edition, and it has since gone through three more. The foreword to the first edition confidently presented the covenant as the beginning of "a global treaty on environmental conservation and sustainable development." The 1999 edition reinforced IUCN's intention that the covenant would ultimately evolve into a binding convention:

> We are constantly asked about the future of this Draft Covenant. [. . .]
> A consensus is growing, favouring a framework agreement like that of the Draft Covenant [. . . .] We have, accordingly, resolved to continue the promotion of an integrated umbrella agreement and be patient until there is sufficient support to go forward.

Starting its retreat, by its 2003 edition, IUCN was describing the covenant as a "'living document' until [. . .] adopted as a basis for multilateral negotiations." The most recent (2010) edition contains not one word on the covenant's future as an international agreement. It is presented simply as a "'living document' regularly updated to reflect the development of international law and practice."537

Other potential directions for new international biodiversity law have also fizzled out. The CBD, a framework convention meant to be implemented by protocols on a diverse range of issues, has produced only two protocols, neither of which tackle the most urgent and dangerous threats to biodiversity. The 2003 Cartagena Protocol on Biosafety deals with risks to human health and the environment from the handling, transport, and use of living modified organisms. The 2010 Nagoya Protocol on Access to Genetic Resources and the Fair and Equitable Sharing of Benefits focuses on access and benefit-sharing issues, and on transfer of technologies. IUCN's ELC played a major advisory role in the drafting of the protocols' texts and their negotiations, and has published explanatory guides to both. But in stark contrast to its former role in the making of the major biodiversity conventions, IUCN was not the catalyst for these protocols, and neither are they key IUCN policy issues.538

Although no further global biodiversity conventions have emerged since the CBD, a significant number of regional agreements for migratory species have been concluded under the Convention on Migratory Species (CMS).

Though protecting fauna and flora species enclosed within sovereign borders is not innately an international issue, protecting migratory species and birds in particular through international cooperation is intuitive. Similar to early twentieth-century conventions for protecting "international animals,"[539] *all* range states need to cooperate, whether developed or developing, to protect species that cross national borders by land or air or that migrate through the international marine environment. Agreements under CMS have been concluded for Eurasian-African waterbirds; albatrosses and petrels; European bats; gorillas; small cetaceans of the Baltic Sea, Northeast Atlantic Ocean, and Irish and North Seas; and, cetaceans of the Mediterranean and Black Seas. Memorandums of Understanding and Action Plans for other species have also been adopted. These agreements are restricted in membership to range states, and although the ELC has contributed to their making and implementation,[540] similar to the CBD protocols, they are not major IUCN policy issues.

The New Colonizers

On the one hand, biodiversity treaty making (except for a few regional migratory species) has come to a standstill; on the other hand, pressures on biodiversity expand and become more complex, and menacing threats lie ahead. If a century ago, hunting of African megafauna was considered the foremost danger facing conservation efforts in Africa, today the phenomenon labeled *land grabs* has replaced it. Land grabbing is the ultimate act of unsustainable use of natural resources, provocatively evoking the wildly outsized human ecological footprint. The global struggle over land and water to feed unsustainable economies and populations operates by exploiting the weakest sectors of human society. Countries that have already exceeded the carrying capacity of their own natural resources are outsourcing food production to developing countries and to Africa in particular. The governments of Ethiopia, Kenya, Mozambique, Sudan and South Sudan, Cameroon, Mali, Egypt, and other African countries are selling or leasing vast acreages to foreign governments and international corporations for industrial agricultural operations. These operations consume not only land but huge amounts of water, leading to accusations that charge African governments with "hydro-colonialism"—dispossessing and excluding local populations not only from their lands but from the water resources located within and flowing through them. Africans who are already suffering from a lack of access to water of adequate quality and quantity are further threatened by land deals orchestrated by their own governments that pose risks to regional freshwater systems. GRAIN, the international NGO based in Barcelona, has been working for over twenty years to strengthen community farming based on local biodiversity. It has extensively researched the implications of land grabbing on African farmers:

> If this land and water grab is not put to an end, millions of Africans will lose access to the water sources they rely on [. . . .] This is already happening in Ethiopia's Gambela, where the government is forcibly moving thousands of indigenous people out of their traditional territories to make way for export agriculture.
>
> The recent wave of land grabbing is nothing short of an environmental disaster in the making. There is simply not enough water in Africa's rivers and water tables to irrigate all the newly acquired land.[541]

Land grabbing is under intense attack by GRAIN and other organizations worldwide. These NGOs have developed remarkable expertise and knowledge on these issues, shared globally through websites that document the deals, the impending threats to local populations, and the ensuing devastation and suffering. Yet even though NGOs have exposed these practices and taken unequivocal positions denouncing them, IGOs remain vacillating on the side. Instead of condemning land grabs outright, FAO has issued "Voluntary Guidelines on the Responsible Governance of Tenure of Land, Fisheries and Forest in the Context of National Food Security." But voluntary guidelines serve to legitimize the practice without committing governments to binding obligations. And despite the implications of land grabbing for the integrity of biodiversity and ecosystems, the governing institutions of the biodiversity conventions—the secretariats, technical and scientific committees, and meetings of the parties—have not condemned land grabs, a key constraint being that the perpetrators themselves are among their member parties.

Biodiversity conventions, direct descendants of hunting and trade conventions, cannot counter the ecological and social devastation orchestrated by powerful coalitions of governments and wealthy corporations. These conventions are still exclusionary mechanisms, this time around for local communities marginalized by corrupt governments that are enticed by the wealth proffered in exchange for their countries' natural resources. Biodiversity conventions stand by helplessly while the devastation goes on, or worse, they play directly into the hands of corrupt governments. As related by an NGO official regarding her organization's participation in multilateral negotiations,

> We can recite a long list of negotiations that we enthusiastically got involved in because we felt that we could achieve some positive results, but in which [. . .] we saw our proposals being stripped of their essential meaning and corrupted into empty promises [. . . .] At the Biodiversity Convention we challenged "biopiracy," and urged the recognition of local communities in the management of biodiversity. We got "benefit-sharing regimes" that do nothing about the monopoly control that corporations obtain on the biodiversity collected from the forests and are essentially about regulating who gets paid for what when genetic resources change hands. They do little to protect local communities from the continuous undermining of their territorial integrity and the biodiversity that they manage.[542]

The end of European rule over Africa did not end the exploitation of its natural resources by foreigners. The issue still remains, staunchly and unwaveringly, the relations between the strong against the weak, and the dilemma is still that of exploitation versus conservation. In a continent carved up into political entities by European conquerors who ignored ethnic and tribal identities, governors and the governed do not necessarily share those identities, and many Africans view their own government as the new colonizers.[543] Although traditionally identified with formal state entities, the colonizer assumes various identities. Non-state actors have also filled the role, and transnational corporations in particular.[544] In a painful reminder of Europeans dispossessing them of their lands and their biodiversity, foreigners continue to steal the natural resources of Africans. This time around they are abetted by independent African governments, hungry for foreign currency that is temptingly offered by transnational corporations, the most powerful international actors.[545]

Corporations were the earliest colonizers. Beginning in the sixteenth century, European trading companies were licensed by their governments to administer colonial territories with the clear objective, befitting a corporation, of maximizing profits from the exploitation of their natural resources. As governance by trading companies was replaced with direct governance by European powers, trade and governance were coupled as a mechanism for bringing civilization to the uncivilized. Today's transnational corporations, driving modern colonialism in its new guise of "globalization," trace to those early British, Dutch, and French trading companies that led the pack in colonizing and ravaging non-European lands. To tie the knots even tighter, the creation of the corporation was a legal fabrication devised precisely to promote and facilitate trading operations in non-European lands.[546]

The beginning of the twenty-first century finds Africans worse off than their colonial ancestors. In comparison to today's continental-scale of threats to Africa's biodiversity, endangering the land and water of millions of Africans, colonial threats were more contained and on a smaller scale. Moreover, European rulers as "gentle civilizers" were guided by a civilizing mission cloaking the harshness of colonialism.[547] The dilemma of the historically abused "other" becomes the ultimate concern in halting biodiversity loss. Yet in the face of wealthy and powerful global forces that plunder Earth and its poorest inhabitants in search of vast profits, what hope is there of achieving a system of governance that can withstand their might? Cruelly and ironically, biodiversity loss imperils the poorest sectors of society: people living low-consumptive lives yet utterly dependent on biodiversity for the life-giving goods and services that it supplies, while excluded by their poverty from the protection that biotechnologies afford. These are the tangible victims of biodiversity loss. Biodiversity, an ultimate source of power, an asymmetrically given gift, a scarce good that is critical to feeding a gluttonous world greedy for endless and all-consuming growth, stubbornly resists international regulation. Mephistopheles stands beckoning, for the temptations are too great, the promises of power too enticing; and the immense number of rapacious states condemn, a priori, the well-intentioned solutions that are based on multilateral cooperation.

Wanted: Courageous NGOs

Custom would demand that anyone who holds views such as those here expressed should, in conclusion, do one of two things—either suggest a program as to how the situation can be saved or, admitting its hopelessness, resignedly express the belief that we are moving towards the twilight of civilization. —*Fairfield Osborn*, Our Plundered Planet[548]

In light of the immense power of international governance structures, coupled with the lack of political will to tackle biodiversity loss, changing or restructuring governance is not feasible. Recalling the dilemma of scales from which this book emerged, an alternative demands strengthening local operating systems outside of existing power bases; this option derives from the premise that the key to successful governance of biodiversity lies in those local communities that rely on it for their livelihood and sustenance. Most vulnerable to biodiversity loss, these communities are most anxious to protect it simply because for them, this is a question of survival. While acknowledging that the national scale will remain the key governance scale, given the right incentives, local communities could become a transformative power in halting biodiversity loss.

Reminiscent of the original proposal for the World Heritage Convention as a trust or foundation, proposals have recently been put forward that would harness the international scale while transforming it from multilateral to bilateral. James Speth has raised the idea of forging "'compacts' or 'bargains' between the [. . .] the North [. . .] and the South [. . . .] [P]oorer countries would take impressive steps to halt deforestation and biodiversity loss, for example, while rich countries provide financial, political and other support." He further proposes strengthening the Global Environmental Facility by "country-specific compacts, incorporating and linking priority goals of industrial and developing countries."[549] International biodiversity consultant Dr. Tamar Ron calls for focusing on the specific needs of individual countries rather than spreading meager resources throughout the international community at large. As an institutional framework, Ron proposes a central UN structure that would work on an individual basis with relevant countries, focusing on local leadership and ownership over natural resources.[550]

These proposals require shifting biodiversity governance from the prevalent multilateral structure to a country-specific bilateral scale, supporting the present devolving trend from the international to the firmer ground of the *local*. Broad consensus exists that effective biodiversity protection depends on strong community-level governance. Community-based natural resource management (CBNRM) has gained wide recognition as the promise of a more effective governing system for people and their natural resources, geared to redress injustices. A widely acknowledged success story is the Namibia-based CBNRM project run by Integrated Rural Development and Nature Conservation (IRDNC).[551] The organization was originally established to end massive poaching. But instead of punishment, poachers were offered employment, creating a cadre of community-based game wardens. IRDNC went on to successfully persuade the Namibian government to undertake legislative reform, and it enacted a natural resource law that devolved ownership of natural resources to local communities with both consumptive and nonconsumptive rights to wildlife, subject to government regulation. As statutory frameworks, Namibia set up *conservancies*, community-based institutions to manage and protect land and to generate income.[552]

The Namibian experience represents an alternative governing system for biodiversity, managed by local communities linked to their land, its wildlife, and plant life. Biodiversity and other natural resources would be defined as *community* resources rather than *national* resources, and ownership of them would be invested in local communities that are legally empowered to manage them. Empowerment for biodiversity conservation could spark strong civil societies that operate as a counterforce to government, protecting their natural resources as insurance for survival, and holding governments accountable by assuming a watchdog role.

The model of CBNRM in Namibia is based on other African community conservation programs, and in particular, the Zimbabwe CAMPFIRE (Communal Areas Management Programme for Indigenous Resources).[553] CAMPFIRE aimed at transferring rights for wildlife from central governments to local communities. Yet in contrast to the Namibian project, the devolving of authorities has stopped in Zimbabwe at regional levels of rural district councils, rather than reaching local communities as originally planned. In Tanzania as well, local communities have gained legal rights over forests, yet on the whole, the central government keeps a tight hold on the country's natural resources.[554] Thus, although the Namibian CBNRM program is largely credited as a success, critics have expressed grave reservations about community conservation in other African countries, charging that "CBNRM policies affirm colonial dispossession."[555] They level criticism at central governments for their obduracy in refusing to carry out institutional reforms and shift authority to local communities.

Accountability and transparency in government, are, of course, basic requirements for gaining institutional reform, and the more democratic a country's government, the more forthcoming it will be to relinquish ownership of natural resources for the benefit of its local communities. Consequently, although empowering local communities might work under democratic governments, in Africa centralized power, corrupt governments, and weak democratic institutions effectively prevent institutional reform of resource ownership by limiting public challenges to their authority, among other ways.[556] Land grabbing and its promise of wealth comprise a powerful disincentive for governments to undertake legal reform of resource ownership. Because natural resources offer power and opportunities for quick riches, African governments keep firm control of them. Yet in light of the ominous threats looming over Africans today from foreigners' exploitation of their land and water, community conservation programs must not be tossed aside, but strengthened and supported.

In the search for counterforces to the impending land-grab catastrophe, the first that comes to mind is the United Nations. The UN carved out its reputation first and foremost as an intergovernmental human rights organization, expanding to environmental issues with the 1973 establishment of UNEP as the lead environmental IGO. Yet fearful of arousing the wrath of governments, IGOs refrain from firmly confronting states on environmental abuse. Not only IGOs quake before governments and corporations; IUCN and other international conservation organizations do too. Fettered by political and corporate ties and compromised by huge budgets, these "establishment" NGOs choose to remain silent.

In the recent incident concerning the venue for its 2012 World Conservation Congress on the South Korean island of Jeju, IUCN has stubbornly refused to take a stand against government development that is devastating the island's unique biodiversity and, consequently, the lives of the island's inhabitants. Among other allegations, IUCN has been charged with accepting contributions from corporations that carry out the development for the Korean government. Born into the governing establishment for colonial nature, IUCN is today well integrated within the global environmental governance establishment. As a captive of both governments and corporations, IUCN has been accused of being overly deferential to states instead of speaking out against their acts of environmental, ecological, and human destruction. Revealing a dark side to these conferences, local Jeju island communities are angry at IUCN for convening its congress on the island—they correctly view this as a signal of IUCN's collaboration with the Korean government. In an open letter from September 5, 2012, the Emergency Action Committee to Save Jeju Island lambasted IUCN for its refusal to condemn the Korean government's destruction of the island's biodiversity and indigenous communities:

> IUCN leadership still refuses to criticize Korea's destructive naval base, though construction work is killing rare soft corals, numerous endangered species (including from IUCN's Red List), and destroying indigenous communities and livelihoods. [. . .] While continuing to proclaim its

devotion to protecting Nature, including the planet's endangered places and species, IUCN leadership has ignored or whitewashed projects that are assaulting these wonders, and undermining human rights and sustainable livelihoods.

Why is IUCN leadership remaining so silent? [...] A large percentage of the cost of this WCC convention in Jeju is being covered by the very people building the military base. Those would be the Korean government, and several giant global corporations, notably Samsung. Having accepted the funding, it is difficult to criticize the funders.

IUCN's top leadership has apparently determined its best course now is to avert its gaze while the government kills the shrimps and the frogs, destroys the corals, and jails the protesting local farmers. Meanwhile, IUCN can freely proceed with its great meeting next door to save Nature.[557]

To empower local communities to tackle these threats, the challenge remains: how to reach effective strategies for influencing institutional change? The cowardly behavior of existing institutions calls for brave individuals and NGOs, independent of governments and corporations, who are willing to take a stand and speak up against governments that abuse their natural resources with devastating implications for local populations. The basis of their operations would be human rights regimes, which can pursue claims against intransigent governments within the extensive international and regional human rights forums that recognize the rights of individuals and NGOs to submit claims against governments. One example of such a process is the Tanzanian case of the Sukenya Farm dispute over the dispossession of local communities of their communal farming and grazing land. Together with international NGOs, the communities have submitted a claim against the Tanzanian government before the UN Committee on the Elimination of Racial Discrimination.[558]

Empowered local communities and highly motivated and courageous organizations, working through international tribunals to counter government abuse, could create a substantial counterforce to existing institutional structures. The core action would be submitting "environmental human rights claims" against governments for violations of recognized human rights triggered by environmental degradation, such as the right to life, to health, to food and sustenance—and perhaps, a right to biodiversity as well.[559] Thousands of effective, dedicated local NGOs are already engaged in defending their communities from greedy governments and corporations. The challenge is to create the maximum impact by increasing both the quality and the quantity of their work. Although decisions of human rights regimes cannot be enforced as effectively as decisions of national courts, their declaratory worth should not be underestimated, nor their persuasive power in leveraging states' reputational concerns. Naming and blaming abusive countries results in international shaming, which the vast majority of countries would try to avoid at any price.[560] As revealed throughout the narrative related in this book, countries greatly value their reputations. Moreover, a decision of a human rights forum can be used in other international forums as compelling evidence of the government's violations of human and environmental rights.

Drawing again from human rights, to back up this proposal with a firm footing, an environmental watchdog organization similar to Amnesty International is needed. Its primary objective would be the compilation of reports on governments' abuse of their natural environment. The idea was raised in 1987 by IUCN president Monkombu Swaminathan, who called for an "Environment Amnesty" to "bring to public notice prominent cases of damage resulting from the desire of some to make personal profit out of public property."[561] Lawrence Susskind, in his book *Environmental Diplomacy*, proposed a new NGO for monitoring compliance with environmental conventions, which he named "Green Amnesty International." He called for a new institutional structure based on human rights regimes. Countries would sign a protocol similar to the Optional Protocol to the International Covenant on Civil and Political Rights, thus allowing their nationals to submit complaints on violations of environmental conventions. To consider the complaints, Susskind further proposed establishing a UN environmental violations committee based on the UN Human Rights Committee.[562] Yet Susskind's proposal draws on an environmental institutional structure that does not yet exist. In light of international reluctance to join binding treaties, Swaminathan's proposal for a watchdog organization, which would bring cases of environmental abuse by governments to public notice without requiring institutional reform, is more optimistic. Incorporating Susskind's suggestions, the organization would create a network for global monitoring, the members of which would submit reports to a central institution, backed up with on-site visits by independent observers.

Sold out by their own governments, exploited by corporations single-mindedly committed to profits, abandoned by the UN as well as leading conservation organizations, Africans face the great challenge of marshaling forces to regain control of their land, water, and biodiversity. A revolution for fair and just biodiversity governance will entail discarding the colonial legacy imposed on Africa from outside and from within. If elephants could talk, they would admonish, *Beware of elephant treaties that did not protect us but rather delivered us into the hands of our abusers.* Heeding this warning, biodiversity governance will abandon the antiquated and faltering international system crafted by colonizers and civilizers for the plunder of Africa. It will replace that system with governance by individuals, courageously routing the exploiters who loot Africa of her riches. The power of the individual, of the local, utterly dependent on biodiversity for sustenance, for life, would counterbalance the mighty and terrifying forces motivated by greed. The ensuing renewal could mean the difference between a crisis of extinction and a harmonious serenity of biological riches.

Notes

CHAPTER ONE Introduction

1. I use the terms *treaties*, *conventions*, and *agreements* interchangeably. *See* the Vienna Convention on the Law of Treaties, definition of "treaty," at Art. 2(a), Vienna, May 23, 1969, entered into force Jan. 27, 1980, United Nations. 1155 *Treaty Series* 331.

2. E.g. *see* MARK CIOC, THE GAME OF CONSERVATION: INTERNATIONAL TREATIES TO PROTECT THE WORLD'S MIGRATORY ANIMALS 19 (Ohio University Press 2009); AFRICA (Phyllis Martin & Patrick O'Meara eds., Indiana University Press 1995). *See also* JOHN READER, AFRICA: A BIOGRAPHY OF THE CONTINENT 573 (Alfred A. Knopf 1998).

3. *Report of the Preparatory Committee for the United Nations Conference on the Human Environment*, Apr. 6, 1970, A/CONF.48/PC/6, at para. 14; held in New York, Mar. 10–20, 1970.

4. Elinor Ostrom, *Scales, Polycentricity and Incentives: Designing Complexity to Govern Complexity, in* PROTECTING GLOBAL BIODIVERSITY 149 (Duke University Press 1998). *See also* HAROLD JACOBSON & MARTIN PRICE, A FRAMEWORK FOR RESEARCH ON THE HUMAN DIMENSIONS OF GLOBAL ENVIRONMENTAL CHANGE 1 (UNESCO 1990); Ken Conca, *Rethinking the Ecology-Sovereignty Debate, in* GREEN PLANET BLUES 46, 47, 88 (Ken Conca & Geoffrey Dabelko eds., Westview Press 1998); Hayward Alker, Jr. & Peter Haas, *The Rise of Global Ecopolitics, in* GLOBAL ACCORD: ENVIRONMENTAL CHALLENGES AND INTERNATIONAL RESPONSES 134 (Nazli Choucri ed., MIT Press 1993). *See also* INSTITUTIONS FOR THE EARTH: SOURCES OF EFFECTIVE INTERNATIONAL ENVIRONMENTAL PROTECTION 9 (Peter Haas, Robert Keohane & Marc Levy eds., MIT Press 1993).

5. JOHN KUNICH, ARK OF THE BROKEN COVENANT: PROTECTING THE WORLD'S BIODIVERSITY HOTSPOTS (Greenwood Publishing Group 2003); John Kunich, *Losing Nemo: The Mass Extinction Now Threatening the World's Hotspots*, 30 COLUMBIA JOURNAL OF ENVIRONMENTAL LAW 1–133 (2005); John Kunich, *Fiddling Around while the Hotspots Burn Out*, 14 GEORGETOWN INTERNATIONAL ENVIRONMENTAL REVIEW 179–263 (2001). *See also* Francis Situma, Legal Protection of Biodiversity with Reference to Agricultural and Medicinal Plants 135–136 (unpublished doctoral thesis, 1995).

6. CHRISTOPHER STONE, SHOULD TREES HAVE STANDING? AND OTHER ESSAYS ON LAW, MORALS AND THE ENVIRONMENT 82 (Oceana Publications 1996).

7. CHRISTOPHER STONE, THE GNAT IS OLDER THAN MAN: GLOBAL ENVIRONMENT AND HUMAN AGENDA 13 (Princeton University Press 1993).

8. TONY BRENTON, THE GREENING OF MACHIAVELLI: THE EVOLUTION OF INTERNATIONAL ENVIRONMENTAL POLITICS 248–249 (Earthscan and the Royal Institute of International Affairs 1994).

9. Richard Sandbrook, *in* THE FUTURE OF IUCN 51 (M. Holdgate & H. Synge eds., IUCN Publications 1993). *Also see* Wolfgang Burhenne's response, at 85.

10. I address *territorial* conventions in contrast to conventions of the same period that addressed migratory species or species of the global commons, such as the 1911 Convention for the Preservation and Protection of Fur Seals 37 Stat. 1542 (July 7, 1911), adopted by the United States, Great Britain, Russia, and Japan, to regulate their hunting; or the 1916 Convention for the Protection of Migratory Birds US-Gr. Brit. 39 Stat. 1702 (August 16, 1916), adopted by the United States and Great Britain (on behalf of Canada).

11. The terms *colonial confrontation* or *colonial encounter* are used recurrently in the scholarship. *See* ANTONY ANGHIE, IMPERIALISM, SOVEREIGNTY AND THE MAKING OF INTERNATIONAL LAW 197–198 (Cambridge University Press 2007) and MARTTI KOSKENNIEMI, THE GENTLE CIVILIZER OF NATIONS: THE RISE AND FALL OF INTERNATIONAL LAW 1870–1960 (Cambridge University Press 2002).

12. E.g. the 1949 Lake Success conference and the 1968 Biosphere Conference.

13. Interview with Dr. Tamar Ron, biodiversity conservation consultant working in Africa, June 21, 2011. *See also* WILLIAM BEINHART & LOTTE HUGHES, ENVIRONMENT AND EMPIRE 62 (Oxford University Press 2007). *See generally* JEAN PAUL HARROY, AFRIQUE, TERRE QUI MEURT: LA DEGRADATION DES SOLS AFRICAINS SOUS L'INFLUENCE DE LA COLONISATION (M. Hayez 1944). *See also* Paul Sarasin, who blamed civilization and "the white race" for the global destruction of nature: PAUL SARASIN, WELTNATURHUT, trans. from German into English as GLOBAL PROTECTION OF NATURE (E. Birkhauser 1911). For early twentieth-century accounts of the unique diversity of African mammals and the danger of extinctions, *see* Major R. W. G. Hingston, *Proposed British National Parks for Africa*, 77(5) GEOGRAPHICAL JOURNAL 2–3 (May 1931) (hereafter Hingston); Henry R. Carey, *Saving the Animal Life of Africa—a New and a Last Chance*, 7(2) JOURNAL OF MAMMALOGY 73–85 (May 1926).

14. JOHN MACKENZIE, THE EMPIRE OF NATURE: HUNTING, CONSERVATION, AND BRITISH IMPERIALISM 202 (Manchester University Press 1988). *See also* a 1931 publication of IOPN, proudly noting that "the Office has already been able to furnish various colonial governments with valuable information, allowing them to prepare [. . .] new legislation concerning game laws, regulations for national parks, game reserves," "The International Office for the Protection of Nature, 1931" in the Harold Jefferson Coolidge Papers, HUGFP 78. Harvard University Archives, Cambridge, Massachusetts (hereafter HJCP/HUA), 78.10, box 27, folder: Van Tienhoven, at 11.

15. KOSKENNIEMI, *supra note* 11, at 127: "For Westlake, it was absurd to think of native

possession in terms of sovereignty [. . . .] Sovereignty was a purely European notion." ANGHIE, *supra note* 11, at 30–31, 35–36, 38.

16. *See generally* KOSKENNIEMI, *id.* at 127, 102, 131. ANGHIE, *id.* at 35–36.

17. ANGHIE, *id.* at 38. *See also* DECOLONIZING NATURE: STRATEGIES FOR CONSERVATION IN A POST-COLONIAL ERA 3 (William Adams & Martin Mulligan eds., Earthscan 2003).

18. Defined as "transnational networks of knowledge-based communities that are both apolitically empowered through their claims to exercise authoritative knowledge and motivated by shared causal and principled beliefs," Peter Haas, *Do Regimes Matter: Epistemic Communities and Mediterranean Pollution Control*, 43 INTERNATIONAL ORGANIZATION 377–403 (Summer 1989).

19. *See generally* the IUCN website at www.iucn.org. Generally on the work of IUCN, *see also* MARTIN HOLDGATE, THE GREEN WEB (Earthscan 1999); BARBARA LAUSCHE, WEAVING A WEB OF ENVIRONMENTAL LAW (IUCN Environmental Law Program 2008).

20. *See Report of the International Committee on National Parks, in* Proc. 7th Sess. Gen. Ass. (IUCN 1960), at 97. *See also* ROBERT BOARDMAN, INTERNATIONAL ORGANIZATION AND THE CONSERVATION OF NATURE 148 (Indiana University Press 1981).

21. Secretariat of the Convention on Biological Diversity (2010), *in* GLOBAL BIODIVERSITY OUTLOOK 3 MONTREAL. Available at http://gbo3.cbc.int.

22. Millennium Ecosystem Assessment, 2005, ECOSYSTEMS AND HUMAN WELL-BEING: BIODIVERSITY SYNTHESIS 30 (World Resources Institute), at www.millenniumassessment.org.

23. Hobley, secretary of SPFE, to Coolidge, American Committee, Aug. 7, 1930. American Committee for International Wild Life Protection/World Conservation Society (hereafter ACIWLP/WCS) box 4, folder: Hobley.

24. The term *developing countries*, referring to countries of Africa, Asia, and Latin America, traces back to Walt Whitman Rostow's 1960 book THE STAGES OF ECONOMIC GROWTH: A NON-COMMUNIST MANIFESTO. The term *North-South* appears in the 1983 Brandt Commission report *North-South and Common Crisis. See also* DECOLONIZING NATURE, *supra note* 17, at 12–13.

25. "Given that international law was inherently European, how could it accommodate the new states which belonged to very different cultural traditions? [. . .] International law had served the interests of the powerful Western states. Inevitably, then, the new states would seek to [. . .] change an international legal regime that operated to their disadvantage," ANGHIE, *supra note* 11, at 197–198. And, "In practice, then, good governance is a concept that has developed, at the international level, principally in relation to Third World states, for these are the countries that lack governance. The task of international law and institutions, then, is to promote good governance in these societies [. . . .] My argument is, however, that this initiative merely replicates the 'civilizing mission'," *id.* at 249–250.

26. Abba Mahmood, Food Crisis and the Global Land Grab: The Scramble for African Land (1) (Sept. 8, 2012), http://farmlandgrab.org/post/view/20889 (accessed May 24, 2013).

CHAPTER TWO Colonial Beginnings

27. International Technical Conference on the Protection of Nature (UN Lake Success conference 22–29–VIII-1949); PROCEEDINGS AND PAPERS 17 (UNESCO 1950) (hereafter 1949 Lake Success Conf. Proc.). Available at http://unesdoc.unesco.org.

28. RICHARD GROVE, GREEN IMPERIALISM (Cambridge University Press 1995), at index, "Dessication Theories."

29. *Id.* at 206, 481, and fn. 7. AARON SACHS, THE HUMBOLDT CURRENT: A EUROPEAN EXPLORER AND HIS AMERICAN DISCIPLES 13 (Oxford University Press 2007).

30. "I have stated in the preface to the Zoology of the Voyage of the Beagle, that it was in consequence of a wish expressed by Captain FtizRoy, of having some scientific person on board [. . .] that I volunteered my services," CHARLES DARWIN, GEOLOGY AND NATURAL HISTORY (Henry Colburn 1839), at preface. Darwin called himself the "Naturalist to the Beagle," *id.* Gregory Barton points out that by the middle of the nineteenth century, the high number of botanists that German and English universities were graduating exceeded the job opportunities in those countries. GREGORY BARTON, EMPIRE FORESTRY AND THE ORIGINS OF ENVIRONMENTALISM 35 (Cambridge University Press 2002).

31. GROVE, *supra note* 28, at 123.

32. GROVE, *id.* at 216, 219–221, 225.

33. *Id.* at 256, 258. Grove points out that the opportunities to enact such pioneering regulations were far greater in a small environmentally fragile island with limited water resources, in which the impact of human activities on the environment was swiftly felt, along with legislative precedents successfully promoted under Poivre.

34. David Anderson & Richard Grove, *The Scramble for Eden: Past, Present and Future in African Conservation*, *in* CONSERVATION IN AFRICA: PEOPLES, POLICIES AND PRACTICE 23, 47–48 (Cambridge University Press 1995). *And see* GROVE, *id.* at 454. And continuing the chain of connections, J. D. Hooker was a close friend and supporter of Darwin, *id.*

35. Hence "the relationship between Pappe and Rawson was an important element in the evolution of conservation legislation at the Cape," *id.* at 26.

36. SACHS, *supra note* 29, at 50–53. As noted by Sachs, "the real significance of Humboldt's journey up the Orinoco as well as for modern environmentalism, was that it had shown him nature's most off-putting and threatening secrets and he managed to pull through without demonizing nature," *id.* at 63. BARTON, *supra note* 30, at 16.

37. See GROVE, *supra note* 28, at 374, on Humboldt's "frequent criticisms of the brutality of European colonial rule."

38. *Id.* at 484, fn. 15. *And see*, at 462, "The biota of Europe were simply not perceived as being threatened by rapid ecological change of the kind taking place in India."

39. SACHS, *supra note* 29, at 14.

40. A. R. Wallace, *On the Physical Geography of the Malay Archipelago*, 32 JOURNAL OF THE ROYAL GEOGRAPHIC SOCIETY 234 (1863).

41. A. F. R. WOLLASTON, LIFE OF ALFRED NEWTON 52 (E. P. Dutton 1921), at preface. Available at BOU website: http://bou-online.blogspot.com.

42. *Id.* at 2, 23, 52, 54, 97.

43. *See* J. SHEAIL, NATURE IN TRUST: THE HISTORY OF NATURE CONSERVATION IN BRITAIN 22–26 (Blackie and Son 1976).

44. *Qtd. in* WOLLASTON, *supra note* 41, at 112.

45. *Id.* at 23, 52, 97, 143.

46. Grove credits Newton with persuading the government to gather data on colonial wildlife laws. In 1876 "Whitehall circularized all colonies [. . .] to obtain information on existing models of game and wildlife protection legislation. This search for models was probably made at the instigation of Alfred Newton, Professor of Zoology at Cambridge, and the progenitor of the first British bird protection legislation of the 1860s." *Early Themes in African Conservation, in* CONSERVATION IN AFRICA, *supra note* 34, at 32. *See also* the extract of a letter by Alfred Newton, "[s]o long ago as the 28th January, 1876, [. . .] published in the 'Times' newspaper," on the destruction of birds for the feather and hat industry, *in* PARLIAMENTARY PAPERS: CORRESPONDENCE RELATING TO THE PRESERVATION OF WILD ANIMALS IN AFRICA, CD. 3189 (1906) (hereafter African correspondence) encl.10 in no. 56, "The British plenipotentiaries to the Game Conference to the Marquess of Salisbury," at 102.

47. Charles Darwin & Alfred Wallace, *On the Tendency of Species to Form Varieties; and on the Perpetuation of Varieties and Species by Natural Means of Selection*, 3 JOURNAL OF THE PROCEEDINGS OF THE LINNEAN SOCIETY OF LONDON. ZOOLOGY 45–50 (Aug. 20, 1858).

48. Sir John Kirk, July 31, 1897, African correspondence, *supra note* 46, no.13, at 43. CIOC, *supra note* 2, at 150.

49. C. W. Hobley, *The London Convention of 1900*, New Series Vol. XX JOURNAL OF THE SOCIETY FOR THE PRESERVATION OF THE FAUNA OF THE EMPIRE (hereafter JSPFE) 48 (1933).

50. On the use of the term by "British diplomats," see CIOC, *supra note* 2, at 150.

51. Second International Conference for the Protection of the Fauna and Flora of Africa, London, May 1938, at 1–2; CIOC, *supra note* 2, at 6.

52. Salisbury to Hardinge and Berkeley, May 27, 1896. African correspondence, *supra note* 46, no. 1, at 1.

53. "This desire to preserve the fascinating aspects of wild nature began to take a more acute shape in the last decade of the nineteenth century, and various African administrators, who were naturalists as well as sportsmen, induced their governments to allow them to proclaim certain areas in Africa to be game reserves," H. H. Johnston, *The Preservation of the African Fauna and its Relation to Tropical Diseases*, NATURE (Dec. 7, 1911).

54. *Generally see* African correspondence, *supra note* 46; EDWARD BUXTON, TWO AFRICAN TRIPS: WITH NOTES AND SUGGESTION ON BIG GAME LIFE PRESERVATION e.g. 1–2 (Edward Stanford 1902); *The Dying Fauna of an Empire*, SATURDAY REVIEW OF POLITICS, LITERATURE, SCIENCE AND ART 635–636 (Nov. 24, 1906); WILLIAM HORNADAY, OUR VANISHING WILDLIFE (New York Zoological Society 1913); William Hornaday & Alwin Haagner, *The Vanishing Game of South Africa*, Permanent Wild Life Protection Fund Bulletin No. 10, (Sept. 1, 1922).

55. Bernhard Gissibl, *German Colonialism and the Beginnings of International Wildlife Preservation in Africa*, Suppl. 3 GHI BULLETIN 131, 121–143 (2006); MACKENZIE, *supra note* 14, at 207; CIOC, *supra note* 2, at 23; *Further Correspondence Relating to the Preservation of Wild Animals in Africa*, Part 2/7822, 154. *See* African correspondence, *supra note* 46, no. 56, at 91; no. 55, at 86. *See* correspondence between Lankester and the Foreign Office, June 24, 1901, *id.* no. 100, at 144; *see also* correspondence with the Zoological Society of London, *id.* no. 214, at 335, and no. 216, at 336.

56. JOSEPH CONRAD, HEART OF DARKNESS 15 (Penguin Books 2012).

57. African correspondence, *supra note* 46, encl. 3 in no. 56, "British Central Africa 1894," at 93.

58. *Zanzibar Ivory Trade*, GAZETTE FOR ZANZIBAR AND EAST AFRICA (Sept. 25, 1895).

59. Hingston, *supra note* 13, at 401–422.

60. World Wildlife Fund Global, Threats to African Elephants, http://wwf.panda.org/what_we_do/endangered_species/elephants/african_elephants/afelephants_threats/ (accessed May 29, 2013).

61. Tara Holmes, Will Africa's Elephants be Extinct in 10 Years? (June 19, 2012), www.care2.com/causes/will-africas-elephants-be-extinct-in-10-years.html (accessed Feb. 14, 2013).

62. Threats to African Elephants, *supra note* 60; Michael Glennon, *Has International Law Failed the Elephant?* 84(1) AMERICAN JOURNAL OF INTERNATIONAL LAW 1–43 (Jan. 1990); WILLIAM ADAMS, AGAINST EXTINCTION: THE STORY OF CONSERVATION 73–74 (Earthscan 2004) (hereafter AGAINST EXTINCTION).

63. *See* World Wildlife Fund website, "African Elephants," at http://wwf.panda.org. *See also* Alex Shoumatoff, *Agony and Ivory*, VANITY FAIR 133, 122–135 (Aug. 2011).

64. "Elephant Database, 2012 Continental Totals," reports on a total of 422,955 elephants for the 2012 summary; *cmp.* 2007 total of 472,134 elephants. *See also supra note* 61, reporting that only 400,000 elephants remain in the wild in all of Africa.

65. *Id.*; Gissibl, *supra note* 55, at 125, 126.

66. African correspondence, *supra note* 46, "Regulations for the Protection of Wild Animals in German East Africa," no. 2 at 3–4.

67. *Id.*, no. 3, at 4. The German law was also sent to Southern Nigeria, *id.* no. 4, at 6; Zululand, no. 5, at 6; *see also* Annex 2 Laws and Regulations for the Preservation of Animals (Colonial Office to Foreign Office), no. 5, at 9.

68. *Id.*, no. 8, at 30, Salisbury to Lascelles, Jan. 19, 1897 (the quotes regarding the German proposal are from Salisbury's letter to Lascelles); Gissibl, *supra note* 55, *generally* and at 126, 130; CIOC, *supra note* 2, at 34–40.

69. *Id.*, Sharpe to Salisbury, Sept. 9, 1896, no. 7, at 26, 27. *See* von Wissmann's response: "I doubt the correctness of Mr. Sharpe's statement that the main blame for the extinction of big game in Africa rests with the natives, and not Europeans. I have too often seen how every European who possesses a gun on board a Congo steamer fires in the most reckless fashion," *id.*, von Wissmann, encl. in no. 10, at 34, 35.

70. *Id.*, no. 7, at 26, 27. Sharpe in his letter dated Sept. 9, 1896, was apparently addressing the "copy of Regulations which have recently been issued in German East Africa [. . .] inquiring whether I am of opinion that any similar Regulations could usefully be issued in this Protectorate." In reply, Sharpe opined that only international cooperation can solve the problem of the ivory trade. It is thus unclear whether the need for international cooperation was recognized separately by both the Germans and the British at around the same time, or whether the Germans first reached this conclusion. In any case, it is clear that the trigger for the "international arrangement" was von Wissmann's regulations.

71. *See* von Wissmann's letter to Baron von Richtofen, Apr. 2, 1897, *id.*, no. 10, at 34–35. Colonial Office to the Foreign Office, July 29, 1897, "on the subject of a proposed Conference between the Powers having African interests, with a view to the preservation of elephants and other African fauna," no. 12, at 42.

72. *Id.*, Foreign Office to Colonial Office, no. 15, at 44. *See also* Salisbury's letter to Lascelles in Berlin, Mar. 3, 1898, *id.*, no. 16, at 45. *See also* 'Draft of suggested bases for Deliberations of an International Conference for the Protection of Wild Animals, Birds, and Fishes in Africa," Salisbury to Lascelles, Apr. 4, 1899, *id.*, no. 33, at 57; and Lascelles's reply, to which he attached the Germans' confirmation of the program, Aug. 7, 1899, *id.*, no. 37, at 62. On further references to the Brussels Act, *see* "Memorandum by Sir John Kirk," *id.*, no. 13, at 42. On the controversy surrounding the use of modern firearms by natives, *see id.*, no. 181, at 252. *See also* CIOC, *supra note* 2, at 16.

73. *Id.*, "The British Plenipotentiaries to the Game Conference," in a letter to Lord Salisbury, May 22, 1900. Signed Hopetoun, Clement Hill, Lankester, no. 56, at 91.

74. *Id.*, Salisbury to Geoffray, French ambassador, Jan. 9, 1900, no. 49, at 80. French suspicions of a new convention are understandable in light of the 1892 Congo Basin Convention between France, Belgium, and Portugal, in which they agreed among

themselves on duties on ivory traded in the territories they controlled. CIOC, *supra note* 2, at 16, 36–39.

75. Art. I. The territorial coverage was bounded "[o]n the north by the 20th parallel of north latitude [. . .] on the South by a line following the northern boundary of the German possessions in Southwestern Africa, from its western extremity to its junction with the river Zambesi, and thence running along the right bank of that river as far as the Indian Ocean." *Id.*, no. 55, at 87. *See* CIOC, *id.* at 34.

76. *See* the report of the British plenipotentiaries (Hopetoun, Hill, Lankester), referring to the limited territorial coverage of the convention: "The fact that the [. . .] Convention [. . .] excludes large territories in which the Governments of Great Britain, Germany and Portugal hold possessions gave rise to apprehensions on the part of the latter Power that its commerce might suffer unless the various Administrations of those territories accede to the Convention. The Representative of Portugal, therefore, signed with a reservation that his Government would delay its ratification until such accession had been obtained." *Id.*, no. 56, at 91–92. *See also* CIOC, *id.* at 34.

77. *Id.*, Art. II, no. 55, at 87.

78. *Id.*, Art. II, at secs. 1–4.

79. *Id.* at secs. 6–10. In other words, traditional African hunting methods. *See* Buxton, *id.*, African correspondence, no. 181, at 252, regarding the controversy over traditional African hunting methods versus the use of modern weapons. Buxton was against the use of modern weapons by Africans, arguing that once they get hold of guns, "there is an end of the game." *Cmp.* CIOC, *supra note* 2: "the delegates reaffirmed the provisions of the Brussels Conference, which forbade the supply of modern arms [. . .] to African blacks. This too ensured that the onus of the treaty fell harder on the indigenous populations than on the Europeans. The convention deprived African blacks of their right to use traditional hunting methods without lifting the ban on the use of European weaponry," at 35. "Since the vast majority of indigenous hunters could not afford these licenses [. . .] this stipulation [. . .] turned subsistence hunting into poaching," *id.*

80. *Id.* at secs. 11–12. Art. II, Art. IV, *id.*, no. 55, at 87.

81. *Id.* Schedules I–V.

82. *Id.*, Art. II, at sec. 11.

83. CIOC, *supra note* 2, at 16, 38.

84. *Id.* at 36–40.

85. *See* Carey, *supra note* 13, discussing the reasons for the failure of the 1900 Convention: "because the machinery of enforcement, including a *permanent* body to keep watch on conditions, has never been set up." He called for "a *permanent* international body to make inter-colonial regulations," and proposed that the League of Nations establish a commission in Africa to protect its wildlife which is in danger of extinction, at 79.

86. African correspondence, *supra note* 46, no. 69, at 115. The self-governing colony of

Natal expressed willingness to accede to the convention, at 126, as did the self-governing colony of the Cape of Good Hope, at 127; Colonial Office to Foreign Office, Sept. 25, 1900, no. 80, at 123.

87. *Id.*, no. 62, at 159, Salisbury to Hardinge, June 20, 1900.

88. *Id.*, Hardinge to Salisbury, Aug. 7, 1900, no. 76, at 120. Hardinge to von Liebert, German East Africa, Aug. 7, 1900. After von Wissmann left his colonial position, the German government's enthusiasm for the 1896 game ordinance ebbed and was replaced by a more lenient one; *See* Gissibl, *supra note* 55, at 128. Yet the Germans did comply with Hardinge's request, *id.*, no. 87, at 129.

89. *Id.*, no. 73, at 117; *id.*, no. 75, at 119; *id.*, no. 77, at 121.

90. *Id.*, Somaliland, no. 89, at 129; no. 94, at 140; Sierra Leone, Nov. 1901, no. 108, at 153; Northern Nigeria, no. 111, at 159; Southern Nigeria, no. 202, at 287; Lagos, no. 205, at 301. *Id.*, Uganda, no. 119, at 176. British Central Africa, no. 121, at 177; Uganda, no. 124, at 184; British Central Africa, no. 135, at 195; no. 200 at 285, July 24, 1905; no. 206, at 305, Aug. 24, 1905. *See also* the report of the plenipotentiaries, *supra note* 76.

91. *Id.*, Art. II. 7, 8, no. 55, at 86. *Id.* at 208. Harry Johnston remarked on the wanton hunting by armed Africans: "it is an example of what can occur when semi-civilised natives have access to guns and gunpowder," African correspondence, *supra note* 46, no. 181, at 255. The situation did not seem to have changed much by 1931. In discussing the implementation of the 1900 Convention in Northern Rhodesia, Hobley noted that one factor for "undue slaughter of wild life" was "the widespread possession of firearms among the natives," Hobley, *London Convention*, New Series Part XX JSPFE 49, 33–49.

92. "The Europeans made it illegal for Africans to acquire modern weaponry—and then demonized them for using 'primitive' hunting techniques. They usurped pastoral and agricultural space [. . .] and then looked askance when Africans relied on [. . .] "bush meat" [. . . .] They turned traditional hunting grounds into [. .] parks and [. . .] reserves—and then complained when Africans continued to hunt there," CIOC, *supra note* 2, at 16.

93. African correspondence, *supra note* 46, Wilson to the Earl of Elgin, Apr. 4, 1906, Entebbe, Uganda, no. 222, at 355.

94. *Id.*, no. 194, at 176. *See also* Lord Delamere to Sir Clement Hill, Aug. 12, 1900, supporting the idea of enclosing land for reserves, but also noting, "The hardship seems to come in more in the case of land round stations or forts where people have been accustomed to shoot for some time and have to live," *id.*, no. 74, at 117.

95. *Id.*, Sharpe to Salisbury, no. 7, at 27; and no. 53, at 83. *See also* comments of von Wissmann, who disagreed with Sharpe's position that the Africans were to blame, and put the blame squarely on Europeans, von Wissmann to Richthoven, Apr. 2, 1897, *id.*, no. 10, at 34. *See also* Lord Delamere to Sharpe, complaining about new regulations that apparently restricted European hunting to allow native hunting, and arguing for a government monopoly on elephant killing, Aug. 12, 1900, no. 74, at 113.

96. *Id.*, SPFE meeting with the secretary of state for the colonies, no. 225, at 375.

97. The Kenya colony Southern Reserve, established in 1900, was "[a]t a later date [. . .] handed over to the Masai and without any provision therein for the recognition of the area as a permanent sanctuary for wild life," Hobley, *supra note* 49, at 34. Similarly, the Kafue Reserve in Northern Rhodesia, which besides 35,000 ungulates "also contains a few thousand meat-loving natives addicted to hunting," *id.*, African correspondence, *supra note* 46, at 39.

98. E.g. the game law in the Nigerian colony, Hobley, *id.* at 40, 43, and regarding the situation in Sierra Leone and Basutoland, that the game regulations apply to alien residents but not to natives, at 46. For verification of this, see letter from the governor of Sierra Leone to Lyttelton, the colonial secretary, May 15, 1905, no. 190, at 271. See also Hobley, *id.* at 47, 48.

99. Vol. I JSPFE 70, extract from Lord Cromer's *Report for Egypt and the Sudan for the Year 1903*.

100. Hingston, *supra note* 13, at 403. The "spread of civilization" as the underlying cause for loss of game was also raised in the *Report on Southern Nigeria*: "the inevitable result of the spread of civilization and the increase in population" as one of the "main causes leading to the destruction of wild animals," African correspondence, *supra note* 46, no. 204, at 298.

101. Carey, *supra note* 13, at 76.

102. E.g. "The Society has been formed for encouraging the protection of the wild fauna in all British possessions. The members regard it as one of the heritages of the empire which, if it be once lost, can never be replaced," Vol. I JSPFE 10 (1904); an "inheritance of the Empire," Vol. II JSPFE 7 (1905); and "an Imperial inheritance," Vol. II JSPFE 9 (1905). See also *Report of the Executive Committee*, New Series Part XI JSPFE 6 (1930).

103. Gissibl, *supra note* 55, at 122. And "the convention [. . .] claimed imperial stewardship over African nature and asserted that wildlife preservation was part of Europe's civilizing mission on the continent," *id.* "We regard the fauna [. . .] as an Imperial inheritance, and we think that if the game were to be killed out, especially if species were to become lost, it would be an Imperial loss," African correspondence, *supra note* 46, no. 181, at 249.

104. African correspondence, *id.*, no. 181, at 249. *See also* Lord Curzon's remarks at the meeting, *id.*, no. 225, at 375. "Positivists developed an elaborate vocabulary for denigrating non-European people, presenting them as suitable objects for conquest [. . .] all in furtherance of the civilizing mission, the discharge of the white man's burden." ANGHIE, *supra note* 11, at 38. *See also* KOSKENNIEMI, *id.* at 127; "indigenous populations were, for the most part, removed from the protected areas [. . .] indigenous populations being only slightly above the wildlife in the minds of many colonists," CIOC, *supra note* 2, at 19.

105. Gissibl, *supra note* 55, at 126.

106. *Report of the Executive Committee*, New Series Part XI JSPFE 6 (1930).

107. *See* Vol. I JSPFE 10 (1904), in which SPFE explains its means of operation by collecting information generated by colonial administrators. A copy of the convention appears in the first volume of SPFE's journal, published in 1904, at 29. Strengthening the links between the convention and SPFE, Sir Clement Hill and E. R. Lankester, both signatories to the 1900 Convention, were also founding members of SPFE, *id.* at 1–4. *See also* CIOC, *supra note* 2, at 40. RICHARD FITTER & PETER OTT, THE PENITENT BUTCHERS 8 (Collins 1978). Although it was originally called the Society for the Preservation of the Wild Fauna of the Empire (SPWFE), the word *wild* was removed after World War I, *id.* at 9.

108. FITTER & OTT, *id.*; David Prendergast & William Adams, *Colonial Wildlife Conservation and the Origins of the Society for the Preservation of the Wild Fauna of the Empire (1903–1914)*, 37(2) ORYX 252, 251–260 (2003).

109. Including Lankester. He was also one of the three British signatories to the convention at the 1900 Plenipotentiaries Conference. *See* African correspondence, *supra note* 46, no. 56, at 91. *See also* Vol. I JSPFE 1–4 (1904). *See also* FITTER & OTT, *id.* at 8.

110. *Id.*, JSPFE, at 5.

111. *Id.*, JSPFE, at 1–4 (list of founding members): "Its list of members is now of considerable influence and volume [. . .] [and] attest the fact that our great administrators are alive to the Imperial obligation of zealously guarding from wanton destruction the marvelous varieties of life [. . .] still to be found within [. . .] His Majesty's Dominions Beyond the Seas." S.H. Whitbread, *The Year*, annual report for 1906, Vol. III JSPFE 10 (1907).

112. African correspondence, *supra note* 46, no. 181, at 249–257.

113. *Id.* at 249. Buxton complained in particular about the lack of information coming from the Nigerian protectorate.

114. African correspondence, *id.* *See* Sierra Leone, no. 190, at 271; Gold Cost, no. 194, at 274; Gambia, no. 196, at 278; Southern Nigeria, no. 204, at 294; Northern Nigeria, no. 207, at 306; Uganda, no. 210, at 319; Somaliland, no. 211, at 322, containing suggestions "to further ensure the protection of wild animals as contemplated in the "International Convention for the Preservation of Wild Animals"; Lagos, no. 212, at 330, and no. 213, at 334.

115. Vol. III JSPFE 14–19 (1907); African correspondence, *id.*, notes 228, 229, 230, 233, 235, 386, 387, 391.

116. FITTER & OTT, *supra note* 107, at 16–17.

117. Vol. III JSPFE 10, 88 (1907).

118. *See* Sarasin's account of these events *in* SARASIN, WELTNATURHUTZ. Global Protection of Nature "Paper read at the VII International Congress of Zoologists in Gratz Aug. 16th 1910 and at the 93d Conference of the Schweiz.Naturf.Gessellschaft in Basel, Sept. 15th 1910. Translated from the German," at 2–6 (copy of English translation

150 *Notes to Chapter Two*

on file with author). Sarasin outlined "a global organization of the protection of nature formed by national leagues and an international commission standing above them," at 10.

119. *Id.* at 7. For a description and background on the advisory commission, *see* REPORT ON THE CONFERENCE FOR THE INTERNATIONAL PROTECTION OF NATURE 61–62, 75–80, 86–93 (Johann Buttikofer ed., 1946), Swiss League for the Protection of Nature (Basle, June 30–July 7, 1946). *See also* "The International Office for the Protection of Nature," *supra note* 14, at 6–7, HJCP/HUA 78.10, box 27, folder: Van Tienhoven.

120. "Advancement of the Protection of Nature, from Dutch Newspaper *Handelsblad*, August 31, 1936, sent by P.G. Van Tienhoven," HJCP/HUA 78.10, box 27, folder: ACIC Colleagues and Friends: P.J. Van Tienhoven Netherlands International Commission for Nature Protection, 1934–1940; *id.*, 78.10, box 25, folder: ACIC Correspondence, 1931–1937.

121. "In considering the protection of nature, two different aspects should be borne in mind: protection in metropolitan countries and protection overseas. The first was a domestic problem for each country, and had few international aspects. The second was much more far reaching and often concerned man's welfare—even his very existence," words of Dr. Ramsbottom, UK representative, INTERNATIONAL CONFERENCE FOR THE PROTECTION OF NATURE 154 (Brunnen, June 28–July 3, 1947) (Johann Buttikofer ed.), Proceedings, Resolutions and Reports. Basle: Provisional International Union for the Protection of Nature, Acting Agency: Swiss League for the Protection of Nature (hereafter 1947 Brunnen conference).

122. Sarasin, *supra note* 118, at 1–2, 17–18.

123. Van Tienhoven to Coolidge, July 18, 1946, HJCP/HUA 78.14, box 45, folder: Van Tienhoven. *See also* 1947 Brunnen conference, *supra note* 121, at 47. *See also* "International Union for the Protection of Nature, Established at Fontainebleau 5 October 1948," (M. Hayez), summary of the conference, at foreword; BOARDMAN, *supra note* 20, at 32.

124. Sarasin, *supra note* 118, at 16.

125. BOARDMAN, *supra note* 20, at 32–33; G. A. BROUWER, THE ORGANISATION OF NATURE PROTECTION IN THE VARIOUS COUNTRIES (1931), "Published by the Cooperation of the Writer and the Netherlands Committee for International Nature Protection" (former name of the IOPN). The 1938 edition was a "Special Publication of the American Committee for International Wild Life Protection, No. 9."

126. "The International Office for the Protection of Nature," *supra note* 14, at 7.

127. William Goodenough, Prince Reginald de Croy, Albert Kitson & C. W. Hobley, *Proposed British National Parks for Africa: Discussion*, 77(5) GEOGRAPHICAL JOURNAL, Hobley at 425, 423–428 (May 1931).

128. Convention Relative to the Preservation of Fauna and Flora in Their Natural State, Nov. 8, 1933, 172 L.N.T.S. 241, entered into force Jan. 14, 1936. Available at http://eelink.net and www.ecolex.org.

129. Roderick Neumann, *Ways of Seeing Africa: Colonial Recasting of African Society and Landscape in Serengeti National Park*, 2(2) ECUMENE 149–169 (1995). ("The plan for an international agreement was the product of [. . .] [SPFE]. The Governor was informed

that [. . .] Caldwell, would tour the African colonies as the initial step in developing an international agreement"), at 153; RODERICK NEUMANN, IMPOSING WILDERNESS 123 (University of California Press 1998).

130. See Hingston, *supra note 13; see also Report of the Executive Committee to the General Meeting*, New Series Part XII JSPFE 10 (June 2, 1930). *See also id.*, NEUMANN, at 123–124. *See also id., Ways of Seeing Africa. See also* CIOC, *supra note 2*, at 47–50.

131. Hingston, *id.* at 405; on the four threats *generally*, starting from 402.

132. *Id.* at 401, 406.

133. *Id.* at 402.

134. *Id.* at 406.

135. *Id.*

136. *Id.* at 413.

137. CIOC, *supra note 2*, Chapt. 1, 14–56.

138. The following account of the 1931 conference is the report on the conference as it appears in New Series Part XV JSPFE 43 (1931).

139. Hingston, *supra note 13*.

140. EARL OF ONSLOW, SIXTY-THREE YEARS: DIPLOMACY, THE GREAT WAR AND POLITICS 193 (Hutchinson 1944).

141. Account of the 1931 conference, *supra note 138*, at 44, 45–46.

142. *Id.* at 45.

143. *Id.* at 48; *see also* 45.

144. Neumann, *supra note 129*, at 124, 125. *See also* CIOC, *supra note 2*, at 49.

145. Neumann, *id.* at 128.

146. ONSLOW, *supra note 140*, at 193.

147. Art. 8.2 declares, "No hunting or other rights already possessed by native chiefs of tribes [. . .] by treaty, concession, or specific agreement [. . .] are to be [. . .] prejudiced by the [. . .] preceding paragraph." Convention Relative to the Preservation of Fauna and Flora in Their Natural State, *supra note 128*.

148. Keith Caldwell, *The International Conference for the Protection of the Fauna and Flora of Africa*, New Series Part XXII JSPFE 45–52 (May 1934). *See also* CIOC *supra note 2*, at 52. But *see* subsequent criticism on the short negotiating period, *in* 1949 Lake Success Conf. Proc., *supra note 27*: "Several speakers then expressed the view that both the African and Western Hemisphere treaties had been drafted and enacted too hurriedly," at 153. *See also* BOARDMAN, *supra note 20*, at 146.

149. African correspondence, *supra note 46*, no. 191, at 273. *See also Report of the Executive Committee*, New Series Part XI JSPFE 6 (1930), at *supra note 102*.

150. E.g. *see Report of Executive Committee to General Meeting*, New Series Part XII JSPFE 5–11, 6 (1930). MARK BARROW, NATURE'S GHOSTS: CONFRONTING EXTINCTION FROM THE AGE OF JEFFERSON TO THE AGE OF ECOLOGY 149, 152 (University of Chicago Press 2009*). See also infra* text accompanying note 169.

151. Coolidge in particular was a supporter. *See also* the report of van Tienhoven on the

1938 Second International Conference for the Protection of the Fauna and Flora of Africa, "Matters of Moment," June 1, 1939, ACIWLP/WCS, box 5, folder: Van Tienhoven.

152. The idea of an Asian convention was under discussion by 1936; *see* article in the Dutch newspaper *Handelsblad*, Aug. 31, 1936, *supra note* 120. *See also* letter from Onslow to Coolidge, Jan. 21, 1942, HJCP/HUA 78.10, box 26, folder: ACIC Correspondence 1942. *See also* letter from Maurice to Coolidge, Oct. 4, 1939, on the cancellation of the conference, *id.*, box 25, folder: ACIC Correspondence, 1939 (2 of 2).

153. *See* letter from Maurice, SPFE secretary, to Coolidge, Oct. 4, 1939, *id.*; *see also* letter from Onslow to John Phillips, May 31, 1938, ACIWLP/WCS, Correspondence, 1930–1940, box 5, folder: Onslow. *See also* FITTER & OTT, *supra note* 107, at 5.

154. Fauna and Flora International, http://www.fauna-flora.org/about/our-history/ (accessed Feb. 18, 2011).

155. On Coolidge generally, *see also* HOLDGATE, *supra note* 19, at 14, 107; BOARDMAN, *supra note* 20, at 33. *See also* Victoria Drake, The Pioneering of Harold Jefferson Coolidge, American Conservationist (undergraduate thesis, Harvard, 1983), HJCP/HUA 78.16, box 16, folder: HJ Coolidge: Thesis.

156. For a detailed account, *see* BARROW, *supra note* 150, at Chap. 5.

157. BARROW, *id.* at 138.

158. 1911 Convention for the Preservation and Protection of Fur Seals, July 7, 1911, 37 Stat. 1542.

159. 1916 Convention for the Protection of Migratory Birds, August 16, 1916, U.S-Gr. Brit., 39 Stat. 1702. For a review of international bird conservation conventions, *see* ROBERT BOARDMAN, THE INTERNATIONAL POLITICS OF BIRD CONSERVATION, BIODIVERSITY, REGIONALISM AND GLOBAL GOVERNANCE (Edward Elgar 2006).

160. *See* Coolidge Oral History on the American Committee, HJCP/HUA 78.10, box 40, folder: Transcription of Boone and Crockett Club Oral History (hereafter Coolidge Oral History), at 27–28. For a description of a much criticized hunting trip of Roosevelt to Africa, *see* BARROW, *supra note* 150, at 144; MACKENZIE, *supra note* 14, at 219.

161. Coolidge Oral History, *id.* at 28. More accurately, the date was Dec. 1929. Phillips to Hobley, Oct. 15, 1935. *id.*

162. ONSLOW, *supra note* 140, at 193. Hobley's visit came on the background of growing concern over African fauna. *See* letters between Roosevelt and Coolidge, HJCP/HUA 78.10, box 2, folder: Boone and Crockett Club, 1929–1942; *See also* BARROW, *supra note* 150, at 147.

163. ONSLOW, *id.* at 194.

164. Coolidge Oral History, *supra note* 160, at 28.

165. Regarding the date, *see* "American Committee for International Wild Life Protection Activities During 1934, Secretary's Report, December 13, 1934." "This meeting marks the fifth anniversary of the founding of the American Committee

for International Wild Life Protection," HJCP/HUA 78.10, box 26, folder: ACIC, John C. Phillips, 1930–1983. In 1974 the organization was restructured as the American Committee for International Conservation (ACIC).

166. Burnham urged "the necessity of America taking a hand in game preservation" in Africa, Coolidge Oral History, *supra note* 160, at 28. *See also* Harold Coolidge, "Notes on Conservation Activities in 1968" ("I recall that our initial meeting was largely sparked by a strong report from [. . .] Burnham"), Dec. 2, 1968, at 1, HJCP/HUA 78.10, box 2, folder: Clubs: Boone & Crockett, 1929–1942. *Id.* at 42. *See* John Phillips article *The Work of the American Committee for International Wildlife Protection*, *id.*, 78.10, box 26, folder: ACIC, John Charles Phillips, Publications, at 54.

167. Coolidge Oral History, *supra note* 160, at 28.

168. And some of them were racists as well, e.g. the eugenicists Madison Grant and Henry Fairfield Osborn, co-founders of the American Committee and authors of THE PASSING OF THE GREAT RACE. Grant went on to notoriety for exhibiting the Congolese pygmy Ota Benga at the Bronx Zoo alongside apes.

169. *See* letter from Dr. Tordis Graim of IOPN to Betty Hone, assistant secretary of the American Committee, Apr. 27, 1934, ACIWLP/WCS, box 1, 1930–1940 Series Correspondence, A-Z; van Tienhoven to Coolidge, Oct. 14, 1946, HCJP/HUA 78.10, box 27, folder: Van Tienhoven, 1934–1940.

170. *See The Work of the American Committee for International Wildlife Protection*, *supra note* 166, at 56.

171. WILDLIFE RESTORATION AND CONSERVATION: PROCEEDINGS OF THE NORTH AMERICAN WILDLIFE CONFERENCE CALLED BY PRESIDENT FRANKLIN D. ROOSEVELT: WASHINGTON, D.C., FEBRUARY 3–7, 1936 51, 51–56 (1936). Available at www.archive.org.

172. "Hemisphere approach" in "Memorandum" 3, HJCP/HUA 78.10, box 30 (notes for L. Gricom by HCJ Jr.); "International Protection Article for the Bulletin of the Pan American Union," box 2, folder: Coolidge, ACIWLP/WCS

173. Coolidge to Madison Grant, Nov. 2, 1933, ACIWLP/WCS, Correspondence, 1930–1940, box 3, folder: Madison Grant.

174. *See* Coolidge Oral History, *supra note* 160, at 32, 43, 45. Phillips participated in both the First International Conference for the Protection of the Fauna and the Flora of Africa, which adopted the 1933 London Convention, and the second international conference in 1938: PROCEEDINGS OF THE SECOND INTERNATIONAL CONFERENCE FOR THE PROTECTION OF THE FAUNA AND FLORA OF AFRICA, LONDON, MAY 1938 (May 24–27, 1938) (hereafter 1938 London Conference).

175. BARROW, *supra note* 150, at 163–164.

176. Coolidge Oral History, *supra note* 160, at 34–35.

177. Phillips considered his participation in the negotiations for the 1933 Convention "the most important single thing outside of our publications that this committee has done," BARROW, *supra note* 150, at 152, 189.

178. Onslow to Phillips, May 31, 1938, ACIWLP/WCS, Correspondence, 1930–1940, box 5, folder: Onslow.

179. Coolidge Oral History, *supra note* 160. But the idea for the convention was discussed even earlier; *see* 1935 Coolidge letter to Julian Huxley, discussing the chances of negotiating a convention similar to the 1933 London Convention, with Latin American countries, ACIWLP/WCS, box 4, folder: Huxley. *See also* BOARDMAN, *supra note* 20, at 35. *See* BARROW, *supra note* 150, at 188–189, letter from Coolidge from 1935.

180. Coolidge to Wetmore, Oct. 4, 1938, HJCP/HUA 78.10, box 27 folder: ACIC, Alexander Wetmore, 1934–1942.

181. The 8th International Conference of American States, in Lima, Peru, adopted Res. 38, Dec. 1938. Convention on Nature Protection and Wildlife Preservation in the Western Hemisphere, Oct. 12, 1940, 56 Stat. 1354, 161 U.N.T.S. 193 (entered into force May 1, 1942).

182. Roosevelt was referring to G. A. Brouwer's 1931 book THE ORGANISATION OF NATURE PROTECTION IN THE VARIOUS COUNTRIES, which had been republished by the American Committee in English in 1938. Roosevelt to Coolidge, Dec. 23, 1938, HJCP/HUA 78.10, box: 30, folder: Pan American Union, 8th International Conference, Dec. 9–27, 1938.

183. Coolidge to Rowe, Mar. 21, 1939, HJCP/HUA 78.10, box 30, folder: PAU, Rowe, 1938–1940.

184. Pearson to Coolidge, Aug. 31, 1939, *id.*, folder: PAU, Gilbert Pearson. *See also* his letter to Coolidge, Nov. 22, 1939, from Buenos Aires, in which he writes, "You cautioned me carefully, and wisely, about saying little if anything about the plans developing on the proposed treaty matter," *id.*

185. Wetmore to Coolidge, Jan. 23, 1940, *id.*, box 27, folder: ACIC, Alexander Wetmore, 1934–1942.

186. Coolidge to Wetmore, Jan. 26, 1940, *id.*

187. *Id.*

188. Wetmore to Coolidge, Jan. 29, 1940, *id.*

189. Coolidge to Dr. Ross McFarland, June 27, 1941, *id.*, box 26, folder: ACIC Correspondence, 1941.

190. Coolidge to Rowe, Aug. 10, 1939, *id.*, box 30, folder: PAU, Rowe, 1938–1942. Coolidge to Wetmore, Dec. 22, 1939, *id.*, box 27, folder: ACIC, Alexander Wetmore, 1934–1942.

191. Wetmore to Coolidge, July 1, 1940, *id.*, box 27, folder: ACIC, Alexander Wetmore, 1934–1942.

192. 1938 London Conference, *supra note* 174, regarding the "proposed international conference for the Protection of fauna and flora of Tropical Asia and the western Pacific." On the intention to achieve a similar convention for Asia and then a world convention,

see Hemming to Phillips, May 31, 1938, ACIWLP/WCS, 1930–1940, Correspondence, box 4, folder: Hemming. *See also* Onslow to Phillips, June 15, 1938, discussing "the Asiatic and Australasian conference," *id.*, box 5, folder: Onslow.

193. Maurice to Coolidge, Aug. 4, 1938, HJCP/HUA 78.10, box 25, folder: ACIC Correspondence, 1938.

194. Maurice to Coolidge, Oct. 4, 1939, *supra note 152*

195. Van Tienhoven to Coolidge, May 19, 1939, *id.*, box 27, folder: ACIC, Van Tienhoven 1934–40, at 3.

196. Coolidge to Maurice, Oct. 30, 1939, *id.*, box 25, folder: ACIC Correspondence 1939 (2 of 2). *See also* Coolidge to Directors, Boone & Crockett Club, Dec. 9, 1941: "We are keeping lighted the torch which has been handed us by the British Fauna Society and the International office at Brussels," *id.*, box 2, folder: Boone & Crockett Club, 1929–1942.

197. Coolidge to Childs Frick, Oct. 19, 1939, *id.*, box 26, folder: ACIC, 1938–1942; Maurice's letter to Coolidge, Oct. 4, 1939, *supra note 152*.

198. *See* Coolidge's letter to William Phillips, Oct. 22, 1940, asking for his help in urging the US government to ratify the Western Hemisphere Convention; and Philip's answer from Oct. 28, 1940. William Phillips to Coolidge, 78.10, box 25, folder: Correspondence, 1940.

199. E.g. *see* "Memorandum Questions to be Discussed with Dr. Wetmore and Dr. Rowe on Washington Visit February 21st." *See* his appointment as "Technical Adviser to the Secretariat of the Committee of Experts on Nature Protection and Wild Life Preservation," Rowe to Coolidge, Apr. 20, 1940, *id.*, 78.10, box 30, folder: L.S. Rowe. Coolidge to Wetmore, Feb. 14, 1939; Coolidge to Rowe, Aug. 10, 1939; Coolidge to Wetmore, Dec. 22, 1939; *id.*, 78.10, box 27, folder: Alexander Wetmore, 1934–1942.

200. Henry Maurice to Coolidge, Oct. 4, 1939; Coolidge to Huxley, Nov. 3, 1939, responding to Huxley's letter from Oct. 13, in which he had apparently raised the issue of a British observer attending the Western Hemisphere conference, indicating that it would mean also having "to ask for a French and Dutch one," 78.10, box 25, folder: ACIC, Correspondence, 1939 (2 of 2). *See also* Maurice to Coolidge, Apr. 5, 1940, *id.*, box 25, folder: ACIC Correspondence, 1940. *See* Onslow's letter to Coolidge, Sept. 1, 1941, box 26, folder: ACIC Correspondence, 1941; *see* Onslow to Coolidge, Jan. 21, 1942, box 26, folder: ACIC Correspondence, 1942. *See* Coolidge's answer to Maurice, Oct. 30, 1939, HJCP box 25, folder: ACIC Correspondence, 1939 (2 of 2).

201. *See* Coolidge to Onslow, Nov. 28, 1941, and Coolidge to Onslow, *id.*, 78.10, box 26, folder: ACIC Correspondence 1941.

202. Onslow's letter to Coolidge, Sept. 1, 1941, *supra note* 200; and Coolidge to Onslow, Nov. 28, 1941, *id.*

203. Maurice to Coolidge, Oct. 4, 1939, *supra note 152. See* Maurice to Coolidge, Apr.

5, 1940, HJCP/HUA 78.10, box 25, folder: ACIC Correspondence, 1940. *See* Onslow to Coolidge, Jan. 21, 1942, *supra note* 200.

204. Onslow to Coolidge, Sept 1, 1941 *supra note* 200.

205. HJCP/HUA 78.10, box 25, folder: ACIC Correspondence, 1940.

206. Coolidge to Wetmore, Oct. 4, 1938, *supra note* 180, and Oct. 8, 1938, 78.10, box 27, folder: ACIC, Alexander Wetmore, 1934–1942. On Coolidge's view of the American Committee as a quasi-governmental organization, *see also* Coolidge Oral History, *supra note* 160, at 27. But *see also* 1970 letter from W. Murray Todd, executive secretary of the National Academy of Sciences, to Coolidge regarding the future CITES: "I must confess I still am most uneasy about the Union [IUCN] undertaking what is fundamentally an intergovernmental role," Jan. 26, 1970. *Id.*, 78.20, box 2, folder: IUCN–WWF + related Int'l conservation 1970 IUCN HJC President, *infra* note 286.

207. Coolidge to Maurice, Oct. 30, 1939, *supra note* 196, box 25, folder: ACIC Correspondence, 1939, at 3.

208. Coolidge Oral History, *supra note* 160, at 27. BARROW, *supra note* 150, at 166–167.

209. "Hemisphere approach" in "Memorandum" 3, "International Protection Article," HJCP/HUA 78.10, box 30.

210. PREPARATORY DOCUMENTS TO THE INTERNATIONAL TECHNICAL CONFERENCE ON THE PROTECTION OF NATURE, AUGUST 1949, U.S.A. 56 (Secretariat of the IUPN ed., UNESCO 1949), Fontainebleau, France, (hereafter 1948 Conf. Prep. Docs).

211. 1938 London Conference, *supra note* 174, at para. 40; *see also* at para. 29–30. *See also* letter from Coolidge to Maurice, in which Coolidge asks for more information about "the convention dealing with the fauna of the Pacific," June 22, 1939, HJCP/HUA 78.10, box 25, folder: ACIC Correspondence, 1938. *See also* Maurice to Coolidge, Oct. 4, 1939, *supra note* 152.

212. Coolidge to Huxley, Feb. 11, 1935, ACIWLP/WCS, 1930–1940, Correspondence box 4, folder: Huxley. *See also* BARROW, *supra note* 150, at 188. *See also* Hemming to Phillips, May 25, 1935, ACIWLP/WCS, 1930–1940, Correspondence box 4, folder: Hemming. *See also* Hemming to Phillips, Jan. 11, 1935, *id*. *See also* Hobley's suggestion for an "international wild life conference which would deal with southern Asia, Malaysia, Australia, and New Zealand," Hobley to the American Committee, Jan. 23, 1935. *Id.*, box 4, folder: Hobley.

213. Onslow to Coolidge, Sept. 1, 1941, HJCP/HUA 78.10, box 26, folder: ACIC Correspondence, 1941. This was in answer to Coolidge's letter from June 27: "For several years I worked [. . .] to carry out in the new world your suggestion with regard to an international convention for the protection of fauna and flora." *id.*

214. *Id.*, ACIC Correspondence, 1942.

215. Coolidge had apparently been trying to get the newly established UN interested in conservation issues. *See* van Tienhoven to Coolidge, May 28, 1946, *id.*

216. Coolidge to van Tienhoven, May 9, 1946, HJCP/HUA 78.14, box 45, folder: Van Tienhoven.

217. Van Tienhoven to Coolidge, July 18, 1946, *id.*

218. Coolidge to van Tienhoven, July 31, 1946, *id.*

219. Coolidge to de Alba, Jan. 31, 1947, HJCP/HUA 78.14, box 4, folder: American Committee, 1947 and 1950s.

220. Harold Coolidge, *A World Approach to Nature Conservation, in* PROCEEDINGS OF THE INTER-AMERICAN CONFERENCE ON CONSERVATION OF RENEWABLE NATURAL RESOURCES: DENVER COLORADO, SEPT. 7–20, 1948 715, 717–718.

221. 1947 Brunnen conference, *supra note* 121, at 166–167. Originally called the International Union for the Protection of Nature (IUPN), for the reasons behind the change of name, *see* LAUSCHE, *supra note* 19, at 18–19; HOLDGATE, *id.* at 63–65.

222. *Id.* But *cmp.* next speaker, from Argentina, who pointed out that intergovernmental action was not always necessary to solve the problem, *Id.* 1947 Brunnen conference, at 168.

223. "Points Discussed at Expert Panel on Nature Preservation," Friday, Feb. 6, 1948, HJCP/HUA 78.14, box 4, folder: American Committee, 1947 and 1950s. *See also* "Letter from George Brewer, Director of the New York Zoological Society," draft letter to M. Bernard, president of the Swiss League, Feb. 9, 1948, *id.*

224. Letter from Coolidge to UNESCO, Apr. 7, 1948, *id.*, box 6, folder: International Relations, 1947 and 1948 International Unions.

225. Letter from Jean Thomas, acting director of UNESCO, to Coolidge, *id.* That same year—1948—two regional conferences took place, regarding the Americas and the Pacific. "One more task remained and that was to collect data concerning the European and African Continents. The Fontainebleau meeting provided a favourable opportunity for this," resulting in the European and African Symposium. *See* 1948 Conf. Prep. Docs, *supra note* 210, at 15–84.

226. *See* 1949 Lake Success Conf. Proc., *supra note* 27.

227. *See* "Pairing of Law and Science, Huxley's Vision of IUCN" *in* LAUSCHE, *supra note* 19, on Huxley, at para. 1:15: Huxley's vision of IUCN included laws and international conventions along with science as part of nature protection. *See also* Coolidge's letter to Huxley, Dec. 13, 1973: "I clearly recall the Fontainebleau Conference in 1948 when you created a launching pad to start us off," HCJP/HUA 78.20, box 14, folder: IUCN–WWF, 1973, Executive Board.

228. Although UNESCO's initial intention was to negotiate a convention, Eleen Sam of UNESCO noted in a letter to Coolidge that "the Technical Conference [. . .] will not be plenipotentiary and will not negotiate Agreements between Governments. But we hope it will [. . .] draft a World Convention following the findings of the various regional discussions," Aug. 13, 1948. Sam, Natural Sciences Section, UNESCO, to Coolidge, HJCP/HUA 78.14, box 6, folder: 1947 and 1948 International Unions. A "World Convention"

appeared in an Apr. 29, 1948, document titled "Division of Responsibilities and the Table of Preparation for the Fontainebleau Conference," at para 5. *See also* Harold Coolidge, "Conference for the Establishment of the International Union for the Protection of Nature," Fontainebleau, France, Sept. 30–Oct. 7, 1948, European and African Technical Symposium, NS/IUPN/8 Annex VI, at para. IV(A).

229. *Summary Report of the Conference of Fontainebleau, International Union for the Protection of Nature* (M. Hayez), Fontainebleau, France, Sept. 30–Oct. 7, 1948, at foreword.

230. 1948 Conf. Prep. Docs, *supra note* 210, at 16.

231. *Id.* at 32.

232. *Id.* at 56, 59.

233. As to the conclusion "of a world convention on fauna protection [. . .] Mr. Harroy could not envisage this eventuality unless it were implemented by a group of naturalists and jurists with power to carry on the necessary investigations on the authority of [. . .] [IUPN]," *id.* at 62, 68–70.

234. "Preparation of a World Convention to serve as a basis for future international cooperation in the field of the protection of nature and to assist in the development of national legislation by the countries participating in it," 1948 Conf. Prep. Docs, *supra note* 210, at 83.

235. Article I.2 (d). This object of "a World Convention for the conservation of nature" remained in the constitution of IUCN until 1977, in which year an Extraordinary General Assembly was called that decided to delete it. HJCP/HUA 78.20, box 20, folder: 1977 IUCN Adm: Exec. Board (2 of 2).

236. *Supra note* 228, at 551. This resolution was probably the result of Coolidge's statement that "there appears to have been little follow-up by the central agencies of the London African Convention [. . .] or the Western Hemisphere Convention [. . .] to make the provisions in these Annexes as effective as they were intended to be," *id.* at 485.

237. *Id.* at 552.

238. Res. 19, *id.* at 187.

239. Third International Conference for the Protection of the Fauna and Flora of Africa. On the role of IUCN in this conference, *see* Proc. 4th Sess. Gen. Ass. 2, 33, 41–42 46 (IUCN 1954). *See* JOHN MCCORMICK, RECLAIMING PARADISE: THE GLOBAL ENVIRONMENTAL MOVEMENT 43 (First Midland Book Edition 1991). *See* Captain Keith Caldwell, *The Bukavu Conference*, 2(4) ORYX 234–237 (1954). *See* Peter Sand, *Whither CITES? The Evolution of a Treaty Regime in the Borderland of Trade and Environment*, 8(1) EUROPEAN JOURNAL OF INTERNATIONAL LAW 32, 29–58 (1997). Kai Curry Lindahl, *The Conservation Story in Africa during the 1960s*, 6(3) BIOLOGICAL CONSERVATION 170–178.

240. Proc. 3rd Sess. Gen. Ass. 60 (IUCN 1952); HOLDGATE, *supra note* 19, at 17.

241. "Dr. Coolidge urged the establishment of a World Convention for Nature Protection, an objective not realized until the negotiation of the endangered species and world heritage treaties following the 1972 UNCHE," LYNTON CALDWELL, PAUL STANLEY

WEILAND, INTERNATIONAL ENVIRONMENTAL POLICY: FROM THE TWENTIETH TO THE TWENTY-FIRST CENTURY 395 (Duke University Press 1996). In addition to CITES and the World Heritage Convention, the 1992 Convention on Biodiversity manifestly fulfills this vision of a world convention for nature.

242. U.N. Convention on Biological Diversity, June 5, 1992, 1760 U.N.T.S. 142.

243. CIOC, *supra note 2*, at 13, 153.

CHAPTER THREE Decolonialization

244. "M. Van der Goes van Naters, a delegate from the Netherlands, made an address that 'greatly impressed the Assembly,'" Proc. 2nd Sess. Gen. Ass. 19 (IUCN 1950).

245. Coolidge to van Tienhoven, May 9, 1946, HJCP/HUA 78.14 box 45, folder: Van Tienhoven.

246. Julian Huxley, *qtd. in* HOLDGATE, *supra note 19*, at 72, reporting on his impressions of a trip to Africa: "there is widespread African resentment against game as destroying crops or competing with native cattle, and resentment against National Parks and Game Reserves as European inventions and relics of 'colonialism' which occupy land coveted by Africans."

247. Lake Success Conf. Proc., *supra note 27*, at 157.

248. *Id.* at 95.

249. *Id.* at 43.

250. *Id.*

251. *Id.* at 18. Proc. 2nd Sess. Gen. Ass. (IUCN 1950), at 20.

252. Proc. 2nd Sess. Gen. Ass. (IUCN 1950), at 52.

253. *Report of the International Committee on National Parks, in* Proc. 7th Sess. Gen. Ass. (IUCN 1960), at 97. But *see* Joseph Murumbi's (Kenyan government minister) speech to the 1963 8th IUCN General Assembly, at 37: "this wild life [. . .] is a heritage which belongs not only to us in Kenya, but to the world at large." Proc. 8th Sess. Gen. Ass. (IUCN 1963), at 48.

254. "The African Special Project was conceived at Warsaw in 1960 by a working-group which included representatives of IUCN, UNESCO, FAO and CCTA. The purpose of the project was to study the conservation situation in all the middle part of Africa, between the Sahara and the Kalahari, to promote interest in all aspects of conservation of nature and natural resources, and to advise those countries which asked for advice, on specific problems, such as the establishment and management of National Parks," Proc. 8th Sess. Gen. Ass. (IUCN 1963), at 99.

255. Res. 1 and 2, Proc. 7th Sess. Gen. Ass. (IUCN 1960), at 151.

256. Res. 3, Proc. 7th Sess. Gen. Ass. (IUCN 1960), at 151.

257. Proc. 7th Sess. Gen. Ass. (IUCN, 1960), at 48.

258. *See* Proc. 8th Sess. Gen. Ass.(IUCN 1963), report on the IUCN Species Survival

Commission meetings, para. 11, at 115. *See also* "Why would it not be possible to establish the principle of a sense of world responsibility for the care and protection of greatly reduced species, threatened with total extinction?", Coolidge, "Emergency Action for the Preservation of Vanishing Species," 1949 Lake Success Conf. Proc., *supra note 27*, at 479–489, 483.

259. "Remarks for Introduction to Judge Train's Talk before National Parks Association's Conservation Meeting on 12 November 1963," HJCP/HUA 78.14, box 12, folder: Adm: International Relations, 1963 International Unions, IUC: ICNP: General box 45, folder: MI. and private T General.

260. Coolidge to Dr. A Starker Leopold, Jan. 21, 1963, HJCP/HUA 78.14, box 12, folder: Adm: International Relations, 1963 International Unions, IUC: ICNP: General. On the same issue, Coolidge wrote to the president of the US Wildlife Society, "I am sure you and many members of the Wildlife Society are aware of how many countries in the world are looking to the [US] for leadership in matters relating to conservation." *id.*

261. HJCP/HUA 78.14 box 19, folder: Adm: international relations 1966, Area Info: Africa: General. The ivory trade was an issue here as well; *see* undated letter (circa Sept. 1966) from Arthur Riopelle, director of Delta Primate Center, to Fairfield Osborn, director of the New York Zoological Society, *id.*

262. *Id.*, letter from Coolidge to Aleubierre, "General Comisar of the Equatorial Region, Saint Isabel, Fernando Poo, West Africa, March 9, 1966."

263. "[I]t might be useful to put a bug in the ear of our friend Ambassador Duke. If Generalissimo Franco should take an interest in the establishment of the park, I imagine the petty politics would fade very rapidly," *id.*, letter from Coolidge to Osborn, Oct. 11, 1966, referring to Osborn's note from Sept. 30.

264. On the "other," *see* DECOLONIZING NATURE, *supra note 17*, at 59.

265. "Colonizer and colonized: this is the basic dichotomy that has structured the 'civilizing' [. . . .] [T]he relationship between these two roles continuously shifts with history and circumstances," ANGHIE, *supra note 11*, at 318. And at 319: "many Third World states which have been the victims of colonialism have themselves minorities and indigenous peoples within their borders. Imperialism is not by any means a purely Western practice," *id.*

266. Today, Virunga National Park. Letter from Coolidge to Litho, minister of agriculture, Kinshasa, Republic of the Congo, July 20, 1968, HJCP/HUA 78.14, box 27, folder: International Relations 1968 International Unions: IUCN Area Info: Africa: Congo.

267. Proc. 44th Sess. E.B., Morges, Sept. 16 and 17, 1968, para. 44.12.1–2. *Id.*, box 29, folder: International Relations 1968 IUCN Executive Board: 44th Session.

268. *See* Lindahl letter of Aug. 8, 1968, to Coolidge displaying the extent of IUCN influence and the depth of its involvement in Congolese politics. "As far as the Nyakakoma fishing village is concerned [. . .] Nyakakoma had already been occupied by hundreds of fishermen and workers in order to build up the fishing village. I visited

Nyakakoma on August 3 and could confirm these bad news. I did not announce that the concession had been withdrawn, because I thought it preferable that these news should arrive through official Congolese channels. This was the case two days later [. . .] the concessioner, who is a very powerful, dynamic and clever chief, became furious and announced that he will not withdraw from Nyakakoma, that he will raise a new rebellion against Kinshasa [. . .] apparently the concessioner must be driven out by force." HJCP/HUA 78.14, box 27, folder: ADM: International relations, IUCN, Africa, Congo, 1968.

269. African Convention on the Conservation of Nature and Natural Resources, Sept. 15, 1968, 1001 U.N.T.S. 3.

270. Res. 9, Bukavu, Belgian Congo, Oct. 26–31, 1953, Third International Conference for the Protection of Fauna and Flora in Africa, *qtd. in* Proc. 4th Sess. Gen. Ass. (IUCN 1954), at 41. *See also* Burhenne-Guilmin discussing the "68 Algiers Convention, replacing the 1933 colonial treaty," Françoise Burhenne-Guilmin, *Biodiversity and International Law: Historical Perspectives and Present Challenges: Where Do We Come From, Where Are We Going?, in* BIODIVERSITY CONSERVATION, LAW AND LIVELIHOODS, BRIDGING THE NORTH-SOUTH DIVIDE 30 (Michael I. Jefferey, Jeremy Firestone & Karen Bubna-Litic eds., Cambridge University Press 2008, IUCN Academy of Environmental Law Research Studies series).

271. BOARDMAN, *supra note* 20, at 146–149.

272. IUCN gave credit to the ASP for putting "African conservation on its feet": "One of [IUCN's] earliest achievements was the African Special Project, 1960–1964, which the Union operated jointly with FAO, UNESCO and the Commission de Cooperation Technique en Afrique. Nineteen countries cooperated in the Project, which included the famous Arusha Symposium and a detailed survey of technical problems with recommendations for their solution, and which may fairly be claimed to have put African conservation on its feet," "Draft Report on International Conservation," Aug. 18, 1978, Maurice F. Strong Papers: 1948–2000, Environmental Science and Public Policy Archives, Harvard College Library (hereafter Maurice Strong Papers). box 81/776, at para. 18; *see* Proc. 8th Session Gen. Ass. (IUCN 1963), at 63–64.

273. Proc. 28th Sess. E. B., May 11–13, 1963, "Supporting Paper No. 2," HJCP/HUA 78.14, box 11, 1963 ADM: International Relations: IUCN Executive Board, unnumbered para., before para. 2.

274. *Id.* at paras. 2–5.

275. *Id.*, and at para. 18.1; Proc. 27th Sess. E. B., Nov. 24–26, 1962, at para. 7, HJCP/HUA 78.14, box 10, 1962 ADM: International Relations: IUCN Executive Board.

276. Proc. 30th Sess. E. B., Sept. 15–24, 1963, para. 3.a.: "Professor Monod reported that in addition to Professor Harroy, Colonel Cowie and himself, representatives of Dahomey, Ghana, Tchad, Sudan, Ethiopia and Tanganyika had met for discussions. There was undoubtedly considerable interest on the part of the African participants in the possibility of a new Convention."

277. *Id.* at para. 18.3.b.

278. Proc. 28th Sess. E.B, May 11–13, 1963. HJCP/HUA 78.14, box 11, ADM: International Relations 1963 International Unions: the Executive Board. Adm. International Relations 1963, para. 9.

279. Proc. 30th Sess. E.B., Sept. 15–24, 1963, at para. 18.3.b. *Generally regarding* IUCN concern over too strong a European identity, "We must also get away from the impression of IUCN as an European-centered organization. We need new ideas and approaches." Gerardo Budowski, director general of IUCN, Proc. 12th Sess. Gen. Ass. (IUCN 1975), at 244.

280. Proc. 9th Sess. Gen. Ass. (IUCN 1966), at 159, Appendix E, para. (d)(ii).

281. As an example of the competition between FAO and IUCN, *see* Coolidge letter from Oct. 25, 1966: "I do not [. . .] feel that under any circumstances should we slack off in our worldwide activities, although I hear [. . .] that this would give a satisfaction to some of those in FAO who feel that the very existence of the Union tends to narrow the scope of some future hopes for [. . .] the conservation field. The latest word is that the [OAU] is more interested in our version of the African Treaty than the FAO one," HJCP/HUA 78.14, box 21, folder: International Relations, 1966, World Conservation Plan. This was in answer to a letter to Coolidge, Oct. 19, 1966, quoting an FAO official that "IUCN could become a far more important [. . .] organization [. . .] for conservation [. . .] if they were to concentrate initially on European countries," *id.*

282. "Supporting Paper No. 2," *supra note* 273, at para. 8.

283. BOARDMAN, *supra note* 20, at 151. *See also* letter from A. I. Odelola, executive secretary, OAU, to Burhenne, Jan. 3, 1968, "that the FAO has not changed its approach [. . . .] They have got their biennial conference to endorse what Africa believes they did wrongly. Africa does not want a separate Wildlife Convention [. . .] FAO seems determined to put its African Wildlife Convention on the statute books of African Nations irrespective of what the African Nations themselves want." HJCP/HUA 78.14, box 29, folder: ADM: International Relations 1968: IUCN Executive Board: Meetings: 43rd Session.

284. *Id.*, letter from OAU to Coolidge, president, IUCN, Mar. 11, 1968.

285. *Id.*, Proc. 43rd Sess. E.B., May 4–5, 1968, at para. 43.23.1–6. *See also* letter from Coolidge disclosing that he did not want the African countries to know about the FAO-IUCN feud, and that the NGOs and IGOs had to appear united, HJCP/HUA 78.14, box 19, folder: ADM: International Relations 1966 International Unions: IUCN Executive Board. By 1970 a truce had been achieved between the two organizations: "FAO will be unhappy about IUCN intruding [. . .] in areas in which it is already working [. . .] [I]f IUCN is to work in harmony with FAO, incidents such as that of the African Convention must be avoided," Contact Note 14, subject: IUCN-FAO Collaboration, 10th–11th June, 1970, HJCP/HUA 78.20, box 2, folder: 1970 International Relations General: International Relations. *See also* "CONFIDENTIAL: FOR BOARD MEMBERS ONLY" memorandum concerning FAO

comments on the Draft African Convention," and at para. C. d, the mandate entrusted to IUCN by OAU was "to establish an 'O.A.U.' draft and not an 'I.U.C.N.' one," at 2, 78.14, box 24, folder: ADM: International relations 1967, Executive Board 42nd session.

286. IUCN's activism in the area of international law was not free of criticism. *See* letter from W. Murray Todd to Coolidge, *supra note* 206.

287. Proc. 9th Sess. Gen. Ass. (IUCN 1966), at 159.

288. U.N. Convention Concerning the Protection of World Cultural and Natural Heritage, Nov. 23, 1972, 1037 U.N.T.S. 151.

289. 1949 Lake Success Conf. Proc., *supra note* 27, at 95.

290. *See* Coolidge Oral History, *supra note* 160, at 46, 47 (in the text, the year indicated is 1955 rather than 1965, a typographical error). *See also* HOLDGATE, *supra note* 19, at 106–107.

291. Dr. Joseph Fisher, president of Resources for the Future, Washington, DC, "New Perspectives on Conservation for the Years Ahead," Proc. 9th Sess. Gen. Ass. (IUCN June 25–July 2, 1966), at 68. HOLDGATE, *id.* at 106. Proc. 9th Sess. Gen. Ass. (IUCN 1966), at 73–74.

292. Proc. 40th Sess. E.B. (IUCN), at para. 40.21.2, Nov. 5–6, 1966, "A Trust for the World Heritage," HUGFP 78.14, box 24, folder: ADM: International Relations 1967 International Unions: IUCN Executive Board: 41st Session.

293. "Remarks by Russell Train, President, the Conservation Foundation, Before the Stony Brook-Millstone Watersheds Association, Princeton, New Jersey," Nov. 11, 1966, HJCP/HUA 78.20, box 2, folder: IUCN–WWF, 1970, World Heritage Trust—early ideas.

294. *Id.*

295. "Address by the Honorable Russell D. Train President The Conservation Foundation, International Congress on Nature and Man, Amsterdam, April 29, 1967," titled "A World Heritage Trust," *id.*

296. Michael Parry quoting Michaela Denis, "Serengeti May Have to Die," EAST AFRICA STANDARD, Aug. 29, 1969, HJCP/HUA 78.14, box 31, folder: Adm: International relations 1969, Tanzania. The title was a play on words with the title of the book SERENGETI WILL LIVE by Bernard Grzimek.

297. *See* Anderson & Grove, *supra note* 34, describing Grzimek as "possibly the most influential European post-war publicist of African wildlife," at 5. But he was controversial as well; *see also* BEINHART & HUGHES *supra note* 13, at 232: the leader for "people-free parks without fully consulting the people concerned." And "Grzimek showed little sympathy for the rights of local Africans," his goal being "to keep the park from being reduced in size at a time when the British government was under pressure from the Masai, who wanted to regain some of their lost grazing space," Mark Cioc, Hunting, Agriculture, and the Quest for International Wildlife Conservation during the Early Twentieth Century (unpublished, n.d., available online), at fn. 21.

298. Grzimek report, Sept. 1, 1969, HJCP/HUA 78.14, box 31, folder: Adm: International relations 1969, Tanzania.

299. *Id.*, letter of Sept. 5, 1969, referring to Nyerere's landmark speech at the 1961 Arusha Conference.

300. *Id.*, Coolidge to Simon, Sept. 8, 1969.

301. Preliminary Draft, "World Heritage Trust, Noel Simon, Oct. 3, 1969," HJCP/HUA 78.14 box 24, folder: Draft Plan, 1967–1972, at 1.

302. Noel Simon to Leonore Smith, the Pacific Science Board in Washington, DC., Sept. 2, 1969, HJCP/HUA 78.14, box 36, folder: ADM: International Relations 1969 World Heritage Trust. *See also supra* text accompanying note 267.

303. Preliminary Draft, *supra note* 301, at 1.

304. *Id.* at 5.

305. *Id.* at 3.

306. "IUCN will give the highest priority to seeking the implementation of the World Heritage Trust as part of the outcome of the 1972 U.N. Conference on the Human Environment," Outline for project no. 1–2, World Heritage Trust, October 1970, Annex I, HJCP/HUA 78.14 box 36, folder: International relations 1969 World Heritage Trust.

307. On the impact of the Vietnam War on the Stockholm Conference, *see* article in 176 SCIENCE 1308, HJCP/HUA 78.20, box 12, folder: 1972 UN Conference on the Human Environment (2 of 2). Regarding its implications for IUCN, Nicholls also noted "that U.S. endorsement of international action initiated by IUCN could do no harm. (I suggested the possibility of reference to the IUCN convention and of the proposed 'Pacific Islands for Science')," HJCP/HUA 78.20, box 7.

308. Contact Note 71/11, World Heritage Trust, Nicholls, Jan. 19, 1971, HJCP/HUA 78.20, box 7, folder: IUCN&WWF, 1971 UNESCO–World Heritage Trust.

309. Cong. Record S. 953 (Feb. 8, 1971), IV. Toward a Better World Environment [. . .] World Heritage Trust. *Id.* A *New York Times* editorial from Feb. 19, 1971, praised the president's initiative: "Among the most daring of the proposed innovations is an international 'heritage' concept for protecting sites of natural, historical and cultural value anywhere in the world—an idea long nurtured by Russell E. Train, chairman of the Council on Environmental Quality." *Id.*

310. *Report of the Preparatory Committee for the United Nations Conference on the Human Environment, Second Session, Geneva, 8–19 February 1971*, A/CONF.48/PC.9, at para. 54. Available at www.unlibrary-nairobi. *See* handwritten letter from Cristina Bruchhausen to Coolidge on a world heritage foundation, Mar. 8, 1971, HJCP/HUA 78.20, box 7, folder: IUCN and WWF, 1971, New York Office at UN. A month later the "foundation" had turned into a "convention." *See also* letter of Bruchhausen to Frank Nicholls, Apr. 19, 1971, on five intergovernmental working groups established by the second session of the Prep Comm. The fifth group on conservation "will be meeting concurrent to the Third session of the Prep Comm and will deal with the World Heritage Convention and two conventions suggested by IUCN on wetlands and islands for science." *Id.*

311. Budowski Statement to the Advisory Committee for the United Nations

Conference on the Human Environment (the Baker Committee), US Dept. of State, Washington, DC, HJCP/HUA 78.20, box 8, folder: IUCN–WWF and related int'l conservation 1971 UNCHE (1 of 2). Nicholls, World Heritage Task Force, "Draft Convention on the World Heritage," Apr. 1971, HJCP/HUA 78.20, box 7: folder: IUCN–WWF and Related international conservation—World Heritage Trust. *See* "World Heritage Task Force," Agenda Paper 1–2 TF.71/4, Apr. 1971, at cover page. Draft Convention of the World Heritage Prepared by IUCN, A/CONF.48/IWGC.I/3, July 1971, New York, Sept. 14, 1971, IWGC.

312. *Supra note* 301, at 2: "it is essential to limit it to a small number of outstanding areas which have been carefully selected according to the most exacting standards."

313. *See* "50th anniversary of Nubia Campaign, UNESCO, Egypt and Sudan have started commemorating the 50th anniversary of the Nubia Campaign, a defining example of international solidarity when countries understood the universal nature of heritage and the universal importance of its conservation," UNESCO website, http://whc.uneo.org, at "news archives."

314. *Report of the Intergovernmental Working Group on Conservation on its First Session*, Oct. 4, 1971, A/CONF.48/IWGC.I/11, at introduction, para. 3.

315. *Id.* at para. 2(a).

316. *Id.* at Part I.A., paras. 7, 9(a).

317. *Id.* at Part I.D., para. 13(a).

318. In the draft tabled at the meeting, IUCN had proposed that "the World Heritage Foundation" "may recognize as part of the World Heritage any natural or cultural site located within the territory of a Contracting State [. . .] provided that the Contracting State agrees to such recognition." A/CONF.48/IWGC.I/3, at note 5 to Art. II: The World Heritage, *supra note* 311.

319. A/CONF.48/IWGC.I/11, *supra note* 314, at Part I.C., para. 11.

320. "[T]he main decision-making should be left to contracting States, advised by a board of experts," *id.* at Part I.D., para. 13(b).

321. The Convention Concerning the Protection of the World Cultural and Natural Heritage, Arts. 8–14, III. Intergovernmental Committee for the Protection of the World Cultural and Natural Heritage (the World Heritage Committee).

322. A/CONF.48IWGC.I/11, *supra note* 314, at Part I.E., para. 15(a), (b), (c).

323. HOLDGATE, *supra note* 19, at 114.

324. HJCP/HUA 78.20, box 12, folder: IUCN–WWF and Related International Conservation 1972.

325. *See* "Statement to the Advisory Committee for the United Nations Conference on the Human Environment" (the Baker Committee), US Dept. of State, Washington, DC, at 5, para. 4, 6 (Nov. 22, 1971).

326. Recommendation 98, UNCHE, Action Plan for the Human Environment.

327. U.N. Convention on International Trade in Endangered Species of Wild Fauna and Flora, Mar. 3, 1973, 993 U.N.T.S. 243.

328. BOARDMAN, *supra note* 20, at 88. *See* LAUSCHE, *supra note* 19, Chap. 6, *The Making of* CITES, at 71–88; on the role of the United States, *see* "U.S. Provides Leadership," at 76–78.

329. Letter from Maurice, SPFE secretary, to Coolidge, Oct. 4, 1939, *supra note* 152.

330. IUPN *Proceedings and Reports of the Third General Assembly, Caracas, Venezuela, Sept. 3–9, 1952* (IUPN 1952), Proc. 3rd Sess. Gen. Ass. (IUCN 1952), Res. 96, at 24.

331. Res. 14, Proc. 7th Sess. Gen. Ass. (IUCN 1960).

332. HOLDGATE, *supra note* 19, at 91.

333. Res. 5, Proc. 8th Sess. Gen. Ass. (IUCN 1963), at 130.

334. "IUCN Executive Board Minutes, Meeting of 11–13 May 1963," Report of the Committee on Legislation, *supra note* 273, at 5.

335. Proc. 9th Sess. Gen. Ass. (IUCN 1966), at 110, Appendix B, para. 4 (i); *see also* Report of the Committee on Legislation, *id.*, noted as Appendix E, at 156., para. (d) (ii).

336. Proc. 10th Sess. Gen. Ass. Vol. II (IUCN 1969), at 48, para. 4.

337. IUCN YEAR BOOK 1970 62 (IUCN, 1971); LAUSCHE, *supra note* 19, at 77.

338. LAUSCHE, *id.* at 75–76.

339. *See* US Code, Title 16, sec. 668cc-5(b), 1970. Pub. L. 91–135, sec. 5, Dec. 5, 1969, 83 Stat. 278. LAUSCHE, *id.* at 76–77, 87, note 32, 33.

340. Proc. 45th Session E.B., June 17, 1969, at para. 45.7A.1, HJCP/HUA 78.14, box 33, folder: ADM: International relations 1969 IUCN Executive Board: Meetings: 45th Session. In June 1969 the lists had not been completed, but were still under revision of the Survival Service Commission.

341. "The Working Group also discussed the draft of CITES, which was the third formal one prepared by IUCN. Kenya's representative objected to it for what he termed its ineffectiveness and potential clash with more restrictive national law. He submitted another draft of the convention [. . . .] The Working Group was informed that the US intended to convene a conference to review the draft in April 1972 [a meeting that was delayed]." A/CONF.48/IWGC.I/11, Oct. 4, 1971, *supra note* 314, at Part II. C., para. 25; *see also* paras. 26, 27. The United States exported bobcat skins and alligator hides; *see* Sand, *supra note* 239, at 32. GREEN GLOBE YEARBOOK 1997: YEARBOOK OF INTERNATIONAL COOPERATION ON ENVIRONMENT AND DEVELOPMENT 19–36; 5–6 (Helge Ole Bergesen & Georg Parmann eds., Fridtjof Nansen Institute).

342. LAUSCHE, *supra note* 19, at 79; BOARDMAN, *supra note* 20, at 91.

343. Statement to the Advisory Committee for the United Nations Conference on the Human Environment (the Baker Committee), US Dept. of State, Washington, DC, at 12, *supra note* 311.

344. *Generally see* Stephen Macekura, *The Limits of the Global Community: The Nixon Administration and Global Environmental Politics*, 11(4) COLD WAR HISTORY, Nov. 2011, at 491. *See* LAUSCHE, *supra note* 19, at 77.

345. HOLDGATE, *supra note* 19, at 277; LAUSCHE, *id.* at 77.

346. Nicholls to Gardner, Feb. 8, 1972, HJCP/HUA 78.20, box 7, folder: IUCN–WWF and related international conservation 1971 UNESCO-World Heritage Trust. *See also* Mar. 4, 1972, letter from the Secretary's Advisory Committee, HJCP/HUA 78.20, box 12, folder: IUCN–WWF + related int'l conservation ACIC/PPS 1972, Conference on the Human Environment.

347. Udall had delivered the keynote address at the 1963 IUCN General Assembly in Nairobi, which had adopted the earliest resolution for a convention. Res. 5, Proc. 8th Sess. Gen. Ass. (IUCN 1963). Other IUCN supporters included Congressman Dingell. "US members of the Commission on Legislation also helped promote IUCN's convention work, including Homer Angelo." LAUSCHE, *id.* at para. 6.32; para. 6:8, at 72; para. 6.32, at 79.

348. Displaying further links between the United States and IUCN in negotiating CITES, *see* letter from Coolidge to Christian Herter, special assistant to the secretary for environmental affairs, Apr. 24, 1973: "I have told you verbally what a splendid work you did in chairing the Washington meeting which developed the Convention in Trade in Endangered Species. I also want you to know how much I appreciate your note of March 5th addressed to Dr. Budowski commenting on the splendid work of Frank Nicholls and Mrs. Burhenne," HJCP/HUA 78.20, box 14, folder: IUCN–WWF 1973 IUCN Domestic Rel: US gov., NGOs individuals. BOARDMAN, *supra note* 20, at 91; LAUSCHE, *supra note* 19, at 79.

349. *See* Lausche, *id.* at 164–165, paras. 12:11–12.15.

350. *See* Sand, *supra note* 239; LAUSCHE, *supra note* 19, at 81–85.

351. Shoumatoff, *supra note* 63, at 132.

352. *Id.*

353. *Id.* And, "In CITES COPs all countries promote first their own commercial interests, then agreements with others for the same, and only lastly they consider the conservation factor," email, Jan. 6, 2012 (sender requested anonymity).

354. "The demand for ivory has surged to the point that the tusks of a single adult elephant can be worth more than ten times the average annual income in many African countries." *See* Jeffrey Gettleman, *Elephants Dying in Epic Frenzy as Ivory Fuels Wars and Profits*, NEW YORK TIMES, www.nytimes.com, Sept. 3, 2012.

355. "[Garamba] Park officials, scientists and the Congolese authorities now believe that the Ugandan military—one of the Pentagon's closest partners in Africa—killed the 22 elephants from a helicopter and spirited away more than a million dollars' worth of ivory"; and "[m]embers of some of the African armies that the American government trains and supports with millions of taxpayer dollars—like the Ugandan military, the Congolese Army and newly independent South Sudan's military—have been implicated in poaching elephants and dealing in ivory," *id.* "According to a report written in 2010 by John Hart, an American scientist and one of the top elephant researchers in Congo, the 'Congolese military are implicated in almost all elephant poaching,' making the military the main perpetrator of illegal elephant killing in D.R.C. The Garamba rangers and a

Congolese government intelligence officer said that they also routinely battled soldiers from the Sudan People's Liberation Army, the military of South Sudan," *id.*

356. 62CD MEETING OF THE STANDING COMMITTEE GENEVA (SWITZERLAND) 23–27 JULY 2012, SC62 DOC.46I (Rev.I), "Elephant Conservation, illegal killing and ivory trade," at 24.

357. Shoumatoff, *supra note* 63, at 128.

358. *Id.*

359. *Id.*

360. "CITES Acts to Curb Smuggling of Elephant Ivory and Rhino Horn" (press release, July 31, 2012). Available at www.cites.org (accessed Aug. 13, 2012).

361. *See* "Summary of EIA recommendations to the 62nd Standing Committee," Environmental Investigation Agency, at 6–7. Available at www.eia-international.org.

362. Section III/B, "Preservation of Zoological or Botanical Species Endemic in Small Islands, Particularly in the Caribbean Sea," Res. 14–19, Proc. 3rd Sess. Gen. Ass. (IUCN 1952), at 66–67.

363. Proc. 9th Sess. Gen. Ass. (IUCN 1966). *Generally see* "[I]t was in the tropical colonies that scientists first came to the realization of the extraordinary speed at which [. . .] Europeans [. . .] could [. . .] destroy the natural environment. Above all the environments of tropical islands played a very prominent part in this development of mental perceptions," RICHARD GROVE, ECOLOGY, CLIMATE AND EMPIRE: COLONIALISM AND GLOBAL ENVIRONMENTAL HISTORY, 1400–1940 1 (White Horse Press 1997), at introduction.

364. Proc. 44th Sess. E.B. (IUCN), HJCP/HUA 78.14, box 29, folder: ADM: Internat'l Relations 1968 Executive Board Meetings: 44th session, Sept. 16 and 17, 1968, at para. 44.9.

365. *Id.* at para. 44.9.3. "Oceanic Islands," Res. 28, Proc. 10th Sess. Gen. Ass. (IUCN 1969).

366. *See* "IUCN, Outline for Project no. 37–1 Conservation of Certain Pacific Islands as Islands for Science, Jan 1971," HJCP/HUA 78.20, box 12, folder: IUCN–WWF + related int'l conservation 1972 IUCN UN Conference on the Human Environment, Stockholm, June 5–16.

367. Bruchhausen to Nicholls, Apr. 19, 1971, *id.* The memo also notes that the committee recommended to the secretariat to study the subject of "genetic pools," a forbearer of the CBD twenty years later.

368. Budowski memo, Oct. 1971, at para. 9(1). HJCP/HUA 78.20, box 6, folder: IUCN–WWF + related Int'l Conservation ACIC/FFPS 1971, at para. 10. Nicholls to Coolidge, Feb. 22, 1971, *id.*, box 7, folder: IUCN-WWF, 1971, Correspondence with or within IUCN staff, Budowski, Nicholls.

369. *Id.* at paras. 19–23.

370. Res. 99.2, UNCHE, "Action Plan for the Human Environment."

371. For more on what happened to this draft convention, *see* letter from Hugh Elliot to Coolidge, Jan. 25, 1973: in answer to a letter from Coolidge "about Pacific islands" (Coolidge left IUCN in 1972), Elliot writes that he is "completely out of touch with island conservation matters [. . .] the result is that I have, for example, no recent information whether IUCN has been able to pursue the promotion of the proposed Convention," HJCP/HUA 78.20, box 14, folder: IUCN–WWF, 1973 IUCN, ADM: Executive Board. *See also* letter from Lenore Smith to Coolidge, Feb. 8, 1973: "we have asked Dieter Mueller-Dombois to delete the item calling for an IUCN paper on the Islands for Science Convention from the Guam Inter-Congress agenda. There is nothing special to be said at this time, and should there be any new developments on the subject we will brief IUCN delegates before the meeting," *id. See also* letter from Elliot to Coolidge, Feb. 21, 1977: "Frank Nicholls who took over the promotion of the Islands for Science project and, in particular, the stimulation of the New Zealand Government to fulfill their promise to call a meeting to establish an international convention on the subject, fell by the wayside so to speak." HJCP/HUA 78.20, box 22, folder 1977 IUCN Commission on ecology. *See also* IUCN *Strategy Report*, Apr. 1977: "A draft convention, prepared by IUCN, on the conservation of certain islands for science was circulated to governments in 1972. The New Zealand government has now indicated its interest in hosting a meeting to conclude such a convention in late 1977 or early 1978," at 9. HJCP/HUA 78.20, box 14, folder: 1973 IUCN Executive Board, at para. 4.2.

372. Proc. 11th Sess. Gen. Ass. (IUCN 1972), at 150.

373. "The Problems of the Human Environment," UNGA 2387 (XXIII) 1733rd plenary meeting, Dec. 3, 1968.

374. 1978 "Draft Report on International Conservation," *supra* note 272, at para. 12. *See also* paras. 30, 32. *See also* Res. 1, "The Proposed 1968 Biosphere Convention," PROC 9TH SESS. GEN. ASS. (IUCN 1966). IUCN's first director, Jean Paul Harroy, complained in 1972 at the Stockholm Conference that no one remembered the 1949 Lake Success conference, BOARDMAN, *supra* note 20, at preface.

375. For recognition of IUCN's role in the Stockholm Conference, *see* Maurice Strong, "The Environmental Challenge to Men and Institutions," speech to IUCN 11th General Assembly, Banff, Canada (Sept. 11, 1972), Maurice Strong Papers, box 29/295.

376. Letter from Philippe de Seynes, undersecretary for economic and social affairs, HJCP/HUA 78.14, box 33, folder: ADM: International Relations 1969 IUCN Conferences: UN on problems of Human Environment.

377. *Id.*, Standish to Coolidge, Mar. 29, 1969. *See also* Maurice Strong's speech, *supra* note 375.

378. Berwick to Coolidge, Mar. 18, 1969, *supra* note 376.

379. *See supra* note 258, on a proposal raised at IUCN 8th General Assembly in 1963. *See also* the proposal raised by Noel Simon in Oct. 1969. *See also* Susan Bragdon, *National Sovereignty and Global Environmental Responsibility: Can the Tension Be Reconciled for the*

Conservation of Biological Diversity? 33(2) HARVARD INTERNATIONAL LAW JOURNAL 381–392 (1992).

380. Berwick to Coolidge, *supra note* 376.

381. Burhenne to Coolidge, Mar. 28, 1969, *id.*

382. Coolidge to de Seynes, Apr. 5, 1969, *id.*

383. Berwick to Coolidge, *id.*

384. Coolidge to de Seynes, *id.*

385. *Id.* at para. 2(a). Coolidge to de Seynes, "Attachment for letter of 5 April to Mr. Phillipe de Seynes."

386. HOLDGATE, *supra note* 19, at 110.

387. *See* letter from de Seynes to Coolidge, Dec. 21, 1966, HJCP/HUA 78.14, box 20, folder: ADM: International Relations 1966 International Unions: IUCN:ICNP Area Info: UN List. *See also* Coolidge letter to Mussard, Apr. 27, 1970, HJCP/HUA 78.20, box 8, folder: IUCN–WWF 1971 UN Conference on the Human Environment—plans (2 of 2).

388. Jean Mussard, the first director of the Human Environment Conference Secretariat, to Coolidge, May 8, 1970, HJCP/HUA 78.20 box 3, folder: 1970 IUCN, Conference on the Human Environment (1 of 2). *See* letter from Coolidge to Budowski, June 18, 1970, HJCP/HUA 78.20, box 2, folder: IUCN–WWF, ACIC/FFPS, 1970, NY office at UN.

389. Letter from Kai Curry-Lindahl, Jan. 22, 1970, HJCP/HUA 78.20, box 2, folder: IUCN–WWF 1970 IUCN General: International relations.

390. *Id.*

391. Coolidge to Curry-Lindahl, Feb. 2, 1970, *supra note* 389.

392. Feb. 2, 1970. HJCP/HUA 78.20, box 2, folder: IUCN–WWF, 1970, ACIC/FFPS, NY office at UN. A further example of competition between organizations is disclosed by Coolidge's reaction to the request of another organization for the use of IUCN data: "I don't like to see us work our neck off and let others get all the credits and kudos for publishing the results. On the other hand, the North American Wildlife Federation is a respected and powerful member of IUCN and we must be willing to cooperate with them on a reasonable basis," Jan. 12, 1972, Coolidge to Budowski, HJCP/HUA 78.20, box 12, folder: 1972 UN Conference on the Human Environment (1 of 2).

393. *See* Contact Paper 70/64, June 24–25, 1970, "IUCN Projects in Environmental Law." HJCP/HUA 78.20 box 2, folder: IUCN-WWF, 1970, ACIC/FFPS, NY office at UN, February 2, 1970.

394. Letter from Feb. 2, 1970, HJCP/HUA 78.20 box 2, folder: IUCN-WWF, 1970, ACIC/FFPS, NY office at UN, February 2, 1970.

395. "IUCN's Representation at the United Nations," HJCP/HUA 78.14, box 33, folder ADM: International Relations 1969 International Unions: IUCN Executive Board Meetings.

396. She even had her own telephone extension; *see* Coolidge to Budowski, June 18,

1970. *Id.* Box 78.20, box 2, folder: IUCN–WWF 1970 IUCN HJCP President—NY Office of UN. Coolidge went on to note that the UN official told him that the UN "will need much help from IUCN"; *see* "IUCN's Representation at United Nations," *id.*

397. Memo from Budowski, Oct. 1971, *supra note* 368, at para. 7.

398. Coolidge to Budowski, *supra note* 388; Coolidge to Suzy Reed, Dec. 17, 1970, HJCP/HUA 78.20, box 2, folder: IUCN–WWF 1970 IUCN HJCP President—NY Office at UN.

399. Contact Note 70/130 29, Sept. 1970, para. 1, HJCP/HUA 78.20, box 3, folder IUCN–WWF + Related International Conservation 1970 IUCN HCJ President, Conference on the Human Environment (2 of 2).

400. Bruchhausen to Nicholls, "Notes made at the Informal Meeting of the Preparatory Committee on the 1972 Conference," Nov. 16, 1970, HJCP/HUA 78.20, box 3, folder: 1970, preparations, Conference on the Human Environment, para. 2 (2 of 2).

401. HJCP/HUA 78.20, box 2, folder: IUCN–WWF 1970 IUCN HJCP President—NY Office at UN. *See also* Contact Note 71/86, Feb. 26, 1971, para. 1.

402. Budowski to Strong, Mar. 9, 1971, *supra note* 368, HJCP/HUA 78.20, box 8, folder: WWF + related Int'l conventions, 1971 IUCN–Int'l relations: UN Conference on the Human Environment (1 of 2), HUGFP 78.20, box 7, folder: IUCN–WWF, 1971, Correspondence Budowski, Nicholls.

403. Memo from Budowski, Oct. 1971, *supra note* 368, at para. 9(2).

404. "[I]t will be impossible for IUCN to carry out special work that may be requested by the Secretariat of the Conference, unless a contractual arrangement with an adequate fee for the work can be established. A precedent for this has already been established by the Secretariat for the Conference providing financial support for IUCN to undertake the tasks with which it has been entrusted," *id.* at para. 9(1).

405. *Id.* at paras. 9(2), 10.

406. DECLARATION OF THE UNITED NATIONS CONFERENCE ON THE HUMAN ENVIRONMENT, at preamble, UNGA 2849 (XXVI) Environment and Development, Initiated by Brazil. *See* NICO SCHRIJVER, SOVEREIGNTY OVER NATURAL RESOURCES: BALANCING RIGHTS AND DUTIES 122 (Cambridge University Press 1997). *Generally see* Macekura, *supra note* 344, 504–508. *See* Bragdon, *supra note* 379, at 383.

407. *See* "Report Submitted by a Panel of Experts convened by the Secretary General of the UNCHE," June 4–12, 1971, Founex, Switzerland, Maurice Strong Papers, box 40/395. *See also* the reports submitted to the panel of experts, "Concepts of International Cooperation," *id.*; "Taxonomy of International Environmental Problems," submitted by C. S. Russell and H. H. Landsberg, *id.* at 40/397.

408. Robert J. Gruszka, bimonthly report, third session of the Prep Comm, to Coolidge, Oct. 10, 1971, HJCP/HUA 78.20, box 8, folder: IUCN–WWF + Related Int'l Conservation 1971 IUCN—Int'l Relations: UN Conference on the Human Environment—plans (1 of 2), at 5.

409. *See* Holdgate's remark at the third session of the Prep Comm about the

importance of differentiating between actions to be undertaken at the national level and those at the international level; he "ruled out forestry resources, for example, as an appropriate subject for international action," *id.* at 3.

410. *Id.* at 7.

411. Schrijver, *supra note* 406, at 2, 3, 37.

412. *See* UNGA Res. 637 C(VII) and 738 (VIII).

413. U.N.Doc. A/CONF.48/PC/.12. Annex I, at 1 (1971), fn. 244.

414. *See generally* SCHRIJVER, *supra note* 406. *See also* Louis Sohn, *The Stockholm Declaration on the Human Environment*, 14(423) HARVARD INTERNATIONAL LAW JOURNAL 485, 486, 492 (1973).

CHAPTER FOUR Disillusionment

415. AGAINST EXTINCTION, *supra note* 62, at 177.

416. Francoise Burhenne-Guilmin and Susan Casey-Lefkowitz, *The New Law of Biodiversity*, 3 YEARBOOK OF INTERNATIONAL ENVIRONMENTAL LAW 30 (World Conservation Union [IUCN] 1992).

417. THE WORLD CONSERVATION STRATEGY (IUCN, WWF, UNEP, FAO 1980). *But see* Grove's criticism of the World Conservation Strategy *in The Scramble for Eden*, *supra note* 34, at 3.

418. *Id.*, THE WORLD CONSERVATION STRATEGY, Chapt. 15, "International Action: Law and Assistance," at para. 3.

419. *Id.* at paras. 5, 7–10.

420. UN Convention on Biological Diversity, June 5, 1992, 1760 U.N.T.S. 142 (hereafter CBD).

421. Res. 15/10, "Genetic Resources," Proc. 15th Sess. Gen. Ass. (IUCN 1981). *See also* G. Kristin Rosendal, *The Convention on Biological Diversity: A Viable Instrument for Conservation and Sustainable Use*, *in* GREEN GLOBE YEARBOOK OF INTERNATIONAL CO-OPERATION ON ENVIRONMENT AND DEVELOPMENT: 1995 69–81 (Helge Ole Bergesen, Georg Parmann & Øystein B. Thommessen eds., Oxford University Press 1995).

422. *See* HOLDGATE *supra note* 19, discussing the 1982 Bali Conference on National Parks: "Cyrille De Klemm [. . .] suggested that a global convention covering all the world's habitats should be prepared [. . .] led to the CBD ten years later," at 168.

423. Cyrille de Klemm, *Conservation of Species: The Need for a New Approach*, 9(1) ENVIRONMENTAL POLICY AND LAW 12, 122; 117–128 (1982).

424. *Id.* at 122.

425. Recommendation 10 of the World Congress on National Parks, Bali, Indonesia, Oct. 11–22, 1982.

426. World Charter for Nature, GA Res. 7, 36 UN GAOR Supp. (No. 51), UN Doc. A/51

(1982). On further historical links, *see* WOLFGANG BURHENNE, WORLD CHARTER FOR NATURE: A BACKGROUND PAPER (E. Schmidt 1983), UNEP-IUCN project.

427. Proc. 12th Sess. Gen. Ass. (IUCN 1975), at 217–222. *See also* BURHENNE, *id.* at 14.

428. *Id.*, Proc. 12th Sess. Gen. Ass., Res. 1, "Charter for Nature," at 147.

429. BURHENNE, *supra note* 426, at 18.

430. *Id.* at 37.

431. *Id.* at 37–38.

432. Res. 16/24, "Wild Genetic Resources and Endangered Species Habitat Protection," Proc. 16th Sess. Gen Ass. (IUCN 1984) Madrid, Spain, Nov. 5–14, 1984, at preamble. Available at http://cmsdata.iucn.org.

433. OUR COMMON FUTURE: REPORT OF THE WORLD COMMISSION ON ENVIRONMENT AND DEVELOPMENT para. 59 (WCED 1987) (hereafter Brundtland Report).

434. E.g. *see* FIONA MCCONNELL, THE BIODIVERSITY CONVENTION: A NEGOTIATING HISTORY 5 (Kluwer Law International 1996), discussing the 14th GC in June 1987.

435. *Id.*

436. UNEP GC 14/26.

437. *See* "Draft articles for inclusion in a proposed convention on the conservation of biological diversity in situ and for the establishment of a fund for that purpose." Attached to UNEP/Bio.Div.1/Inf.1 Oct. 7, 1988, *Report of the Ad Hoc Group of Experts to the Executive Director on Governing Council Decision 14/26. See* UNEP/WG 187/4, Rev. 1, at para. 2: UNEP notes that the "global genetic heritage is the living foundation of the future."

438. MCCONNELL, *supra note* 434, at 4.

439. FROM STRATEGY TO ACTION: HOW TO IMPLEMENT THE REPORT OF THE WORLD COMMISSION ON ENVIRONMENT AND DEVELOPMENT 5 (IUCN 1988), at vii, viii.

440. Res. 17.22, "Development of International Law, Proc. 17th Sess. Gen. Ass (IUCN 1988), at para. 5.

441. MCCONNELL, *supra note* 434, at 5.

442. US House Judiciary Res. 648, 100th Congress, 2nd session, 1988. Melinda Chandler, *The Biodiversity Convention: Selected Issues of Interest to the International Lawyer*, 4 COLORADO JOURNAL OF INTERNATIONAL ENVIRONMENTAL LAW & POLICY 142, 141–174.

443. UNEP/Bio.Div.1/Inf.2, Nov. 13, 1989, PROCEEDINGS OF THE AD HOC WORKING GROUP ON THE WORK OF ITS FIRST SESSION (GENEVA, 16-18 NOVEMBER 1988), at paras. 21, 100 (hereafter Proceedings of First Session).

444. Kal Raustiala, *The Domestic Politics of Global Biodiversity Protection in the United Kingdom and the United States, in* THE INTERNATIONALIZATION OF ENVIRONMENTAL PROTECTION 47–49 (Miranda Schreurs & Elizabeth Economy eds., Cambridge University Press 1997).

445. MCCONNELL, *supra note* 434.

446. Raustiala, *supra note* 444, at 47.

447. *See* "List of Parties," CBD website, http://www.cbd.int/convention/parties/ (accessed May 28, 2013). Veit Koester, *The Biodiversity Convention Negotiation Process and Some Comments on the Outcome*, 27(3) ENVIRONMENTAL POLICY AND LAW 176, 175–192 (1997).

448. *See* "Declarations made at the Nairobi Final Act Conference," MCCONNELL, *supra note* 434, at 179.

449. MUSTAPHA TOLBA & IWONA RUMMEL-BULSKA, GLOBAL ENVIRONMENTAL DIPLOMACY: NEGOTIATING ENVIRONMENTAL AGREEMENTS FOR THE WORLD, 1973–1992 159 (MIT Press 1998).

450. UNEP/Bio.Div.1/2, "Rationalization of International Conventions on Biological Diversity," note by executive director, Oct. 3, 1988, Ad Hoc Working Group of Experts, 1st Session, Geneva, Nov. 16–18, 1988, at para. 1 (hereafter ED Note, Oct. 3, 1988). The scientists' document was attached to UNEP/Bio.Div.1/Inf.1, *Report of the Ad Hoc Group of Experts to the Executive Director on Governing Council Decision 14/26* 1 (hereafter Scientists' Report). *See also* Chandler, *supra note* 442, at 142. For a chronological listing of the many CBD pre-negotiation and negotiation sessions, *see* Koester, *supra note* 447, at 182.

451. The four IUCN officials were Martin Holdgate, Jeffrey McNeely, Kenton Miller, and David Munro. *Id.*, Scientists' Report, *Annex* II, "Lists of Participants."

452. *Id.* at para. 9.

453. *Id.*, "Draft Articles," at 4.2, 4.3, 2.1.

454. *Id.* at paras. 16, 60.

455. ED Note Oct. 3, 1988, *supra note* 450, at paras. 9, 12(a), 15, 21, 25(a), 17(a).

456. UNEP/WG. 187/4, Rev. 1, Meeting of the Ad Hoc Group of Experts, Nairobi, Aug. 29–Sept. 1, 1988, "Draft Note by the UNEP Secretariat concerning Gaps and Overlaps in Existing Conventions on Preservation of Biological Diversity," at paras. 10, 12, 13.

457. *See* Koester, *supra note* 447, at 176.

458. ED Note Oct. 3, 1988, *supra note* 450, at para. 2(a). UNEP had sent out a questionnaire to states on a new convention for biodiversity, and argued that the results demonstrated that the majority of the states that responded supported the proposal. Apparently Brazil was doubtful and wanted to see the documents: "The representative of Brazil requested access to UNEP's analysis of government responses to the ED's letter of 10 September 1987 concerning follow-up to UNEP GC's decision 14/26. In reply, "The Deputy Asst ED said that the analyses undertaken by the UNEP Secretariat were available for consultation but not for reproduction," Proceedings of first session, at paras. 66–67.

459. Koester, *supra note* 447, 184.

460. Draft Art. 19 established an advisory committee on conservation of biodiversity, *supra note* 453. *See also* LYLE GLOWKA, FRANCOISE BURHENNE-GUILMIN & HUGH SYNGE, A GUIDE TO THE CONVENTION ON BIOLOGICAL DIVERSITY 4 (1994).

461. *See* MCCONNELL, *supra note* 434, at 77.

462. *Id.* at 76. *See also* Koester, *supra note* 447, at 176. E.g. *see also* Vandana Shiva, describing the biodiversity crisis from a North-South perspective, *in* VANDANA SHIVA, BIODIVERSITY: SOCIAL AND ECOLOGICAL PERSPECTIVES (Zed Books 1991), at introduction.

463. Proceedings of First Session, *supra note* 443, at para. 23. *See also* the Habitats Directives and the Birds Directives, which form "the cornerstone of Europe's nature conservation policy," at the EC website: http://ec.europa.eu. *See also* the Bern Convention on the Conservation of European Wildlife and Natural Habitats.

464. *Id.* at paras. 25, 71.

465. *Id.* at para. 73.

466. *Id.* at para. 26.

467. *Id.* at para. 29. But *see also* para. 76; the Egyptian representative apparently later agreed to a new convention.

Id. at para. 73.

468. *Id.* at paras. 47, 48, 86.

469. *Id.* at para. 49 (but "generally supported the idea of developing a new convention").

470. *Id.* at para. 37.

471. *Id.* at paras. 21, 68, 100.

472. *Id.* at para. 74, 78; and at paras. 30, 36.

473. *Id.* at para. 109.

474. *Id.* at paras. 68, 77.

475. *Id.* at para. 43.

476. Koester, *supra note* 447, at 183.

477. E.g. Proceedings of First Session, *supra note* 443: Brazil, at paras. 99, 106; Egypt, at para. 105.

478. *Id.* at para 133. And, "A document had been drafted by IUCN which, together with documents of FAO, the World Bank and other agencies, might be taken as a basis for the future work of the Group," *id.*

479. *Id. See* Sheila Jasanoff & Marybeth Long Martello, *On Science and Politics*, in EARTHLY POLITICS: LOCAL AND GLOBAL IN ENVIRONMENTAL GOVERNANCE (MIT Press 2004).

480. *Id.* at paras. 136, 137, 138 (and the representative added as an afterthought, "That did not mean, however, that his country did not appreciate the work of IUCN"), 139.

481. *Id.* at 70.

482. TOLBA & RUMMEL-BULSKA, *supra note* 449, at 138. *See also* Koester, *supra note* 447, who also claims that "[t]he need for a new convention was widely supported," in apparent contradiction of the proceedings themselves.

483. UNEP/Bio.Div.1/3, Nov. 9, 1989, *Report of the AD Hoc Working Group on the Work of Its First Session*, at para. 21.

484. Describing the CBD negotiations, "one Western analyst wryly observed that 'the treaty might just as appropriately have been designated the "Convention on biotechnology transfer"'", MCCONNELL, *supra note* 434, at 47. *See also id.*, interview from July 29, 2010, with Iwona Rummel-Bulska, UNEP official who had served as secretary general of the Biodiversity Intergovernmental Negotiating Committee (INC; MCCONNELL, *id.* at 160), and who emphasized the polarization between the developed countries that did not have much of their own biodiversity left and wanted the developing countries to conserve their own biodiversity; and also that the CBD started out as a conservation agreement and ended up as a rationale use agreement.

485. "Preparation of an International Legal Instrument on the Biological Diversity of the Planet," GC Decision 15/34, 1989 (hereafter GC 15/34), at para. 4.

486. McConnell recounts that climate change was the main issue at this meeting, edging out biodiversity and placing it in a secondary role, and thus the discussion of a new convention on biodiversity was almost postponed. MCCONNELL, *supra note* 434, at 11, 12.

487. MCCONNELL, *id.* at 11. *See also* Rosendal, *supra note* 421, at 73.

488. GC 15/34, *supra note* 485, at para 6.

489. *Id.* at para. 5.

490. UNEP/Bio.Div.1/Inf.3, Sept. 14, 1989, Meeting of UNEP Ad Hoc Senior Advisory Panel of Experts on Biological Diversity, Nairobi, Sept. 19–20, 1989, "Draft Note by the UNEP Secretariat Concerning the Preparation of an International Legal Instrument on the Biological diversity of the Planet," at para. 4.

491. TOLBA & RUMMEL-BULSKA, *supra note* 449, at 139.

492. *Report of the Ad Hoc Working Group on the Work of its Second Session in Preparation for a Legal Instrument on Biological Diversity of the Planet*, UNEP/Bio.Div.2/2, Feb. 1990, at para. 2. This was a recurring refrain: "many people considered it unfair that biodiversity should be seen as the common heritage of mankind. Inequalities and imbalance had to be remedied in order to achieve a more stable new world order." TOLBA & RUMMEL-BULSKA, *id.* at 153, discussing the fourth session of the INC in Sept. 1991.

493. *Report of the AD HOC Group on the Work of its Third Session in Preparation for a Legal Instrument on Biological Diversity of the Planet*, UNEP/Bio.Div.3/12 13, Aug. 1990 (Geneva, July 9–13, 1990), at paras. 18, 31, 35, 38, Annex I.

494. TOLBA & RUMMEL-BULSKA, *supra note* 449, at 140. Regarding the number of countries participating, *see* Koester, *supra note* 447, who points out the small number of countries (nineteen) that participated in all the meetings.

495. *Id.* at 140.

496. Rosendal, *supra note* 421, at 70.

497. MCCONNELL, *supra note* 434, at 26–27.

498. Rec. 18/28, Proc. 18th Gen. Ass. (IUCN 1990), at preamble, paras. 2, 6.

499. McConnell, *supra note* 434, at 84.

500. ANGHIE, *supra note* 11, at 313. "Resolution adopted by the UNGA 3201 (S-VI). Declaration on the Establishment of a New International Economic Order," May 1, 1974, at para. 1. Yet the NIEO did not succeed in changing the international legal order that it had set out to accomplish, *id.* at 11, 211–220, 245, 313.

501. Res. 16/24, "Wild Genetic Resources and Endangered Species Habitat Protection," at preamble, *supra note* 432.

502. *Id.* at para. 1(b).

503. *See* GLOBAL BIODIVERSITY STRATEGY 43 (WRI, IUCN & UNEP 1992).

504. *See* Burhenne-Guilmin & Casey-Lefkowitz on states' unhappiness with the term *common concern* as well, *supra note* 416, at 25.

505. E.g. Haas, *Do Regimes Matter?*; PETER HAAS, SAVING THE MEDITERRANEAN (Columbia University Press 1990).

506. Raustiala, *supra note* 444, at 56, 47.

507. Koester, *supra note* 447, at 178. *See* MCCONNELL, who notes that the major problem was that there was no draft text, *supra note* 434, at 24. *See* Tolba's account of the session, TOLBA & RUMMEL-BULSKA, *supra note* 449, at 145, 148–150.

508. McConnell, *supra note* 434, at 146. *See also* TOLBA & RUMMEL-BULSKA, *id.* at 154–155.

509. TOLBA & RUMMEL-BULSKA, *id.* at 159.

510. McConnell, *supra note* 434, at 47.

511. *Id.* at 61–62.

512. Koester, *supra note* 447, at 179. *See also* David Bell, *The 1992 Convention on Biological Diversity: The Continuing Significance of US Objections at the Earth Summit*, 26 GEORGE WASHINGTON JOURNAL OF INTERNATIONAL LAW & ECONOMY 522, 480–537 (1992). *See also* TOLBA & RUMMEL-BULSKA, *supra note* 449, at 157, that the May 1992 session was attended by a record 101 governments, disclosing the growing significance that they attributed to it.

513. As related by MCCONNELL, *supra note* 434, at 83. *See also* Koester, *id.* at 179.

514. MCCONNELL, *id.* at 75, 83, 84.

515. The US delegation pointed out to the meeting "that the London Summit Declaration did not commit any of the G7 to completing work on the convention in time for Rio," *id.* at 84.

516. Koester, *supra note* 447, at 179. On the dispute between Brazil and Kenya on the name of the convention, *see* MCCONNELL, *id.* at 73–74; TOLBA & RUMMEL-BULSKA, *supra note* 449, at 155.

517. "Brazil was interested in UNCED, not biodiversity," MCCONNELL, *id.* at 94; and at 90, regarding "Brazil, anxious not to tarnish the Earth Summit with a failure."

518. *See* Myanna Lahsen, *Transnational Locals: Brazilian Experiences of the Climate Regime, in* JASANOFF & MARTELLO, *supra note* 479, at 151–172; and "Brazil led the

opposition of less-developed countries [. . .] to the first international environmental initiative, the 1972 [UNCHE]," at 156.

519. "Whatever their motivation for signing, be it a desire to be "politically correct," a belief that acceptable changes could yet be effected, or simply a confidence that the Convention was the best way to ensure and improve the Earth's biological diversity, other developed countries did not oppose the Convention publicly," Bell, *supra note 512*, at 534–535.

520. Koester, *supra note* 447, at 183.

521. JEFFREY A. MCNEELY, CONSERVATION INTERNATIONAL, WORLD WILDLIFE FUND & WORLD BANK, CONSERVING THE WORLD'S BIOLOGICAL DIVERSITY 20 (IUCN 1990), and *generally* at 68–69. In 1990 IUCN was still thinking along the lines of a traditional nature conservation agreement.

522. *Id.* at 25, 29.

523. GLOBAL BIODIVERSITY STRATEGY, *supra note* 503.

524. "Genetic resources have traditionally been treated as though they were a common heritage of humankind—free to all who could use them [. . . .] The growing importance of biotechnology has forced a reassessment of the ownership issue. Simply put, biotechnology has made genetic resources much more valuable and called into question the wisdom of treating them as free goods," *id.* at 43.

525. A/CONF.48/PC/15, *Report of the Secretary General*, Prep. Comm. 4th Sess., Mar. 6–17, 1972, at para. 56.

526. *Id.* at para. 47.

527. "Do we really need international law when national resources are at stake? Is it not a diversion? [. . .] Legal agreements do not stick anywhere [. . . .] Perhaps we have been seduced into thinking we are making progress by the disease I call 'conventionitis,'" *supra note* 9 and accompanying text.

528. As an example of IUCN-states competition, *see* the 1978 incident concerning the Convention on the Conservation of Antarctic Marine Living Resources, minutes of 5th meeting of Bureau of IUCN, Nov. 7–8, 1978, para. 5, 76/732, Maurice Strong Papers, Council Paper UC.78/52, subject: IUCN position on Southern Ocean management.

529. E.g. *see* Ken Conca, *Rethinking the Ecology-Sovereignty Debate*, *in* GREEN PLANET BLUES: FOUR DECADES OF GLOBAL ENVIRONMENTAL POLITICS, chapt. 5 (KEN CONCA & GEOFFREY DABELKO EDS.,WESTVIEW PRESS 4TH ED. 1998); KEN CONCA, GOVERNING WATER: CONTENTIOUS TRANSNATIONAL POLITICS AND GLOBAL INSTITUTION BUILDING 181–182 (MIT Press 2006); LAWRENCE SUSSKIND, ENVIRONMENTAL DIPLOMACY: NEGOTIATING MORE EFFECTIVE GLOBAL AGREEMENTS 130 (Oxford University Press 1994); THE GREENING OF SOVEREIGNTY IN WORLD POLITICS 24–25 (Karen Litfin ed., MIT Press 1998). *See* Kal Raustiala, *The Role of NGOs in International Treaty-Making* (Sept. 16, 2011). DUNCAN HOLLIS, THE OXFORD

GUIDE TO TREATIES (Oxford University Press 2012); UCLA School of Law Research Paper No. 11–31, at 6, available at http://ssrn.com.

530. "Greetings by Dr. Patrick de Rham, UNESCO," Proc. 12th Sess. Gen. Ass. (IUCN 1975), at 234. *See also supra* text accompanying note 405, at 146.

531. *See* DECOLONIZING NATURE, *supra note* 17, at 19.

CHAPTER FIVE Epilogue and Renewal

532. JAMES GUSTAVE SPETH, RED SKY AT MORNING: AMERICA AND THE CRISIS OF THE GLOBAL ENVIRONMENT 2 (Yale University Press 2nd ed. 2005).

533. *Id.* at 8.

534. THE FUTURE OF IUCN, *supra note* 9, at 93.

535. Brundtland Report, *supra note* 433, at sec. 5.2. "A Universal Declaration and a Convention on Environmental Protection and Sustainable Development," at para 86.

536. "Development of Environmental Law," Proc. 17th Sess. Gen. Ass., Rec. 17:22, at para. 3.

537. Meeting on the Draft Covenant on Environment and Development in Bonn, Jan. 14–15 (Jan. 21, 2010) Available at www.iucn.org (accessed May 15, 2013).

538. On IUCN's role as a catalyst, *see* Nicholas Robinson, *IUCN as Catalyst for a Law of the Biosphere: Acting Globally and Locally*, 25 ENVIRONMENTAL LAW 250 (2005).

539. Berwick to Coolidge, Mar. 18, 1969, HJCP/HUA 78.14, box 33, folder: ADM: International Relations 1969 IUCN Conferences: UN on problems of Human Environment.

540. *See* New Agreement Governs the Relationship between the IUCN Environmental Law Centre and the CMS Family, Sept. 5, 2011. Available at www.iucn.org (accessed May 15, 2013).

541. Squeezing Africa Dry: Behind Every Land Grab Is a Water Grab (June 11, 2012). Available at www.grain.org (accessed May 15, 2013).

542. Erna Bennett, commenting on the role of NGOs in intergovernmental negotiations, quoted in an article in SEEDLING in 2002: "playing the game by the enemy's rules has achieved nothing but to show us how we got to where we are. But it has not shown us how to get out." Available at www/grain.org/seedlings_files/seed-10-07.pdf (July 2010), at 9–10 (accessed June 5, 2013).

543. "Re post-colonialism: many communities in ex-colonized independent countries view their current governments as the real post-colonialists. This is a result of [. . .] colonialism creating countries with no ethnic coherence. The minority ethnic groups often view themselves (and often correctly so) as being colonized and deprived in the same way the whole country was previously colonized, and the natural resources within their lands, used by central governments, and often even by individuals in power, through corruption. In any case—and in any country—developed and developing and even where

there is democracy—there is often no identity of interests between the government and the citizens, or at least not with ALL the citizens. Often ex-colonized countries would use the arguments of sovereignty and of recovering the country's interests, as a mean[s] to defend the extraction of the countries' natural resources for the good of a certain ethnic group within the country at the expense of others, or even only for the good of a small layer of elite," email interview, Jan. 6, 2012 (interviewee requested anonymity).

544. As examples of "colonizing" corporations, *see* John Vidal, *How Food and Water Are Driving a 21st-century African Land Grab*, THE OBSERVER, Mar. 7, 2011. Available at www.guardian.co.uk; Lorenzo Cotula et al., *Land Grab or Development Opportunity: Agricultural Investment and International Land Deals in Africa* (FAO, IIED & IFAD 2009).

545. SPETH, *supra note* 532, at 72. Demonstrating that the influence of corporations is not limited to African countries, Mark Hertsgaard points out that despite popular spins as to the remarkable environmental consciousness of the Clinton-Gore team in the White House, and despite Al Gore's book EARTH IN THE BALANCE: ECOLOGY AND THE HUMAN SPIRIT, the president and vice president were controlled by corporate interests. "[O]nce they entered the White House, the environmental proposals the Clinton administration advanced in its first few months [. . .] [were] abandoned at the first sign of opposition from corporate interests," MARK HERTSGAARD, EARTH ODYSSEY: AROUND THE WORLD IN SEARCH OF OUR ENVIRONMENTAL FUTURE 281 (Broadway Books 1998).

546. "Until the latter half of the nineteenth century large trading companies, such as the British East India Company and the Dutch East India Company, had driven the colonial enterprise," ANGHIE, *supra note* 11, at 141: "[T]he MNCs [multinational corporations] were in many respects successors to entities such as the Dutch and British East India Companies [. . .] Grotius, the father of international law, had also served as the lawyer for the Dutch East India Company, and had written several of his most important works as a justification for advancing their interests," *id.* at 224. *See also id.* at 252–253.

547. *See* KOSKENNIEMI, *supra note* 11.

548. FAIRFIELD OSBORN, OUR PLUNDERED PLANET 194 (Little, Brown and Co. 1948), at conclusion.

549. SPETH, *supra note* 532, at 174.

550. Dr. Tamar Ron, A Proposed Alternative Institutional Approach to Meeting International Biodiversity Targets, Dec. 10, 2010 (accessed May 15, 2013). Available at www.iucn.org.

551. Rachelle Adam, interview with Dr. Tamar Ron, Jan. 12, 2012. "Integrated Rural Development and Nature Conservation (IRDNC)." Available atwww.openafrica.org.

552. *Id. See also* interview with Garth Owe-Smith, co-founder of IRDNC, www.youtube.com/watch?v=AQdqERZTYjk (accessed May 15, 2013); interview with John

Kasaona, director of IRDNC, www.viewchange.org/videos/ted-john-kasaona-how-poachers-became-caretakers (accessed May 15, 2013).

553. COMMUNITY RIGHTS, CONSERVATION AND CONTESTED LAND: THE POLITICS OF NATURAL RESOURCE GOVERNANCE IN AFRICA 9 (Fred Nelson ed., Earthscan 2010), *generally*, at preface.

554. *Id.* at 4.

555. James Murombedzi, *Devolving the Expropriation of Nature: The "Devolution of Wildlife Management in Southern Africa*, in DECOLONIZING NATURE, *supra note* 17, at 140.

556. *Supra note* 553, at preface.

557. "Open Letter #3, To: IUCN Leadership, Participants, and Global Environmental Organizations, From: Emergency Action Committee to Save Jeju Island," August 2012, https://app.e2ma.net/app/view:CampaignPublic/id.0 (accessed May 15, 2013).

558. COMMUNITY RIGHTS, CONSERVATION AND CONTESTED LAND, *supra note* 553, at 286.

559. LINDA MALONE & SCOTT PASTERNACK, DEFENDING THE ENVIRONMENT: CIVIL SOCIETY STRATEGIES TO ENFORCE INTERNATIONAL ENVIRONMENTAL LAW 9, 12 (Island Press 2006).

560. *See* SUSSKIND, *supra note* 529, Oran Young on how countries consider shaming worse than actual sanctions, at 113.

561. HOLDGATE, *supra note* 19, at 211.

562. SUSSKIND, *supra note* 529, at 114–117.

Index

1900 London Convention (Convention for the Preservation of Wild Animals, Birds and Fish in Africa): and the African elephant, 24–25; background of, 18–24; colonial tool for Africa, 28–29, 56–57; contents of, 25–26; as a as a hunting convention, 26–27; SPFE and implementation of, 29–30. *See also* African elephant

1933 London Convention (Convention Relative to the Preservation of Flora and Fauna in Their Natural State): background, 33–36; as a colonial tool for Africa, 56–57; contents of, 37–38; Hingston's report and, 36; and IUCN, 122; and ivory, 36, 38; as a model for biodiversity conventions, 57; and replaced by the 1968 African Convention, 64, 67. *See also* the American Committee; Coolidge; national parks; SPFE

1946 Basle Conference, 51

1947 Brunnen Conference, 51–52

1968 African Convention (African Convention on the Conservation of Nature and Natural Resources), 64–67; and the IUCN–FAO dispute, 66–67, 72, 121, 162n283

Adams, William, 98, 125
Advisory Commission for International Protection of Nature, 31, 32

Africa: and CITES, 75; and the colonial biodiversity crisis, 4–5, 18–19; and a colonial ethos, 26–29, 129–30; as the object of colonial international law, 10, 28–29; and international biodiversity law, 5–6, 18, 97; and IUCN, 59–64, 67, 96–97, 121; and the WHC, 67

African elephant, 12, 19–21; and the 1900 London Convention, 24–25; and the 1933 London Convention, 38; and CITES, 79–82; and Grzimek, 163n297; and Hingston's report, 34–35; proposed domestication of, 22; requiring international cooperation, 22

African fauna/wildlife: and American Committee, 41–42; and Boone and Crockett Club, 40–41; CITES and, 75–76; and the civilizing mission, 27–28, 38, 49; devastation by colonialism, 5–6, 19–24, 28–32, 36, 148n100; Coolidge and, 40–42; as an imperial heritage, 6, 28; and international conservationism, 18, 32–33, 97; and IUCN, 8, 60–61; and national parks as separation mechanisms, 11, 34–36, 39, 54; and Sarasin, 32; and the SPFE, 30–31, 35, 37–39; and van Tienhoven, 32–33. *See also* Hingston

African Special Project (ASP), 60, 64, 87, 159n254, 161n272

Albert (King of Belgium), 30

Albert National Park, 53

Allen, Glover M., 43
American Committee (American Committee for International Wild Life Protection): and the 1933 London Convention, 42–43; and Africa, 41, 59; background of, 41–43; and the civilizing mission, 48–49; and global inventory of species, 43; and SPFE, 41, 48–49, 67, 122, 155n196; and the Western Hemisphere Convention, 44, 47–49
Amnesty International, 136
Arusha Conference (Symposium on the Conservation of Nature and Natural Resources in Modern African States), 64, 76, 161n272; Arusha Manifesto, 69

Banks, Sir Joseph, 14
Bernard, Charles, 53
Berwick, Joe, 86–87
biodiversity: 2010 biodiversity target, 1; and asymmetric global distribution, 4; and colonialism, 5–6, 8–12, 31–33, 64, 97; and the international agenda, 4, 10, 116; as a land-use issue, 2; national versus global scales of, 3–4, 12, 57, 75, 84–85, 178n527; origins of the term, 2; and vulnerable human populations, 9, 36, 131–32
Biosphere Conference (Intergovernmental Conference of Experts on the Scientific Basis for Rational Use and Conservation of the Resources of the Biosphere), 85
Brundtland Report (Our Common Future: Report of the World Commission on Environment and Development [WCED]), 102–4
Budowski, Gerardo: and the Islands convention, 84; and IUCN, 162n279; and the Stockholm Conference, 89–90, 91–92

Bukavu conference (Third International Conference for the Protection of the Fauna and Flora of Africa), 55, 64; and the Bukavu recommendations for revising the 1933 London Convention, 65
Burhenne, Wolfgang, 77, 79, 87, 140n9
Burnham, John, 41
Buxton, Edward North, 29–30

Caldwell, K. F., 33, 150–51n129
Caldwell, Lynton K., 90
CAMPFIRE (Communal Areas Management Programme for Indigenous Resources), 197
Cartagena Protocol on Biosafety, 133
CBD (Convention on Biological Diversity): and the 1900 and the 1933 conventions, 98, 99; background, 99–100, 102–4; and changing state behavior, 117–18; and developed countries, 116–17, 118–19; and developing countries, 116, 118–19; early negotiations, 105–12; and IGOs, NGOs; and reputation, 121; IUCN and negotiations of, 112–16; and state reputation, 119–21; US role in, 104–5, 119–20
CBNRM (Community-based natural resource management), 132–33
China: and delay in CITES plenepotienary conference, 78; and the ivory trade, 80–82
Cioc, Mark, 56
CITES (Convention on International Trade in Endangered Species): and the 1900 and 1933 conventions, 80; and Africa, 75; background, 74–77; and colonialism, 80, 82, 84; and the conflict between trade and protection of endangered species, 80; and the elephant crisis, 80–82; and

IUCN, 85; IUCN and implementation of, 79; Richard Leakey and, 79–80; and the Stockholm Conference, 85–88, 92; US role in negotiations of, 77–79; and a world convention for nature, 55–56, 75

civilizing mission, 6–7, 9, 131; and the American Committee, 48–49; imperial heritage and, 28; international law and, 6, 29, 49, 68, 141n25; IUCN and, 61, 63; and SPFE, 29, 38, 49

CMS (Convention on the Conservation of Migratory Species), 99, 127–28

colonial constructivists, 6–8, 14

colonialism: and devastation of African fauna, 27–29; as a driver of biodiversity loss, 4–6; and ecological epistemic communities, 7, 13–14; impact of on elephants, 80, 82; and environmental advocacy, 14, 16–17, 30; and globalization, 130–31; impact on indigenous people, 9; and international law, 8, 125; land grabbing as, 11; and slavery, 9; and trade in fauna, 5

colonial legacy, 8–12; of the CBD, 116; of global governance for biodiversity, 124–25; of IUCN, 116, 123–25; overcoming the, 125, 137

common heritage: biodiversity as a, 108; CBD negotiations and rejection of by developing countries, 101, 112–17; discarded by UNEP in favor of "national resource," 111, 114; genetic resources as a, 99, 102, 117; IUCN and, 11, 117; origins in an "imperial heritage," 28, 111; vs. the PSNR principle, 94; world heritage as part of, 72

Congo Basin Convention (1892), 25, 145n74

convention for Asia and Australia, 39, 44, 46, 49–50, 154n192

Convention for the Preservation and Protection of Fur Seals (1911), 40, 140n10

Convention for the Protection of Migratory Birds (1916), 40, 140n10

Convention on Conservation of Certain Islands for Science, 82–85; epilogue, 169n371; international lists and the authority to determine their contents, 83, 127; and the limits of international law, 84–85; on preventing development of islands, 83, 84, 116; rejection of by states, 84; and the Stockholm Conference, 85, 86, 87, 90, 92, 123, 234n307, 235n310

Coolidge, Harold Jefferson: and the 1933 London Convention, 42–43, 44; and the 1968 African Convention, 66; and African national parks, 40, 44, 60, 61–63; and the American Committee, 40–41; background of, 39–41; Boone and Crockett Club, 41; and CITES, 78, 86, 167n348; and a "civilizing mission," 48–49; and the Convention on Conservation of Certain Islands for Science, 83, 169n371; Equatorial Guinea under Spanish rule, 62, 160n263; Harper-Allen report, 43; influence of colonialism on, 48–49, 61–62; and international conventions, 86–88; involvement in Congolese civil war, 63, 160n268; as IUCN president, 56, 61, 66, 68, 83, 86; legacy of international organizations and conventions, 40; and the Ngorongoro incident, 69; and the Stockholm Conference, 86–90, 170n392; turf war with FAO over the 1968 African Convention, 65–67, 162n281, 162n285; turf war with SPFE over Western Hemisphere Convention, 47–48; and the Western Hemisphere Convention,

44–46; "A World Approach to Nature Protection," 51; and a world convention for nature, 50–56, 88, 99, 158n241; and the World Heritage Convention, 67–68, 78
Covenant on Environment and Development, 126–27

Darwin, Charles, 13, 14; and Alfred Newton, 17; and Humboldt, 16; and Wallace, 17, 18, 142n30, 142n34
dilemma of scales, 2–5, 12, 131; Africa's biodiversity and postcolonial shift to national scale, 57

elephant treaties: and CITES, 80; and colonialism, 12, 75, 118, 125, 137; and European countries, 80; and modern international conservation law, 12, 125; and trade in African fauna, 75, 82, 125
Emergency Action Committee to Save Jeju Island, 134
epistemic communities, 7, 117–18
Ethiopia, 25, 123, 128, 129
Extinct and Vanishing Mammals of the Old World, 43
Extinct and Vanishing Mammals of the Western Hemisphere, 43

FAO (UN Food and Agricultural Organization): and the African Special Project, 159n254, 161n272; and the CBD negotiations, 109–10, 121; and IUCN and the 1968 African Convention, 66–67, 72, 121, 162n281, 162n283; and landgrabbing, 129; use of international law for reputational concerns, 97
Fisher, Joseph, 67–68
Fontainebleau conference (Conference for the Establishment of the International Union for the Protection of Nature [1948]), 52–53, 85

Gardner, Richard, 78, 90
genetic resources: and 1981 IUCN GA resolution, 99; and 1984 IUCN GA resolution, 102; and access to, 108, 111, 112–14, 116–17; and the Brundtland Report, 104; and early CBD negotiations, 112–14; and colonialism, 113; as the common heritage of mankind, 99–100, 103, 117, 178n524; and developing countries, 105, 108, 113; and the FAO, 121; and IUCN, 117, 122; ownership of, 114, 117; and UNEP, 106
global governance for biodiversity: colonial roots of, 10–12, 56–57, 124–25; and conferences, 1, 126; and conservation organizations, 9, 56, 124; and developing countries, 10, 124–25; and IUCN, 134; and local communities, 131–36; rethinking current structures of, 12; scales of, 2–4, 131–32. *See also* international conservation conventions; international cooperation for nature
GRAIN, 129
Green Amnesty International, 136
Gruszka, Robert, 93–94
Grzimek, Bernard, 69

Hardinge, Arthur Henry, 25
Harroy Jean Paul: and the 1968 African Convention, 161n276; and Africa as a "common heritage of natural resources," 59, 60; as colonial governor of Rwanda-Burundi, 56; as IUCN's first secretary general, 54; and the Stockholm and Lake Success conferences, 169n374; and a world convention for nature, 158n233
Hingston, Major R. W. G: 1930 trip to

Africa, 33; and 1931 report *Proposed British National Parks for Africa*, 33–36; and the African elephant, 20, 34–35.
Hobley, C. W. (secretary of the SPFE): and 1930 visit to the US, 41, 152n162; on Africans and hunting, 18, 147n91, 148ns97–98; on national parks, 33; on a wildlife conference for Australasia, 156n212
Holdgate, Martin, 78, 174n451
Hooker, Sir William, 15
Humboldt, Alexander von, 16, 143n37, 142n36
hunting: and the 1900 Convention, 23–26, 31–33; and the 1933 Convention, 35–38, 54; banned in US national parks, 62; European vs. African hunters, 26–28, 146n79, 147nn91–92, 147n95, 148n97, 147n95; and German colonial regulations, 21–22; as key colonial threat to African wildlife, 53–54, 57, 128; regulation of by treaties for seals and migratory birds, 140n10; SPFE and, 30, 39
Huxley, Julian: and an Asian convention, 50, 154n179; and international law for nature, 157n227; and postcolonial African resentment of game and parks, 159n246; as UNESCO's first director general, 53; and the Western Hemisphere Convention, 154n179, 155n200; and a world convention, 53–54; 99

imperial heritage, 6, 53; and the 1900 convention, 28–29, 148n103; and a "common heritage, 111; and IUCN, 63, 106 (early draft articles for the CBD); and SPFE, 38, 148nn102, 103
Inter-American Conference on Conservation of Renewable Natural Resources (Setpember 1948), 51
International Congress for the Protection of Nature (1931), 35
international conservation law and conventions: African fauna as catalyst of, 5–6, 8, 10–12, 18, 33, 50; and colonial law, 4–8, 10–12, 29, 31–33, 56–57, 125; as entry points for conservation organizations, 29–30, 38; as governance tools for developing countries, 8, 10–11, 74–75, 106–7, 111, 125; and Harold Coolidge, 42–43, 47, 50; instrumental versus normative use of, 6, 22–23, 39, 123; limits of, 12, 84, 98–99, 118, 125–26; rejection and recreation of by developing countries, 8, 77, 94–97, 103–5, 108–18, 122–23. *See also* international organizations; IUCN; SPFE
international cooperation for nature: and the 1900 convention, 18; for the elephant and the ivory trade; 5, 22–23, 25, 145n70; Coolidge and, 42, 44; between Great Britain and Germany, 19, 75; John Phillips and, 42; Onslow and, 36, 50; origins in colonialism, 32–33, 50; and the Stockholm Conference, 88, 93–95; and a world convention for nature, 50, 158n234
internationalization: of African biodiversity, 94; and Brazil, 110; and CITES, 75; and the WHC, 67, 74
international organizations: as agents for change, 57, 123; challenging traditional views of, 8–9, 124; and colonial roots, 7, 48, 56–57; competition amongst, 89; and international conventions, 6–7, 67, 122–23; relations with governments and corporations, 48, 134–35. *See also* American Committee; FAO; IUCN; Sarasin, SPFE; UNESCO; van Tienhoven

IPCE (International Parliamentary Conference on the Environment), 79
IRDNC (Integrated Rural Development and Nature Conservation), 132–33
IUCN (International Union for Conservation of Nature): and the 1933 London Convention, 55, 122; and the 1980s biodiversity decade, 98; and the 2012 World Conservation Congress, 134–35; colonial origins of, 7–8, 56, 62–63; and concern over Africa, 5, 8, 59–64, 97; as creator of biodiversity conventions, 4, 54–56, 67, 86, 122–23; disillusionment with international conventions, 8, 97, 99–100, 121–25; failure to change states' behavior, 117–18, 123–24; and NGO status as an obstacle in the CBD negotiations, 110; overlapping relationships with US officials, 78–79; and the Stockholm Conference, 86–92; and the US State Department and CITES, 119; and a world convention for nature, 54–55
ivory trade: and the 1900 Convention, 21–23, 25; and the 1933 Convention, 36; and CITES, 80–82; under colonialism, 5–6. *See also* African elephant

Jeju island, South Korea, 134

Kenya: and the CBD negotiations, 120; and CITES, 77, 123, 166n341; and land grabbing, 128
Klemm, Cyrille de, 99–100, 102, 172n422
Koester, Veit, 105, 107, 119, 175n482

Lake Success Conference (International Technical Conference on the Protection of Nature): and a focus on Africa, 59–60; as distinguished from the Stockholm Conference, 85; number of states participating in, 94; and the origins of the WHC, 67; and the world convention for nature, 52–55
land grabbing, 11, 129
Lankester, Edwin Ray, 19, 149n109
Leakey, Richard, 79–80
Liberia: barred from negotiating the 1900 Convention, 29, 34, 123
Lima Conference (Eighth International Conference of American States, 1938), 44–46
Lindahl, Kai Curry: and the Congo civil war, 268n160; and the Stockholm Conference, 89

Maurice, Henry, 46, 49
Mauritius, 14–15; and Edward Newton, 17
McConnell, Fiona: on the CBD negotiations, 104, 108, 112–13, 115, 119–20; on climate change edging out biodiversity as key issue, 176n486
Mobutu, President of Zaire, 100

Nagoya Protocol on Access to Genetic Resources and the Fair and Equitable Sharing of Benefits, 127
Namibia, 81, 132–33
national parks: and the 1933 convention, 33, 35–39; and the African Special Project, 226n254; as a colonial conservation institution, 26, 194n14; and exclusion of Africans, 28, 34–35; former colonial parks in Africa, 10–11, 62–64; and IUCN intervention in the Congo, 63–64; and IUCN–UN project for, 88; a world convention for, 88. *See also* Coolidge; Hingston
Newton, Alfred, 16–18, 31, 143n46,
Newton, Edward, 17

Ngorongoro, 68–70, 72, 74
Nicholls, Frank, 70–71, 78, 164n307
NIEO (New International Economic Order), 96, 116
Nixon, Richard, 68, 71, 78
North American Wildlife Conference (1936), 42
Nyere, Julius, 69

Onslow, Earl of, 35–37, 41; and the Western Hemisphere Convention, 44, 48; and a world convention for nature, 50, 99
Osborn, Fairfield, 13, 131

Pan-American Union, 44–45, 47, 51
Pappe, Ludwig, 32
Pearson, T. Gilbert, 40, 45, 154n184
Phillips, John, 41–43, 44
Poivre, Pierre, 14–15, 142n33
Preparatory Committee for the International Conference for the Protection of the Fauna and the Flora (1932), 36–37; Report of the Prepatory Committee, 62
Principle 21 to the Stockholm Declaration, 95–96
PSNR (Permanent Sovereignty over National Resources) principle, 58, 61, 94–95

Ramsar Convention on Wetlands of International Importance, and the Stockholm Conference, 83, 84, 86, 90, 92, 164n310
Raustiala, Kal, 117–18
Rawson, Rawson, 15, 142n35
Reagan, President Ronald, 104
reputation: and Brazil, 120–21; and conservation organizations, 9, 67; and FAO, 67, 121; and IUCN, 62, 67, 108; and Kenya, 120; and SPFE, 30–31, 39, 67; and the UN, 97, 134; and UNEP, 120
Rio Summit (UN Conference on Environment and Development, UNCED), 85, 98, 105 118–21
Ron, Tamar, 132, 140n13
Roosevelt, Theodore, 41, 45
Roosevelt, Theodore, Jr. 45
Rosendal, G. Kristin, 115
Rummel-Bulska, Iwona, 105, 176n484

Salisbury, Robert Cecil, Lord, 19, 22–23, 25
Sandbrook, Richard, 2, 123
Sarasin, Paul, 31–33, 40, 41–42, 51, 53, 140n13, 150n118
Seynes, Philippe de, 86–88
Sharpe, Alfred, 22–23, 76, 145nn69–70, 147n95
Shoumatoff, Alex, 79–80
Simon, Noel, 69–70
South Korea, 134–35
Speth, James Gustave, 126, 132
SPFE (Society for the Protection of the Fauna of the Empire): and the 1900 convention, 29, 149n107; and the 1933 convention, 33–39, 43, 150n129; and Africa, 6, 30–31, 33–38; and the American Committee, 41–44, 46–49, 155n196; and planned "Australasia" conference, 50, 68; background of, 29–30; and international law and conventions, 33, 38–39, 43–44, 47–50, 122; and IUCN, 56, 122; and King Albert of Belguim, 30–31; overlapping role with British government, 29–30, 37–39, 48, 149n111; and the Western Hemisphere Convention, 39, 44–49; and a "world convention for nature," 49–50, 54; and WWII, 46–47, 218n196. *See also* African fauna; imperial heritage; reputation

Index 189

Stockholm Conference (UN Conference on the Human Environment (UNCHE)): and China, 78; and colonialism, 130; compared to the Rio Summit, 118; on a continuum of environmental conferences, 4–5, 85–86; and developing countries, 92–96; and IUCN, 86–92, 94, 96, 169n375; launching the UN as the global environmental leader, 96–97; and "three levels of activities," 83, 91, 118; and the Vietnam War, 71, 164n307. *See also* Coolidge; Principle 21; PSNR principle

Stockholm Declaration, 93, 95–96

Strong, Maurice, 90–91, 96, 118

Susskind, Lawrence, 136

Swaminathan, Monkombu, 136

Swiss League for the Protection of Nature, 31, 51–52, 53

Talbot, Lee, 78–79

Tanganyika, 33, 35, 60, 161n276

Tanzania: and biodiversity and local communities, 133; and the Ngorongoro crisis, 69–70; and the WHC, 72, 74

Tienhoven, Peter van, 31–33, 34; and IOPN, 42; and the Western Hemisphere Convention, 46; and a world convention for nature, 51

Tolba, Mustapha, 105, 114, 118–20

Train, Russell: and IUCN and postcolonial Africa; and overlapping relations with US and IUCN, 78; and the WHC, 63, 67–70, 74, 164n309

Trust for the World Heritage, 68–71

Udall, Stewart, 78, 167n347

Ultimate Responsibility for the Preservation of African Species, 61, 70, 86

UNCSD (UN Conference on Sustainable Development, Rio+20), 85

UNEP (UN Environmental Programme): and 1988 scientists' report on biodiversity, 105–7; and biodiversity as a common heritage or resource, 103, 111–12, 113–14, 250n437; and CBD deadline, 105, 118–21; cooperation with IUCN, 102–3, 110–11; GC decision 14/26, 102–3, 104; GC decision 15/34, 112–13; and government support for CBD, 107–8, 174n458; as initiative of the Swedish government, 89; and US, 104–5; as outcome of the Stockholm Conference, 90; replacing IUCN in drafting the CBD, 110, 112; and reputational concerns, 120–21, 134

UNESCO: and the African Special Project, 61, 159n254; and early CBD negotiations, 109–10, 113; and cooperation with FAO, 88–89, 109–10; and the Fontainebleau conference, 52–54, 85; and Julian Huxley, 53–54; and the Lake Success conference, 13, 52–53, 59, 67, 85, 94; and the WHC, 67, 71–74; and a world convention for nature, 52–55, 157n228. *See also* World Heritage Convention

United States: and the CBD and biotechnologies, 104–5, 113; and preventing conclusion of the CBD negotiations, 119–21; and China, 78; and IUCN and CITES, 77–79, 86, 166n341, 167n348; and promoting the future CBD, 96, 102–3, 104–5, 108–10, 117–18; and the WHC, 68, 70–71, 73–74; as world conservation leader, 68, 73–74, 96, 102, 123

UNSCCUR (UN Scientific Conference on the Conservation and Utilization of Resources), 53

Wallace, Alfred Russel, 16–17, 34
Western Hemisphere Convention (1940 Convention on Nature Protection and Wild Life Preservation in the Western Hemisphere): and colonial civilizing mission in Latin America, 45, 48–49; conflict over exclusion of European-held territories, 47–48; and Harold Coolidge, 43–47, 50; IUCN and implementation of, 55, 122, 151n148, 224n236; and the Lima Conference, 44–45; and John Phillips, 44; and William Phillips, 44, 155n198; and the Smithsonian Institution, 44, 46; and SPFE, 39, 43, 48, 67; and territorial coverage of, 47–48; and van Tienhoven, 46; and Wetmore, 63; and a world convention, 50
Wetmore, Alexander, 44–46, 48
White House Conference on International Cooperation, 67
Wissmann, Major Hermann von, 21–22, 145n69, 145ns70–71, 147n88, 147n95
World Charter for Nature, 100–101, 110; and a "World Manifesto on the Protection of Nature," 55

World Conservation Congress (2012), 134–35
World Conservation Union. *See* IUCN
"world convention for nature," 49–56; and the CBD, 55; and CITES, 55–56, 75; as a vision of conservationists, 31–32, 39, 42–43, 50–52, 88, 99–100, 157–58nn228, 233–35, 241
World Heritage Convention (Convention Concerning the Protection of the World Cultural and Natural Heritage, WHC), 67–74; and a "common heritage, 67–68; IUCN–UNESCO conflict, 67, 71–72; and the Ngorongoro crisis, 68–70; and Richard Nixon, 71; and the Stockholm Conference, 83, 85–86, 90; as a tool for post-colonial Africa, 64, 74–75; and US leadership role, 73–74, 78
WWF (World Wildlife Fund), 20

Yellowstone National Park, 34, 71

Zaire, 31, 100–101
Zanzibar Gazette, 20
Zimbabwe, 133